Implicit Bias

Implicit Bias

An Educator's Guide to the Language of Microaggressions

Theresa M. Bouley
Anni K. Reinking

ROWMAN & LITTLEFIELD
Lanham • Boulder • New York • London

Published by Rowman & Littlefield
An imprint of The Rowman & Littlefield Publishing Group, Inc.
4501 Forbes Boulevard, Suite 200, Lanham, Maryland 20706
www.rowman.com

6 Tinworth Street, London, SE11 5AL, United Kingdom

British Library Cataloguing in Publication Information Available

Library of Congress Cataloging-in-Publication Data

Names: Bouley, Theresa Marie, author. | Reinking, Anni K., 1985– author.
Title: Implicit bias : an educator's guide to the language of microaggressions / Theresa
  M. Bouley, Anni K. Reinking.
Description: Lanham : Rowman & Littlefield, [2021] | Includes bibliographical
  references. | Summary: "In this book the authors offer an educator's guide to using
  culturally responsive teaching as an antidote to microaggressions"—Provided by
  publisher.
Identifiers: LCCN 2021026583 (print) | LCCN 2021026584 (ebook) |
  ISBN 9781475855876 (Cloth : acid-free paper) | ISBN 9781475855883
  (Paperback : acid-free paper) | ISBN 9781475855890 (ePub)
Subjects: LCSH: Discrimination in education—United States. | Minorities—
  Education—United States. | Multicultural education—United States. | Educational
  equalization—United States. | Teaching—Social aspects—United States. | Culturally
  relevant pedagogy—Social aspects—United States.
Classification: LCC LC212.2 .B68 2021 (print) | LCC LC212.2 (ebook) |
  DDC 370.1170973—dc23
LC record available at https://lccn.loc.gov/2021026583
LC ebook record available at https://lccn.loc.gov/2021026584

♾ ™ The paper used in this publication meets the minimum requirements of American
National Standard for Information Sciences—Permanence of Paper for Printed Library
Materials, ANSI/NISO Z39.48-1992.

Contents

Prologue   xi

1 Biases and Stereotypes   1
- Bias   3
   - Explicit Bias   4
- Implicit Bias   4
- Ladder of Inference   6
- Figure 1.1 The Ladder of Inference   6
- The Language of Stereotypes: Macroaggressions   8
- Cycle of Socialization   10
- Figure 1.2 Cycle of Socialization   10
- Figure 1.3 One Word, Chapter 1   14

2 The Impact of Implicit Bias and Microaggressions   15
- Forms of Microaggressions   16
- Types of Microaggressions   16
- Table 2.1 Types of Microaggressions   17
- Social-Emotional Development and the Mind-Body Connection   18
- The Language behind Microaggressions   20
- Table 2.2 Microaggression Messages   21
- Implicit Bias and Teacher-Student Expectations   23
- Figure 2.1 One Word, Chapter 2   27

3 Multicultural Education: An Antidote for Implicit Bias
and Microaggressions   29
- Culturally Relevant Pedagogy and Culturally
    Responsive Teaching   30
- Figure 3.1 Seven Principles of Culturally Responsive Teaching   31

- Social Identity Wheel   33
- Figure 3.2 Social Identity Wheel   34
- Intersectionality   35
- The Hidden Curriculum   36
- Status Quo   38
- Figure 3.3 The Culture Tree   40
- Figure 3.4 Diversity Is and Is Not   41
- Figure 3.5 One Word, Chapter 3   42

4 Section 2   43

5 Racial Microaggressions   47
- Figure 5.1 Macro, Micro, Impact, ABE   48
- Figure 5.2 Macro, Micro, Impact, ABE   49
- Table 5.1 Reflection of Terminology   50
- Racial Microaggressions   51
  - Cultural Appropriation   51
  - Invisibility   52
  - Second-Class Citizen   53
  - Othering from the Dominant Privilege   55
  - Dehumanization   57
  - Perpetual Foreigner   58
  - Model Minority   59
- Figure 5.3 Macro, Micro, Impact, ABE   60
- Figure 5.4 Macro, Micro, Impact, ABE   61
- Discipline   62
  - Hair Discrimination   62
  - Zero Tolerance   63
  - Suspension/Expulsion   64
- Figure 5.5 One Word, Chapter 5   64
- Table 5.2 Reflections and Intentions   65
- Resources   65

6 Gender, Gender Identity/Expression, and Sexual Orientation
       Microaggressions   67
- Figure 6.1 Macro, Micro, Impact, ABE   69
- Table 6.1 The Gender Equality Law Center: Gender Stereotypes 71
- Figure 6.2 Macro, Micro, Impact, ABE   72
- Gender Role Bias   72
- Gender Bias   72
- Gender Identity and Gender Expression   74
- Sexual Orientation Bias   74

- Table 6.2 Sexist, Gender Expression/Identity, Sexual
  Orientation Examples   75
- Figure 6.3 Macro, Micro, Impact, ABE   76
- Figure 6.4 Macro, Micro, Impact, ABE   78
- Figure 6.5 One Word, Chapter 6   81
- Table 6.3 Reflections and Intentions   81
- Resources   82

7 Religious, Spirituality, and Non-Religious Microaggressions 83
- Figure 7.1 Macro, Micro, Impact, ABE   84
- Figure 7.2 Macro, Micro, Impact, ABE   85
- Endorsing Religious Stereotypes   86
- Exoticization   86
- Pathology of Different Religious Groups   87
- Assumption of One's Own Religious Identity as the Norm   88
- Table 7.1 Microaggression Messages   89
- Assumption of Religious Homogeneity   89
- Denial of Religious Prejudice   89
- Assumption of Religion   90
- Figure 7.3 Macro, Micro, Impact, ABE   90
- Figure 7.4 Macro, Micro, Impact, ABE   91
- Discipline   92
- Figure 7.5 One Word, Chapter 7   93
- Table 7.2 Reflections and Intentions   94
- Resources   94

8 Economic Microaggressions   95
- Figure 8.1 Macro, Micro, Impact, ABE   96
- Figure 8.2 Macro, Micro, Impact, ABE   98
- Table 8.1 Reflection Table   98
- School Transience/Mobility   99
- Frequent Absenteeism   99
- Little to No Family/Parent Communication   100
- Cultural Capital   101
- Economic Shaming   102
- Lack of Openness to Building Relationships   102
- Figure 8.3 Macro, Micro, Impact, ABE   103
- Figure 8.4 Macro, Micro, Impact, ABE   105
- Discipline   108
- Figure 8.5 One Word, Chapter 8   109
- Table 8.2 Reflections and Intention   109
- Resources   110

9   Ability, Disability, and Ableism Microaggressions   111
     - Figure 9.1 Macro, Micro, Impact, ABE   112
     - Figure 9.2 Macro, Micro, Impact, ABE   114
     - Othering   114
     - Minimization/Belittling   115
     - Fixing or Praying for You   116
     - Placing on a Pedestal   116
     - Figure 9.3 Macro, Micro, Impact, ABE   117
     - Figure 9.4   117
     - Discipline   118
     - Figure 9.5 Macro, Micro, Impact, ABE   119
     - Table 9.1 Edited Summary of Disability Microaggressions
         in Schools   120
     - Figure 9.6 One Word, Chapter 9   123
     - Table 9.2 Reflections and Intentions   123
     - Resources   124

10   Linguistic Diversity and Microaggressions   125
     - Figure 10.1 Macro, Micro, Impact, ABE   126
     - Figure 10.2 Macro, Micro, Impact, ABE   128
     - "Standard" English   128
     - Table 10.1 Common Linguistic Microaggressions   129
     - Ability   130
     - Race/Ethnicity and Language (Intersectionality)   131
     - Dialect/Accent   131
     - Discourse Styles   132
     - Figure 10.3 Macro, Micro, Impact, ABE   133
     - Loss of Native Language   133
     - Deficit Focus   134
     - Figure 10.4 Macro, Micro, Impact, ABE   135
     - Table 10.2 Examples of Hurried Expectations vs. High
         Expectations   136
     - Figure 10.5 One Word, Chapter 10   140
     - Table 10.3 Reflections and Intentions   141
     - Resources   141

11   Family Diversity and Microaggressions   143
     - Figure 11.1 Macro, Micro, Impact, ABE   144
     - Getting Married   145
     - Getting Divorced   145
     - Family Dynamic Multiplicity   146
     - Figure 11.2 Macro, Micro, Impact, ABE   147
     - Single-Parent Families   147

- Women "Do It All"   148
- Families of Color   149
- Table 11.1 Reflection on Terminology   150
- Exclusion   151
- Assumed Disadvantage   152
- Family Intersectionality   153
- Figure 11.3 Macro, Micro, Impact, ABE   154
- Figure 11.4 Macro, Micro, Impact, ABE   156
- Table 11.2 Inclusive Language for Families   157
- Figure 11.5 One Word, Chapter 11   158
- Table 11.3 Reflections and Intentions   159
- Resources   159

12 School-Wide Approaches to Creating an Equitable, Anti-Bias
    Education: Administrator Accountability   161
- Microaggressions Interrupted   162
- Figure 12.1 Tool: Interrupting Microaggressions   164
- School-Wide Anti-Racist, Anti-Bias Climates   164
- Table 12.1 Holistic Approach Dimensions   165
- Figure 12.2 Implementing Anti-Racist Policy in Schools   167
- Discipline   167
- The Danger of Social-Emotional Learning (SEL) Programs   168
- The Critical Role of School Administrators   170
- Educator And Student Engagement: Making Time For Talk   173
- Resources   175

Bibliography   177

About the Authors   195

Prologue

Experiencing multiple microaggressions has been referred to as death by a thousand paper cuts. —Shanna K. Kattari, 2017

It is difficult to live in America and not hear of the deaths of multiple people of color (POC) that we witnessed through social media and/or captured by police body cameras. In an article updated on March 28, 2021, on the Washington Post website, where they log every fatal shooting by an on-duty police officer in the United States, it was found that

> although half of the people shot and killed by police are White, Black Americans are shot at a disproportionate rate. They account for less than 13% of the U.S. population, but are killed by police at more than twice the rate of White Americans. Hispanic Americans are also killed by police at a disproportionate rate (The Washington Post, 2021).

The murder of George Floyd on May 25, 2020, appears to have been the tipping point that sparked the already growing movement to end racial profiling, injustice, and inequity in the United States.

Like many other deaths, George Floyd's death was documented for all to see on social media. It is estimated that the George Floyd video, along with other race-related videos were viewed 1.4 billion times between May 25 and June 5, 2020 (Blake, 2020). Additionally, there was a sharp increase in Twitter traffic from May 27 to June 4, 2020, with the hashtag #protest in relation to Floyd's death (Blankenship & Reeves, 2020).

As the nation watched the last eight minutes and forty-six seconds of Floyd's life on video, the already escalating unrest was ignited and the Black Lives Matter (BLM) movement was propelled further into the mainstream.

It was immediately apparent that this time was different, Floyd's death was different, and the nation's response was different as the nation saw its highest level of protests since the inception of #BLM #BlackLivesMatter.

Before Floyd's killing, the Women's March of 2017 held the record for American protests at 4.7 million. By mid-June 2020, three weeks after Floyd's death, polls showed nearly twenty-one million Americans had participated in a BLM protest (CIVIS Poll) and the protesting would continue for months. Then between March 2020 and March 2021, with the uptick in violence and crimes against Asian Americans, the racial discourse surrounding implicit bias continued.

But, why now? Many believe that the pandemic played a role as more people were unemployed or home and paying closer attention. Floyd's death also came after the deaths of Ahmaud Arbery and Breoanna Taylor, making it "the last straw" and helped many white Americans to see that his death was part of a larger issue concerning the treatment of Black people, specifically at the hands of police officers.

It is evident to many, including the authors of this book, that post Floyd's death there is both a heightened awareness of racial inequities and injustices and a heightened determination and dedication to move this country toward a more anti-racist society. As a result, more white Americans, who are also participating in BLM protests in unprecedented numbers, are exploring what it means to be a racist, and how we might work together to develop anti-racist ideas, policies, people, and an overall society.

Since we collectively witnessed Floyd's death through videos and recounts of the incident throughout the trial, more businesses are looking to create anti-racist workplaces, more schools are exploring how to develop anti-racist curriculum and pedagogy, and there is increased pressure for anti-racist policies to be put in place from police forces to government offices. It appears antiracism terminology is making waves. When discussing the term "anti-racist," it is important to note that the term does speak to the racist institutions, actions, and structures in American society, but it also brings in the intersectionality of all oppressed identities.

Author, educator, and anti-racist activist Ibram Kendi defines race as "A power construct of blended human difference that lives socially." Kendi sees racism as, "A powerful collection of racist policies that leads to racial inequity and is substantiated by racist ideas" and a racist idea as "any idea suggesting that a one racial group is inferior or superior to another racial group in any way." Lastly, Kendi defines a racist person as "one who is supporting a racist policy through their action or inaction or expressing a racist idea" (Kendi, 2019, pg. 19).

Conversely, antiracism, according to Kendi, is "a powerful collection of anti-racist policies that leads to racial equity and is substantiated by anti-racist ideas."

An anti-racist idea is, "Any idea suggesting that the racial groups are equal in all their apparent differences." And an anti-racist person is "one who is supporting an anti-racist policy through their actions or expressing an anti-racist idea."

Kendi believes that becoming an anti-racist is a personal journey and one that is best supported by asking oneself, or another, what these terms mean to them. In this way, an anti-racist person is someone who is mindful of his/her actions, or inactions, as well as the impacts she/he may have on others. This is not just the actions or inactions in the realm of race, but in the intersectionality of identities that are often "othered" in America.

An anti-racist is not perfect. An anti-racist does have biases. What makes an anti-racist an anti-racist? An anti-racist is open and able to see the impact of their own biases on others which creates work toward change. In other words, an anti-racist is someone who is intentionally assessing their biases and behaviors, where they originated, the impact they may have on others, and how they may substantiate or perpetuate racist policies and ideas.

Within the wider work of social justice and multicultural education, the term microaggression, coined by Harvard psychiatrist Chester Pierce in 1970, has taken off in recent years with the increased focus on implicit bias, specifically when Secretary Hillary Clinton used the term in a presidential election speech in 2016.

Originally, Pierce used the term microaggression to describe the numerous assaults or abuses he encountered daily as an African American man. Much later psychologist Derald Wing Sue (2010) defined microaggressions as "brief, everyday exchanges that send denigrating messages to certain individuals because of their group membership," which he also relates to his experiences as an Asian American man.

The notion that implicit bias, unconscious racist ideas, or stereotypes toward people is transmitted or communicated as microaggressions became popular in recent years, and the term microaggression became commonly used. Kendi notes that the rise of the term "microaggression" came at a time when some believed having our nation's first Black president meant we were entering a "post-racial era" and "the word "racism" went out of fashion in the liberal haze of racial progress" (p. 46). However, as a respected activist, Kendi goes on to state his objection to the term:

> I do not use the term "microaggression" anymore. I detest the post-racial platform that supported its sudden popularity. I detest its component parts—"micro" and "aggression." A persistent daily low hum of racist abuse is not minor. I use the term "abuse" because aggression is not as exacting a term. Abuse accurately describes the action and its effects on people: distress, anger, worry, depression, anxiety, pain, fatigue, and suicide. What other people call racial microaggressions I call racist abuse? And I call the zero-tolerance policies preventing and

punishing these abusers what they are: anti-racist. Only racists shy away from the R-word—racism is steeped in denial. (p. 46)

Kendi's viewpoint resonated deeply with the authors of this book. The development of new terms to, consciously or unconsciously, soften the impacts of systemic social and racial justice is not new. Nor is the tendency for many to look at our country as beyond the racial era, or deny that racism still exists. We also admit that while we have titled this book *Microaggressions as the Language of Implicit Bias: An Educator's Guide to Creating a Transformative Environment*, we ignored to examine the etymology of the word "microaggression" and how it fails to capture the immense impact that on-going daily acts of abuse have on the recipient, and groups.

Once the authors became familiar with Kendi's work and his strong aversion to the term "microaggression," or any term that was developed to make "it easier to talk about or around the R-word" (p. 47), we, the authors, gave serious thought to how we might modify our work to not distract from or minimize the abuse that millions of students receive daily, rendering their classrooms and schools unsafe. After much reflection and discussion, we chose to continue but to contextualize our work with this cautionary prologue.

We chose this route for one primary reason, access. Access for individuals who are starting their journey toward a culturally integrated, social justice pedagogy and educators who have started and are continuing their journey. Additionally, access for readers to understand that creating anti-racist environments is not only about race.

Individuals of varying diverse identities also experience microaggressions. For example, a religious microaggression occurs when an assignment is due on a religious holiday that is not celebrated by the Eurocentric "mainstream" such as Yom Kippur, Ramadan, or Eid. Or, a family microaggression occurs when a family tree project is assigned without thinking through the difficulties it would present for students who are in foster care, adopted, or have other family dynamics that would prevent the family project from being completed, or from being a positive experience.

Our goal in writing this book is to support teachers in heightening their awareness of the many ways their own biases are transmitted to students, families, and colleagues, and how dangerous the impact is on student learning and overall development. It is only then that they can teach in a more inclusive, culturally competent manner.

As of 2017–2018, approximately 80 percent of America's school teachers are white, with 76 percent women, and most middle class, monolingual, and able-bodied. Yet, the majority of public-school students are minorities (52 percent) who are English language learners (10 percent), living in poverty

(20 percent) or from low-income homes (51 percent) (National Center for Education Statistics, 2020).

Furthermore, in 2015, the United States crossed the threshold of a majority minority newborn population. Derman-Sparks, LeeKeenan, and Nimmo (2015) stated,

> slightly more than half of all babies born in the United States today are a racial or ethnic minority, a threshold first crossed in 2015. Racial and ethnic minorities are expected to make up more than half of the total U.S. population in coming decades. They currently make up about 40% of the overall population, with the share projected to increase to 56% by 2060, according to the Census Bureau projections. (2015)

Therefore, the preschool class of 2020 is the first time the racial and ethnic majority minority threshold has been crossed in the school environment (Derman-Sparks, LeeKeenan, & Nimmo, 2015; Krogstad, 2019). Inevitably, the student demographic will continue this trajectory of "majority minority."

Out of this great dichotomy, a phenomenon known as the cultural gap between students' lived experiences and teachers' lived experiences, it is easy to surmise that many students and their families experience culture shock in schools. It is also easy to imagine how even well-intentioned educators may not see the many ways in which their lack of understanding, or misunderstandings, of students would be transmitted in their daily interactions.

We believe the terms implicit bias and microaggression may feel more accessible to educators than "racist ideas and abuse," even though we use microaggression and implicit bias with reservation. It is also important to note that we view the concept of microaggressions as not about the intent, but the impact.

What Kendi would call racial abuse, we will call racial microaggression, knowing that abuse and microaggression are not synonymous but accessible to a wider range of educators and readers. However, if you, as a reader, are in a place to take the next step in your journey, please read our term "microaggression" as "abuse" throughout this book.

We also agree with Kendi that one cannot be anti-racist without also being anti-sexist, anti-heterosexist, anti-classist, and so on. While in this book we address race and racial bias/microaggressions, we also focus on bias and subsequent microaggressions based on gender, sex and sexuality, religion, socioeconomic status, ability, language and culture, and family structure. We explore the plethora of ways in which these biases are transmitted in schools, and their widely damaging impacts.

Our focus, overall, is on how educators can create more inclusive and safe learning environments by becoming more self-aware, and aware of what it means to be an anti-racist educator. This book has certainly taken us on a journey, and we invite you to journey with us. However, on this journey we must also state community agreements. The community agreements the authors strive to embrace during workshops or courses are:

- Be brave,
- Be honest,
- Be vulnerable,
- Be okay with non-closure.

And, if you are reading this book with a group, during discussions it is also good practice to consider these three additional community agreements or norms:

- Assume good intent,
- Speak from the "I,"
- Confidentiality.

Reflection: Read the following quote. Then, set a timer for three minutes and write. Write everything that comes to mind as you reflect on the quote: "Inclusion means the structure is made for everyone. Transformation is actually what we need to be doing. Don't focus on inclusion into a broken system, but transform the broken system so that inclusion is inevitable" (Reinking, 2021).

Chapter 1

Biases and Stereotypes

Starting at a young age, people will discriminate between those who are like them, their "ingroup," and those who are not like them, their "outgroup." . . . Taken to the extreme, this categorization can foster an "us-versus-them" mentality and lead to harmful prejudice.

—Psychology Today, 2021

When our students walk into classrooms and schools all over the United States, they are walking into environments where the main goal is to create a safe, welcoming, equitable, and inclusive environment for all. However, many practices and communication strategies inadvertently create unwelcoming and unsafe environments. How? Through biases, both implicit and explicit.

Biases, unconscious and conscious, impact graduation rates, social-emotional development, self-concept, and suspension rates of students. Many researchers find that inequality is perpetuated in American classrooms today through biases, often stemming from well-intentioned educators or peers (The Graide Network, 2018). That is the key idea, well-intentioned. It is the hope that educators do not intentionally and consciously create unsafe and unwelcoming environments for students, but it happens. Therefore, it is important to understand the difference between intent versus impact. Essentially, your intent may be good, but what really matters is the impact of those actions or inactions on the person affected.

The research on teacher bias impacting student success or failure stems back to the 1960s when Harvard professor Robert Rosenthal completed an experiment to gauge how teachers' expectations affect student performance (The Graide Network, 2018). This seminal study is the basis for research focused on biases and stereotypes in the classroom. Essentially Rosenthal found that any factor that causes a teacher to have higher expectations for some of their students and lower expectations for others is bound to create results that match (The Graide Network, 2018). In other words, students sense the high and low expectations and fulfill that prophecy through conscious or unconscious actions, thoughts, and self-concepts.

Therefore, the findings from the Rosenthal study support the notion of the self-fulfilling prophecy, or "an individual's expectations about another person or entity eventually result in the other person or entity acting in ways that confirm the expectations" (Jussim, 2016, para. 1). Basically, a teacher acts in a certain way or says statements that indicate to the student that they are met with lowered (or higher) expectations. The student, then, lives up to the perceived expectation.

Hand in hand with this definition is the self-fulfilling prophecy and stereotype threat. The self-fulfilling prophecy is the concept of confirmation bias, which is when an individual takes in new information and interprets the information to confirm one's existing beliefs (Jussim, 2016). An example of this might be a teacher assuming a female student will not be successful in Algebra 2 concepts purely based on the idea that "girls are bad at math." Although the student receives high scores on most of her assignments, the one time that she receives a below average score, the teacher uses that information to confirm the bias of "girls are bad at math."

As outlined in *Whistling Vivaldi* by Claude Steele (2011), individuals who have been taught through socialization what their identity/identities can or cannot do, unconsciously act on those through a self-fulfilling prophecy. This concept is known as stereotype threat. Essentially, a stereotype threat is a "socially premised psychological threat that arises when one is in a situation or doing something for which a negative stereotype about one's group applies" (Steele, 1997, p. 617). In other words, a stereotype threat is when people feel as if they are at risk of consciously or unconsciously confirming a stereotype about their own identity group. This internalized stereotype threat is associated with all types of identities and can undermine successful performance on tasks and activities. The phenomenon of stereotype threat has been studied for decades and very clearly impacts student performance.

In essence, "teachers' belief in their students' academic skills and potential is a 'vital ingredient for student success' because it is linked to the students' beliefs about 'how far they will progress in school, their attitudes toward school, and their academic achievement'" (The Graide Network, 2018, para. 10). Educators' beliefs are critical to developing inclusive and equitable classroom environments.

Another concept under the umbrella of bias is known as blind spot bias. This is important to be aware of because "research finds everyone has a bias blind spot" (Rea, 2015, para 1). But what is a bias blind spot? A bias blind spot is a phenomenon where people are less likely to detect bias in themselves than others. Or, in other words, "believing you're less biased than your peers" (Rea, 2015, para 2).

However, "people seem to have no idea how biased they are. Whether a good decision-maker or a bad one, everyone thinks they are less biased than their peers" said Carey Morewedge, an associate professor of marketing at Boston University (Rea, 2015, para 9). This concept supports the idea that everyone is capable of bias, but we usually only see it in others.

Therefore, being aware of blind spot bias is an essential piece of personal reflective processing. There are several side effects to blind spot bias. One is the inability to evaluate personal bias which, as educators, impacts the learning environment for all students. Other side effects include a decrease in the ability to listen to others' advice and the likeliness, or unlikeliness, of learning from training (or books like this). Therefore, regardless of your self-esteem, intelligence, or actual ability to make unbiased decisions, blind spot bias impacts your life and your actions in and out of the classroom. This is regardless of age, race, ethnicity, gender, sexuality, religion, language, and any other intersectionalities of your identity.

Reflection: Reflecting on the terms "stereotype threat" and "bias blind spot," how might you actively engage in personal reflection to be an agent of change for your students?

BIAS

While there are various examples of bias in the classroom, we will first discuss what a bias is and then the two main types of bias: explicit and implicit.

To begin, a bias is both a verb and a noun. As a verb, bias means that something causes you to feel or show inclination for or against one person or a group of people. As a noun, bias means prejudice in favor of or against a person or group of people. That means we can have a bias for what is called "in group" or individuals who share our identity or a portion of our identity, and we can have a bias against people who may not share our identity or fulfill qualities that we view as unpleasant.

It is important to understand, however, that some of our biases are conscious (explicit) and some of our biases are unconscious (implicit). Either way, it is our duty as educators to ensure that our biases do not negatively impact any student in our classroom or school environment. This can be met through self-reflection and other strategies that will be provided in this book. However, the first step is awareness and acceptance that you do have biases, we all do.

Explicit Bias

What is an explicit bias? Explicit biases are those attitudes and beliefs we have about specific people or a group of people that is at our conscious level, or in other words, racist beliefs that result in abuse. Because explicit biases are at the awareness level, they may create feelings of embarrassment, fear, or shame due to the desire to be politically correct when discussing -isms. Conversely, some individuals may take pride in their explicit biases by acting upon and stating the biases through jokes, discriminatory or exclusionary practices, or violence.

As stated by Kimberly Papillon, Esq.,

> In the case of explicit or conscious, the person is very clear about his or her feelings and attitudes, and related behaviors are conducted with intent. This type of bias is processed neurologically at a conscious level as declarative, semantic memory, and in words. Conscious bias in its extreme is characterized by overt negative behavior that can be expressed through physical and verbal harassment or through more subtle means such as exclusion (n.d., para. 1).

While this book discusses biases in the field of education, the legal system is also a system that incorporates explicit biases into their practices. Understanding explicit biases embedded in the legal system can provide a sociopolitical and historical context to societal acceptance of those biases. As a microcosm of society, this acceptance will definitely impact schools' ability to provide a safe, welcoming, and equitable environment for all students.

For example, in an article by Jessica A. Clarke (2018), it is stated that

> the law does not need empirical methods to identify bias when it is marching down the stress in Nazi regalia, hurling misogynist invective, or trading in anti-Muslim stereotypes. Official acceptance (through court decisions) of such prejudices may be uniquely harmful in normalizing discrimination (p. 505).

Taking this concept even further, it has been found that in court hearings "employment discrimination cases prevent juries from hearing evidence of explicit bias" (Clarke, 2018, p. 505), such as in the case of police shootings based on the explicit biased fear of Black bodies.

IMPLICIT BIAS

While explicit biases are conscious, there are also implicit biases, which are unconscious. Implicit biases are the attitudes or stereotypes that affect our understanding, actions, and decisions in an unconscious manner (The Kirwan

Institute, 2012). Implicit biases are activated involuntarily, without awareness or intentional control and can be either positive or negative. Since race is a social construct, everyone is susceptible to racist beliefs at an unconscious level.

The term implicit bias was first coined by social psychologists Mahzarin Banaji and Tony Greenwald in 1995 in a paper focused on their theory of implicit social cognition. Essentially, they stated that social behavior is largely influenced by unconscious associations and judgments, specifically implicit social bias (Cherry, 2020).

Kimberly Papillon, Esq. discusses the great impact implicit bias can have on teaching and learning,

> Implicit or unconscious bias operates outside of the person's awareness and can
> be in direct contradiction to a person's espoused beliefs and values. What is so
> dangerous about implicit bias is that it automatically seeps into a person's affect
> or behavior and is outside of the full awareness of that person (n.d., para 2).

Implicit biases are those attitudes and beliefs that we have about specific people or groups of people that are at our unconscious level. Most of our biases are at this level, especially without deep reflection or introspection. Since implicit biases are unconscious we cannot disclose them because we are unaware of them. This is what makes implicit biases so dangerous, the lack of awareness at the conscious level, and what makes self-reflection and awareness so important.

Regardless of what implicit bias is in action and word, the process of unconsciously judging individuals or groups of people is a normal behavioral phenomenon (De Houwer, 2019). While many people want to believe they are not susceptible to biases or stereotypes, reality and science argue that making associations and generalizations with things in our world is the way our human brain works, such as the phenomenon of confirmation bias described earlier. Therefore, everyone has implicit biases, but it does not mean that we are prejudiced or inclined to discriminate; our brain is simply working as it was designed to make associations and generalizations (Cherry, 2020).

As imagined, implicit biases influence not only our day-to-day lives but also how schools and classrooms are designed. We are all influenced by our environment, which is an environment where we are all "racism breathers" (Delpit, 2013). A society where children are born to love, but are taught hate through curriculum, interactions, and historical factors that impact how our society functions within a hierarchy state based on identity, or as Kendi would state a hierarchy based in racism.

In summation, explicit and implicit biases can be represented in a visual depiction, another iceberg. The portion with the iceberg above the water, the part that is seen, is representative of the explicit biases we are aware of and see. The portion of the iceberg below the water, the part we cannot see, is representative of the implicit biases, which are unconscious or sometimes oblivious to us. The part under the water, the implicit biases, are hard to see without intentional investigation, reflection, and questioning. This is the part of the iceberg we, as educators, need to work on becoming aware of and fighting against.

LADDER OF INFERENCE

Associated with the idea of bias is the theory/concept known as the Ladder of Inference, displayed in figure 1.1.

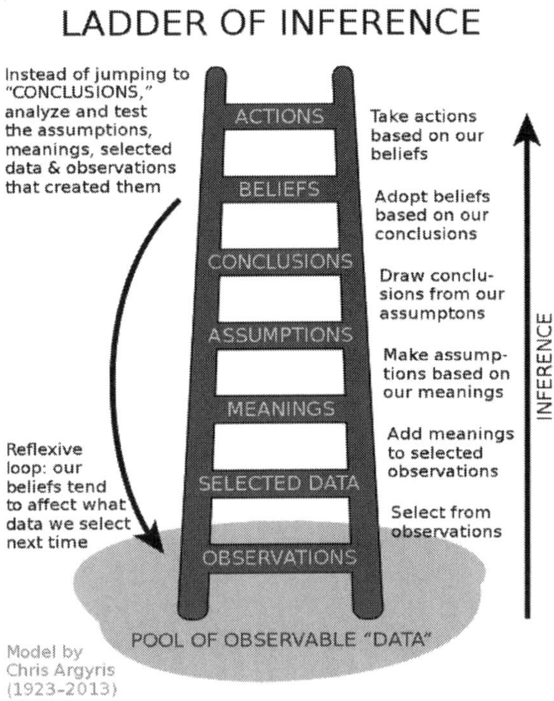

LADDER OF INFERENCE

Instead of jumping to "CONCLUSIONS," analyze and test the assumptions, meanings, selected data & observations that created them

ACTIONS — Take actions based on our beliefs

BELIEFS — Adopt beliefs based on our conclusions

CONCLUSIONS — Draw conclusions from our assumptons

ASSUMPTIONS — Make assumptions based on our meanings

MEANINGS — Add meanings to selected observations

SELECTED DATA — Select from observations

OBSERVATIONS

Reflexive loop: our beliefs tend to affect what data we select next time

INFERENCE

Model by Chris Argyris (1923-2013)

POOL OF OBSERVABLE "DATA"

Figure 1.1   The Ladder of Inference. *Source*: Model Developed by Chris Argyris (blog, trainerswarehouse.com).

The Ladder of Inference was coined by Chris Argyris (1982) and used by Peter Senge (2006) in *The Fifth Discipline: The Art of Practice of Learning Organization*. This ladder or theory displays the fact that our beliefs have a big impact on what we select from reality. This can lead using our knowledge of reference to make assumptions, rather than look at the reality through the eyes of the other individual or group. Essentially, this way of thinking which all humans do instinctively, can create a vicious cycle.

The ladder can be used in several ways. As we are discussing the Ladder of Inference, keep these two questions in mind:

1. Challenge personal beliefs/actions.
2. Challenge other's beliefs/actions.

Before diving into how the Ladder of Inference coincides with biases and the Actor Observe Framework, it is important to define four characteristics of bias:

1. Purposeful reflection is needed to combat biases; however, everyone possesses biases regardless of intentional self-growth.
2. Everyone is wired to categorize new information, hence engaging in bias.
3. Biases have real-world effects on behavior, such as in a classroom setting or school environment.
4. Biases are malleable and can be unlearned with work, reflection, and action (Staats, Capatosto, Tenney, & Mamo, 2017).

Therefore, by understanding the automatic process depicted by the Ladder of Inference, we can see growth can occur and biases can be unlearned.

The automatic process of moving quickly up the Ladder of Inference utilizes the wired brain function known as the reflexive system. This portion of the brain is deviated to automatic processing, which is often unconscious or implicit (National Center for Cultural Competence at Georgetown University, n.d.a). However, when we consciously push against actions and words based on prejudiced biases, we are using our reflective system that asserts our values, such as all people/children deserve to be in an environment that is safe, welcoming, and equitable.

So, how can well-meaning people have bias? Cognitive psychology provides insight into this paradox. It has been found by cognitive psychologists that when humans are faced with "understanding, processing, and acting on complex information, cognitive systems work to simplify the effort. These systems use categories and stereotypes rather than the individual details of the situation in an effort to reduce the cognitive load" (National Center for Cultural Competence at Georgetown University, n.d.a).

Confounding this paradox is the fact that when humans are in a stressful situation, the learning brain turns "off" and the instinct or old survival brain turns "on." This intensifies our move toward stereotyped assumptions that are outside of our conscious awareness, but may be in direct contrast to our conscious beliefs and values.

The self-protective, unconscious, reflexive process that operates quickly, within milliseconds, is our brain moving up the Ladder of Inference. The bits of information used to make judgments are based in experiences or beliefs embedded from a young age through early socialization. Through the Ladder of Inference, feelings, beliefs, and attitudes about the individual or group are then imposed on a person. Toward the top of the Ladder of Inference, when the cycle is able to begin again, bias takes over especially in times of stress, and is expressed in affect, body language, and/or differential treatment.

Overall, understanding the reflective and reflexive systems, as well as the Ladder of Inference, is not an excuse or "pass" to be discriminatory, but it provides context and a place to understand the reality, and where growth needs to take place.

The Ladder of Inference can also be partnered to the Actor-Observer Framework, which states that people tend to explain their own behavior with situation causes and other people's behavior with person-centered causes (Jones & Nisbett, 1971). For example, minority students who are struggling with academic achievement as compared to their equivalent white peers in college courses may be described by the observers as lazy, low expectations, lack of motivation, or assumed family obligations.

However, when speaking directly to the minority students (i.e., the actors), it was discovered that campus wide marginalization of minority students impacted their academic success (Steele, 2011). The solution, in turn, becomes organizational change rather than further marginalization of the observed actors. This framework supports the concept of the Ladder of Inference because the inferences the observer makes are based on stereotypes, experiences, or even confirmation bias when in situations with historically marginalized populations.

Reflection: Refer back to two questions about the Ladder of Inference. How can knowing about the Ladder of Inference be used to:

1. *Challenge personal beliefs/actions.*
2. *Challenge other's beliefs/actions.*

THE LANGUAGE OF STEREOTYPES: MACROAGGRESSIONS

Biases and microaggressions are complex and are a result of the -ism breathing we all do within our society (Delpit, 2013). Biases and microaggressions are connected through the simple truth: microaggressions are the language of implicit bias. This entire book is based on the microaggressive actions and nonactions (verbal, nonverbal, motions, noises, or the nonexistent acknowledgment) individuals experience daily within the education system.

As defined by Columbia University's Derland Wing Sue (2010), a microaggression is a prejudice that leaks out in many interpersonal situations and decision points through slights, insults, indignities, and denigrating messages. However, microaggressions are not the only type of aggression, albeit abuse, experienced in society, there is also the experience of macroaggressions or the language of stereotypes.

Macroaggressions, the actions of stereotypes, are defined as large-scale or overt aggression toward those of a certain race, culture, gender, and so on focused on identities of individuals or group members. While macroaggressions are not yet recognized in the Merriam-Webster dictionary, society, especially marginalized groups, have known and experienced macroaggressions for generations. Macroaggressions are the overt actions that support prejudices. One of the many examples of overt actions is setting policies around types of hairstyles allowed in schools or workplaces.

While there is a dearth of scholarly information on macroaggressions, as compared to microaggressions, researchers Druery, Young, and Elbert (2018), discuss the influx of macroaggressions in the United States between the years of 2016 and 2020. Examples cited focus on the power of language inciting hateful actions to groups of people. As stated in their research, examples show up in institutions, on social media, and through language.

For example, Chastity Jones was fired from her job for wearing locs, Rachel Sakabo was fired from an upscale hotel after she refused to cut her locs, and Zendaya (actress) was criticized on the red carpet for her faux locs (Finley, 2016; Greene, 2017). Each of those situations shows how "implicit bias constantly rears its ugly head when it comes to black hair" (Finley, 2016, para. 12).

Specifically referring back to Chastity Jones' case, "The Alabama Court of Appeals voted 3–0 to dismiss the discrimination lawsuit, thus upholding the 2013 Jones decision (ibid.). However, we consider this legal decision a macroaggression due to the legal precedent it sets—that the natural state in which a woman grows her hair is unacceptable in our society" (Druery, Young, & Elbert, 2020, p. 76).

Another example we have seen in recent history is when Malia Obama, one of the daughters to President Obama and Michelle Obama, was accepted to Harvard. On the social media platform, *Fox News*, people were commenting overtly racist comments, a form of macroaggression, stating that Malia needs to get a "colored disease" like AIDS. While the comments by themselves are microaggressions, the sheer number of the overtly racist, aggressive, and defamatory comments creates the macroaggression impact (Druery, Young, & Elbert, 2020).

Regardless if it is a microaggression or macroaggression, the actions and words all stem from the socialization process we all experience. In other words, it stems from our Cycle of Socialization.

CYCLE OF SOCIALIZATION

One question we may ask ourselves is, how do we develop implicit biases or how do microaggressions become part of our lives? As stated by Lisa Delpit (2013) in her book, *Multiplication is for White People: Raising Expectations for Other Peoples' Children,* we are "racism breathers." In another description of our unconscious development of implicit biases, as depicted in a video put out by the Freedom Project Wa (2019), two narrators state,

> we have all grown up in a culture with media images, news images, conversations we heard at home, our education. Think of it as a fog we have been breathing our whole life. We never even realized it, what we are taking in. And that fog causes association that leads to biases.

An example they use in the video is a socialized association between Black men and violence. Through racist ideas, concepts, and embedded mindsets received through interactions in our society, we implicitly make the association between Black men and violence. This process of learning through "breathing the fog" can be outlined using Bobbie Harro's (2000) Cycle of Socialization.

In figure 1.2, the Cycle of Socialization is presented.

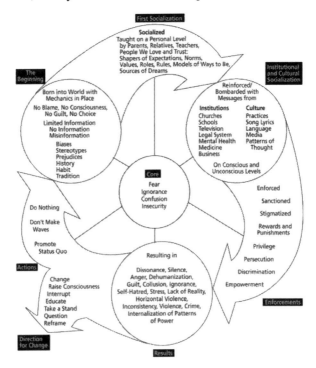

Figure 1.2   Cycle of Socialization. *Source:* https://depts.washington.edu/fammed/wp-content/uploads/2018/06/Cycle_ofSocializationHandout.pdf.

In this cycle it is evident that the core of our socialization is led by fear, ignorance, confusion, and/or insecurity. These concepts turn the wheel, or are the precipice for either stagnation, which would continue the cycle of bias, or change to interrupt the status quo. We have the choice to continue the stagnation of oppressive thoughts, actions, and environments, or decide to change to create an equitable and safe space for all individuals.

The outside of the cycle consists of three circles starting at the beginning, moving to institutions and culture, and ending with the result. Overall, the Cycle of Socialization "helps us understand the way in which we are social-ized to play certain roles, how we are affected by issues of oppression, and how we help maintain an oppressive system based upon power" (Adams, Bell & Griffin, 1997, para. 1).

The first circle represents the beginning of our life, what we are born into. At this point in our life, we do not have control of the messages we are receiving or the people we are around. We either are born into privilege or not, which is often accompanied by racial profiling, lack of power, and discrimination. Furthermore, as soon as we are born, we are embedded in the socialization process, which is represented by the first (top) arrow.

Are we given a pink blanket or a blue blanket? Are we given white baby dolls or black baby dolls or no baby dolls but only trucks? Am I allowed to wear a dress or not allowed to wear a dress? Do I hear positive words regarding differences or negative words regarding differences? What are the subtle or not so subtle rules of gender, race, and other identities that are being communicated in the first years of socialization? What we learn in our first experiences with socialization is our family or community view of "right" or "good" and "wrong" or "bad." Will we have consequences if we rebel and/or be praised if we conform?

After the first circle and arrow in the cycle is the second circle and arrow. "The second circle represents the institutions that help shape our views and beliefs, and help instill within us prejudice or acceptance" (Adams, Bell, & Griffin, 1997, para. 4).

How does the institution and history of medicine impact us if we decide to go to the doctor when we are sick? How does the institution and history of education impact us if we have positive or negative experiences? How does media, song lyrics, or the practices of the legal system impact our view of the world, our implicit biases, and our prejudices for or against a group of people or institution? How does social media and what peers or acquaintances post impact our views, experiences, and socialization?

Extending from the second circle is the second arrow which repre-sents how ideas, beliefs, and behaviors are instilled into the systems and into our thought processes. These are the concepts of institutional and structural racism, gender dynamics in the workplace, and overall complacency.

As is illustrated in the Cycle of Socialization, going against the status quo is not easy because we are rewarded for doing "good" according to the Eurocentric view of good, and punished for being bad, or going against the Eurocentric view by rebelling or questioning oppressive societal norms.

The third and final circle in the cycle represents "the devastating result upon all of us that this self-perpetuated cycle of oppression produces" (Adams, Bell, & Griffin, 1997). We internalize and act on the oppressive ideologies of silence, dehumanization, and power. Stemming from this final circle, we have a choice. We have the choice to do nothing and continue to perpetuate the cycle of oppression or we can do something, speak out, learn, reflect, and push against the oppression in our society.

This relates directly to Kendi's work of enacting change as part of being or becoming anti-racist. However, if we continue with the cycle and to not "break off" we are continuing the "fog" of marginalization (i.e., racism). We can push back on the fog of implicit bias and stereotypes through activism. Therefore, throughout this book, you will be given the opportunity to reflect, change, and dive deep into the fog we are all breathing in our society.

Reflection: Reflect and process your socialization through each of the steps within the Cycle of Socialization. A short video located here, https://www.youtube.com/watch?v=mPp7uaGYdDw, also provides grounding in this process of reflection. Use the example below to assist in the process.

A brief personal reflection example:

The Beginning: I was born into a family that had generational wealth, generations of Christian beliefs, generations of landowning, generations of "helping the other," and generations of living in the Midwest in communities that were homogeneously white. The biases of body image, othering people of color, and a history of wealth influenced me from the beginning. I was born into privilege: access to education privilege, economic privilege, racial privilege, and religious privilege.

These three identities, identities I had no choice in upon birth, provided me advantages throughout life. I was born into privilege and the dominant culture in many of my identities.

Arguably, these identities led to my medical privilege. When I was born to my white mother, I had the umbilical cord wrapped around my neck, reportedly so tight that the doctor had a hard time getting his finger between my neck and the cord. Knowing the statistics of Black maternal and infant death at birth compared to white mothers and babies makes me wonder that if my skin and my mother's skin was a different color, would I have made it past day one? (Statistics: "Black babies died at a rate of 10.97 per 1,000 births— more than twice the rate for white, Asian or Latin newborns" (Lakhani, 2020). "Black maternal mortality rate is 2.5 times higher than white" (Boyd-Barret, 2020).)

First Socialization: From my experiences and interactions through socialization, I was taught that we "help the other," which generally meant people who were poor and people of color in our community. I grew up with migrant workers transitioning in and out of my community yearly, which also socialized me to develop a view of Mexican children and families. A continued first experience in my family was also focused on body image and "othering" people who were obese through comments or jokes. So, what were the expectations I learned? Stay healthy with your weight, help people who are different from you (socioeconomic and race), and, to be honest, "our way is the best way" to live life.

Institutional and Cultural Socialization: I experienced churches that were homogeneously white. I experienced schools that were homogeneously white for most of the year (outside of when the migrant children would attend school). I experienced only white doctors, white business people, and the Midwest hospitality practices. These experiences were reinforced through recognition of my white and socioeconomic privilege.

Results: Eventually this resulted in a lack of reality at a young age, especially for the experiences of peers. Looking back, I realize that some of my peers were experiencing adversity and I was not aware of that at the time. They were experiencing foster care, poverty, domestic violence, and questions about their own sexuality. This ignorance resulted or played out in a way of silencing and dehumanization through jokes, invitations (or no invitations) to parties, and an overall lack of reality for what was going on around me.

So, what have I decided to do? Raise consciousness, question, and take the arrow aimed in the direction of change.

Which arrow are you choosing to take?

Now that we have a collective and foundational understanding of bias and the supporting factors to recognizing impulsive reactions based on stereotypes, the reflection process can begin. As you read each chapter, take notes, write in the book, think about how this information impacts you as an educator, and begin or continue the process of growth with the goal of creating a welcoming, safe, and equitable environment for all regardless of students' intersectional identities.

Throughout the rest of the book, we will discuss microaggressions, with respect to the specific identities of race, gender, religion, economics, ability, linguistic and family dynamics, which is directly related to the social identity wheel, which will be discussed further in a later chapter. We will also discuss culturally responsive teaching as an antidote to microaggressions, and ways to interrupt microaggressions in schools.

As you continue through this book, the authors ask that you keep an open mind and create a practice of self-reflection.

Reflection: One Word. What is your one word to summarize your thoughts or feelings after reading this chapter? What is your one word?

Examples of one word are provided in this word cloud (figure 1.3), which was created by using the words in this chapter.

Figure 1.3   One Word, Chapter 1. *Source*: Created by Bouley & Reinking, 2021.

Chapter 2

The Impact of Implicit Bias and Microaggressions

Microaggressions may present as an innocuous comment or behavior, but have the impact of highlighting a person's "difference" from the majority represented group. Microaggressions can occur anywhere.

—Nicole Vassell, 2020

As already inferred in the book title, microaggressions are the language of implicit bias. The term was originally coined by Chester M. Pierce in the 1970s to describe the "subtle insults and put-downs that African Americans experienced regularly" (Smith, 2020, para. 5). However, in the 2000s Asian American researcher and professor at Columbia University, Derald Wing Sue expanded the definition to include any comment or action that negatively targets groups of marginalized people or individuals. The microaggression can be intentional and/or unintentional verbal, nonverbal, and environmental slights, brush-offs or disrespectful comments. The message microaggression sends is damaging to people predicated exclusively upon the fact that they belong to a disenfranchised group (Lynch, 2019; Sue, Capodilupo, Torino, Burcceri, Holder, Nadal, & Esquilin, 2007).

When discussing microaggressions, it is important to know that the impact of the microaggression has numerous effects on the individual or group. They can negatively impact social-emotional well-being, a strong self-concept, academic success, and a multitude of other factors, many associated with the impact of trauma since microaggressions are traumatic.

Furthermore, it is important to remember that the intent of the offender does not truly matter, but rather what is most important is the detrimental impact of the microaggression on the individual (victim). A very well-intentioned person may emotionally harm another individual through the actions they enact or the words they use. The terms "victim" and "offender" are based on the practice of Restorative Practice within a school. There is no insinuation that a person experiencing a microaggression is powerless through the use of the term "victim," but rather these terms are being used as a way to ground our conversations throughout the book.

FORMS OF MICROAGGRESSIONS

Microaggressions come in three different *forms* of communication styles: verbal, behavioral, and environmental (Smith, 2020). It is important to be aware of and reflect on each form of microaggression.

A verbal microaggression is a comment or question from an offender that is hurtful or stigmatizing to a marginalized individual or group of people, the victim/s (Smith, 2020). An example of a verbal microaggression is a subtle racial slight experienced or witnessed by an underrepresented individual, the victim (Lilienfeld, 2017).

A behavioral microaggression happens when someone, the offender, behaves in a way that is hurtful or discriminatory to a marginalized group of people, the victim/s (Smith, 2020). An example of a behavioral microaggression is ignoring underrepresented individuals (Lilienfeld, 2017).

An environmental microaggression occurs when subtle discrimination occurs within society (Smith, 2020). An example of an environmental microaggression is naming all buildings on a college campus after white individuals (Lilienfeld, 2017). While the direct offender and victim relationship is not as clear with an environmental microaggression as with verbal and behavioral microaggressions, there are still negative impacts that result for the marginalized individual or group.

TYPES OF MICROAGGRESSIONS

According to psychologist Derald Wing Sue and colleagues, there are three *types* of microaggressions which can take any of the three forms. The three types are microassaults, microinsults, and microinvalidations. Table 2.1 outlines the differences between the three and provides examples.

Table 2.1 Types of Microaggressions. *Source:* Created by Bouley & Reinking, 2021 based on the work of Sue (2010).

Type	Definition	Example
Microinsult	Comment or action that demeans a person's identity	Teacher: You speak really good English Asian American Student: Thank you? Implication: Asian American students are not assumed to speak English clearly (Nadal, 2014).
Microinvalidation	Comment or action that excludes or negates a person's thoughts, feelings, or experiences	Teacher: I don't see color. We are all human and that is what we will focus on Implication: Racism does not exist and when you experience racism that is not a true reality (Nadal, 2014)
Microassault	Common or action that explicitly disparages a victim, while not intending to be offensive	Student to student: "That is so gay" Teacher: Silent Implication: Gay means weird. If you are gay, then you are weird (Nadal, 2014).

Microaggressions impact all facets of a student's development and school experience, including the implementation of discipline practices. Let us first reflect on the academic, mind-body connection that is impacted by microaggressions.

Reflection: Think about a time in school when you learned something very well. Maybe you approached the learning with a great deal of confidence, or maybe you weren't confident at all, but someone else believed in you and so you persisted and did not give up until you mastered the task. What role did other people's beliefs play in your learning? Under what conditions do you think you learn best?

There is no question that most of us would say we learn best when we feel confident, are highly motivated, have an interest and/or prior knowledge on the topic. However, if an adult in our life such as a teacher or caregiver does not believe in us, developing motivation, confidence, interest, success, or even knowledge is difficult. The right conditions for optimal learning involve relationships with others who hold us to high expectations, take time to get to know us, and use that knowledge to differentiate ways to support our learning, nudge or challenge us, and ultimately treat us with respect. We learn best when our relationships are based on the four Crucial C's (care, connect, courage, and capable) (Bettner & Lew, 1990), which will be discussed further in the next chapter.

Our reflection to our "optimal learning environment" is also supported by research, which states that when teachers demonstrate respectful and caring dispositions, students are more likely to experience academic success. They are also more likely to develop a positive affect toward learning, and themselves. Therefore, the conditions under which we learn the best are dictated by teacher-student interactions and relationships, the single most important aspect of teaching. Educators, you are the change agents.

However, the dichotomy between the teaching force and student body, the cultural gap as discussed earlier, heightens the potential for teacher-student interactions that are based on misinterpretations, miscommunications, trepidations, and expectations based on implicit/explicit biases.

This results in an increased likeliness that students from marginalized groups are targets of implicit bias and microaggressions in school. These on-going experiences impact students negatively in every developmental domain, from mental and physical health, to academic achievement, to behavior and discipline. Students with marginalized identities suffer at the hands of educator's unconscious associations or biases.

SOCIAL-EMOTIONAL DEVELOPMENT
AND THE MIND-BODY CONNECTION

Over the past thirty years brain research focused on learning has developed tremendously. We now know there is a direct connection between social-emotional development and academic learning. When the brain perceives a threat, it responds by shutting down or off. In fact, not only does the brain makes it difficult for us to think in that moment, we know that these perceived threats can have a direct impact on the wiring of the brain, resulting in a life-long impact. We know for sure that there is a direct connection between the mind and the body.

A threat could simply be a timed test, being randomly called on in class, or participating in a competitive academic exercise. The perceived threat could make it impossible for the student to complete the task. When students consistently have these experiences, they come to equate their classroom as unsafe, which has an impact on every aspect of their development from academic learning to social-emotional development to behavior and overall health.

The most important role of the teacher is to intentionally and consistently work at developing a positive interpersonal classroom environment for all of his/her students. The best way to create a safe interpersonal classroom environment is through positive teacher-student interactions and relationships and reflecting on the four Crucial C's (Bettner & Lew, 1990).

Reflection: On a piece of paper write down two columns, and in one column make a smiley face, in the other column a sad face. On the happy side, write down three teachers who have been your favorites, who have made a positive impact on you. On the sad side, write down three teachers that have negative connotations. Next to each teacher, try to write down three reasons why your experiences with that teacher were positive or negative. What do the reasons have in common? Notice any patterns?

People often name dispositions to explain why they held either positive or negative feelings toward a teacher. Rather than say things like, she really knew her content well or he was a skilled teacher, positive teacher connotations are usually due to dispositions such as she liked me, showed me respect, cared about me, believed in me, was patient, funny and enthusiastic, didn't have favorites, got to know me, and so on.

Negative teacher connotations are often due to polar opposite dispositions, but still dispositional traits nonetheless, such as she didn't like me, never got to know me, treated me differently than others, didn't care, and so on. All of this has to do with teacher-student interactions and relationships, and the critical role their relationships play in establishing a safe, social-emotional environment, one that is conducive to development in all domains.

In addition to the common social-emotional threats that students experience in academic settings and in conjunction with teacher-student interactions, some students may also experience consistent microaggressions due to their culture, race, gender, sex, sexuality, religion, economics, ability, body, language, age, national origin, and so on. These experiences may be unknown to the teacher (implicit bias), but leave the student feeling shame, frustration, misunderstood, sadness, anger, low self-esteem, and more.

Culturally aware and responsive teachers recognize that there may be a myriad of ways in which their interactions with students more similar to themselves may come with more ease and accurate understanding. When a student's social or cultural identity differs from the teacher's cultural gap, a culturally responsive teacher (CRT) is proactive in learning about those differences and shows interest in bettering their interactions. Showing these "signs of caring" is not only important with students, its importance also extends to families (Association of California School Administrators, 2021).

However, when a teacher fails to acknowledge differences or how they may impact interactions, biases are transmitted in numerous ways that students see and feel, but may be unconscious or not recognized by the teacher. These microaggressions create a hostile work environment and have a direct negative impact on a student's social-emotional and academic development.

Even worse, often other students pick up on the teacher's bias, and begin to mimic the behavior. As a result, historically marginalized students often experience implicit bias and microaggressions at the hands of all school personnel, from teachers to students and from administrators to cafeteria workers making school a very difficult place to learn, or even be.

THE LANGUAGE BEHIND MICROAGGRESSIONS

As discussed, the impact of microaggressions can vary from hurtful to abusive and can have negative repercussions to all aspects of development: emotional, social, and academic. While the intent may not be to cause harm, the impact is in fact harmful.

Building on the forms and types of microaggressions, there are also themes or overarching categories of microaggressions. Table 2.2 breaks down the language of microaggressions and provides explicit examples of how implicit biases and microaggressions can be interpreted by underrepresented individuals and groups. As you can see, the impact or message varies; however, the same sentiment is there: you are less then and do not belong "here." In this way, microaggressions are experienced as racist ideas and behaviors and perpetuate the basis of racism, superiority vs. inferiority.

Reflection: What microaggressions have you experienced or seen? Did that impact your relationship or interaction in that environment? How?

The impact of microaggressions has numerous physical and social implications for students and adults alike. It has been argued in academic circles that experiencing microaggressions is considered a traumatic experience, which then associates all of the psychological, physical, and social ramifications of trauma in the lives of students and adults (Moody & Lewis, 2019). Negative impacts such as feeling disconnected, the inability to trust people, the inability to manage strong emotions due to overstimulation of the anxiety hormone released in the brain and body.

At a Diversity Dialogue that took place at Harvard University in November 2019 titled "Mental Health and Ethnicity," it was stated that "microaggressions contribute to an onslaught of injuries to the psyche that may seem unrelenting and can result in everything from depression, fatigue, and anger to physical ailments such as chronic infections, thyroid problems and high pressure" (Gehrman, 2019, para 4).

Microaggressions are like a "thousand little cuts" to our psychological, physical, and mental well-being. And, while many of the examples will be race based, it is important to remember that you do not need to be a person of color to experience the daily onslaught of microaggressions.

The psychological consequences of experiencing microaggressions include anxiety, depression, sleep difficulties, diminished confidence or self-esteem, intrusive thoughts, and/or diminished cognition. Dr. Joy Bradford, a licensed psychologist and host of the mental health podcast, Therapy for Black Girls, spoke to the psychological impact of microaggressions. In an interview with Pfizer, she said, "The experience of having to question whether something happened to you because of your race or constantly being on edge because

Table 2.2 Microaggression Messages

Microaggression	Theme	Implicit Bias	Impact (Message)
Where are you really from?	Alien in own land	Assumption of being foreign-born based on race or ethnicity	You are not an American. You don't belong here (the United States)
You are so articulate and clear.	Ascription of intelligence	People of color are less intelligent than white people	It is unusual for someone from your race to be intelligent
I love that necklace, is it a family heirloom?	Classist	Assuming everyone has generational wealth to pass on heirlooms	Your family is not rich and cannot pass on wealth through material items
All lives matter. There is only one race, the human race.	Color blindness	Since race doesn't affect me (a white person), that it must not be something that impacts anyone	Denying someone's identity and racial/cultural being
Crossing the street when a person of color approaches.	Criminality	A person of color is presumed to be dangerous and deviant purely based on their race.	You are a criminal and are dangerous.
So, who is the man in the relationships?	Heteronormativity	Assuming that all relationships must fall within heteronormative lines and gendered norms.	You must pick a side for your relationship to be a "real" relationship. Your relationship isn't valued since it does not have a man and woman
Smile, it makes you seem more approachable.	Sexism	Stating that male affect and behavior is the standard and everything must fall in line with gendered roles from the 1950s.	You are not being listened to and valued, but rather are present for looks only. It is your role (female) to make people feel comfortable.
You're just being too sensitive. You're always so difficult.	---------	---------	Your statement about the microaggression I just committed is invalidated and not relevant.

(Continued)

Table 2.2 Microaggression Messages (*Continued*)

Microaggression	Theme	Implicit Bias	Impact (Message)
School buildings and team mascots that are predominately White heterosexual upper-class males.	Environmental	Assuming harm cannot take place through pictures and names alone.	You do not belong and are not welcome here. This is not a safe, equitable, and welcoming environment for you.
Pictures in schools that are predominately White heterosexual upper-class males.			
	Denial of Individual Racism		I cannot be racist because I have Black friends.
			I can understand what you experience with racial oppression because it is the same as my gender oppression
	Myth of Meritocracy		People of color are lazy, incompetent, and just need to work harder to get ahead in life
	Pathologizing Cultural Values		Cultural values and experiences are not welcomed and will not be discussed because it has no impact on our interaction
	Second-Class Citizen		You are lesser and do not belong here

your environment is hostile can often leave people feeling invisible, silenced, angry, and resentful" (2020).

Physical consequences of microaggressions are feeling unsafe and/or having actions done to you that are unsafe. For example, the killing of Black bodies at the hands of police officers is a microaggression that has life-ending physical consequences. Dr. Bradford, during the same interview mentioned above with Pfizer, stated, "Additionally, the increased stress related to things like microaggressions in the workplace and experiences with discrimination can lead to physical concerns like headaches, high blood pressure, and difficulties with sleep, which of course impact our mood as well" (2020).

Finally, the social-emotional (also known as social and relationship) impact of microaggressions on victims can result in diminished trust, which ultimately impacts the establishment of rapport and safety between and among individuals and groups. La-Rhonda Harmon, during an interview with Katie Smith (2019) of the Philadelphia College of Osteopathic Medicine, stated,

> In school or the workplace, microaggressions are dangerous because they marginalized and ultimately underutilized talent, impair recruitment and retention, erode an individual's performance, stifle innovation and growth, inhibit teamwork and collaboration, and adversely affect business growth.

Regardless if the microggression's impact is social, psychological, relationship based, physical, or a combination, victims are often made to feel excluded, untrustworthy, and as if they are a second-class citizen or abnormal. It is our duty as educators to ensure learning environments are free of subtle or overt slights to a student's identity.

IMPLICIT BIAS AND TEACHER-STUDENT EXPECTATIONS

One of the most important roles of the teacher is to have high expectations for all students at all times. Research strongly suggests having high expectations positively impacts student performance and growth in all domains. At a basic level, having high expectations is a sign of caring and let's students know you believe in them.

Since it is fair to say that a teacher's high expectations for a student can have a life-lasting impact, it's critical that teachers engage in on-going reflective practices, examining ways their implicit bias impacts their expectations.

In 1968, Robert Rosenthal and Lenore Jacobson conducted experiments in elementary schools where they told teachers the names of students who had "unusual potential for intellectual growth" over the next school year. Even though these students were chosen arbitrarily, when they returned at the end of the year those students scored significantly higher on the posttest than the other students in the class.

These studies demonstrated that a teacher's positive expectations impact academic development positively, and negative expectations have a negative impact. Rosenthal and Jacobson (1968) referred to this discovery as the Pygmalion Effect. The Pygmalion Effect suggests that higher expectations lead to higher performance. Their explanation was that when a teacher has high expectations for a student it directly impacts their own behavior, how they interact and teach that student. They believed when certain behaviors of others are expected, we are likely to act in ways that make the expected behavior more likely to occur (Rosenthal and Babad, 1985).

Reflection: Studies show expectations, low or high, are communicated to students verbally and nonverbally (Babad, Bernieri, & Rosenthal, 1989). How do you communicate to your students that you have high expectations? What are some of your experiences or beliefs that might result in you having lower expectations for some students some of the time? How are your beliefs transmitted? Have you noticed the impact your beliefs and expectations have had on your students?

The Los Angeles County Office of Education (2011), developed a teacher training program in the early 1970s called Teacher Expectations and Student Achievement (TESA). The professional development program was designed to support the academic achievement of all students by heightening teachers' awareness of how their beliefs were transmitted to students in daily interactions and instruction. TESA is designed "to modify the way teachers interact with students through heightened awareness of how perceptions affect their expectations" (para. 2).

The Los Angeles County Office of Education states that numerous studies show that "using TESA interactions enhances student academic performance and gender and diversity awareness. It also improves attendance and classroom climate, and reduces student discipline problems." A great deal of research supports the role teacher expectations plays in student performance (Bennet, Gottesman, Rock, & Cerullo, 1993; Brophy & Good, 1970; Ready & Wright, 2011; Rubie-Davies, 2007).

In TESA, teachers are trained to support the development of each other's awareness by observing one another while teaching and taking specific notes on the TESA Observation Coding Form. With this self-reflection and support teachers can learn how they may be transmitting different expectations for different students, and the impact their behaviors have on student performance.

Reflection: Reflect on your interactions with students and your teaching strategies. Do you call on boys more than girls during math and science? Do you give more wait time to Asian American students than students of other races? Do you accept less writing from African American boys than other students? Is your grouping based on ability for reading or math and or do you have flexible, changing groups? Have you ever had assumptions of how a student will perform based on the performance level of her older sibling? What might a colleague notice if he/she were to observe?

Albert Bandura (1977), is best known for his theory of self-efficacy. Bandura believed that self-efficacy, one's beliefs about their ability to master a task, was strongly correlated with achievement of that task. Bandura found that when an individual was self-efficacious, they were more likely to persist, staying motivated to accomplish the task at hand while exhibiting good coping skills and less stress.

Bandura (1977), believed there are four "sources" of self-efficacy. He believed having mastery experiences as the best way to develop self-efficacy. He also believed that "vicarious experiences provided by social models" developed self-efficacy. Simply put, seeing someone like me achieve the task at hand makes me feel more efficacious that I can do it too. In addition, he found that one's interpretations or misinterpretations of their emotional state was a source of self-efficacy.

For example, when one is self-efficacious their emotional response, maybe the nervousness they feel, energizes them and supports their performance. But when they lack efficacy, that emotional response is debilitating and has a negative impact on their performance. Lastly, Bandura saw "social persuasion" as an important source of self-efficacy. When teachers have high expectations for students and offer verbal persuasion and support, students become more efficacious and are more likely to not only believe they can succeed but also show more persistence, determination, and effort in doing so (Bandura, 1977).

When teachers have either too low or too high expectations for their students, it is called biased expectations (de Boer, Bosker, & Van der Werf, 2010; Timmermans, Kuyper, & Van der Werf, 2015). Low biased expectations can manifest in students as low self-efficacy and not only lead to low performance but become sustaining self-fulfilling prophecies.

Studies have shown that biased expectations tend to be based on student identity such as race, ethnicity, gender, socioeconomic status, and so on (Timmermans et al., 2015). Students who are minorities and/or low income are more likely to experience negative biased expectations from their classroom teacher, thus creating a self-fulfilling prophecy or stereotype threat situation (Gay, 2010; Glock, Krolak-Schwerdt, Klapproth, & Bohmer, 2013).

Geneva Gay (2010) discusses the perverseness and harm of negative biased expectations in her work on CRT. Having high expectations for all students, including students of color, is a relevant theme of CRT. Gay (2002) states,

> Teachers need to understand that culturally responsive caring is action oriented in that it demonstrates high expectations and uses imaginative strategies to ensure academic success for ethnically diverse students. Teachers genuinely believe in the intellectual potential of these students and accept, unequivocally, their responsibility to facilitate its realization without ignoring, demeaning, or neglecting their ethnic and cultural identities (p. 110).

Similar to Gay, the researcher Schunk (2003) sees high expectations as "action oriented" and suggests it involves trust and active engagement with on-going feedback/communication. Ladson-Billings' work on effective teaching practices for African American students found that the teachers who were most successful were ones who understood the role societal views of African Americans played in expectations of students.

De Boer et al. (2018) found there are essentially three proposed interventions for addressing teacher biased expectations:

> The first is to instruct teachers to apply behaviours associated with high-expectation teachers. The second approach is to make teachers aware of the effects of teacher expectations on students and to explain that teacher expectations can be inaccurate and/or biased towards particular groups of students. The third approach focuses on addressing the beliefs of teachers that underlie the biased expectations towards student achievement (p. 182).

The role teacher expectations play on student achievement is well documented in research. Equally well documented is the role implicit bias and stereotyping play in creating biased teacher expectations. Negatively biased expectation is a microaggression that is easily understood and deeply felt by students of underrepresented groups. The consequences are great.

Reflection: One Word. What is your one word to summarize your thoughts or feelings after reading this chapter? What is your one word?

Examples of one word are provided in this word cloud (figure 2.1), which was created by using the words in this chapter.

Figure 2.1   One Word, Chapter 2. *Source*: Created by Bouley & Reinking, 2021.

Chapter 3

Multicultural Education

An Antidote for Implicit Bias and Microaggressions

> *Multicultural education is a philosophical concept built on the ideals of freedom, justice, equality, equity, and human dignity as acknowledged in various documents, such as the U.S. Declaration of Independence, constitutions of South Africa and the United States, and the Universal Declaration of Human Rights adopted by the United Nations.*

—The National Association for
Multicultural Education, 2020

Multicultural educators strive to know and affirm student identities and create classrooms and schools that are based on inclusion and equity, and are safe and welcoming for all. Multicultural, anti-racist anti-bias educators create spaces where social and racial injustices are openly and honestly discussed, problematized, and analyzed. As such, Culturally Responsive Teaching (CRT) is an antidote to implicit bias and microaggressions.

Multicultural education is based on plurality and principles of social justice. The goals of a multicultural education are to affirm students' personal, social, and cultural identities, and also to prepare all students to thrive in a pluralistic world or a world where citizens have more acceptance and understanding toward differences. To be comfortable with difference is to know difference, and a multicultural educator strives to help students understand themselves and others. Furthermore, getting to know individuals who are different from you is one of the most effective ways to break down implicit bias or associations and replace them with more positive associations.

A multicultural, anti-racist educator thinks through the lens of multiculturalism by not engaging in surface-level inclusion (i.e., "celebrating" African Americans in February), but rather engages in a practice that permeates every aspect of teaching, and an ethos that consistently and vocally challenges and advocates for social justice. To do this, it is essential that educators develop both cultural awareness and cultural competence.

Cultural awareness is understanding and knowing one's own cultural identity, as well as the traditions, values, beliefs, attitudes, behaviors, and histories of various cultural groups. Cultural competence is being competent, or skilled, at using that awareness and knowledge to direct one's instruction and interactions with students, families, and colleagues. In higher education we want our teaching candidates to have knowledge, skills, and dispositions toward all aspects of teaching and learning.

An educator who is culturally aware demonstrates the knowledge and disposition of a multicultural educator. An educator who is culturally competent demonstrates the ability and desire to translate that awareness and knowledge into practice and integrates cultural awareness into all aspects of their pedagogical and interpersonal practices.

Thus, as the National Association for Multicultural Education (NAME) purports, the multicultural educator who has developed cultural awareness and competence,

> advocates the belief that students and their life histories and experiences should be placed at the center of the teaching and learning process and that pedagogy should occur in a context that is familiar to students and that addresses multiple ways of thinking (The National Association of Multicultural Education, 2021).

All multicultural education should start with developing teacher self-awareness. This is especially important when discussing implicit bias and micro/macro aggressions. Educators are human, and as humans we have all been socialized to believe certain social constructs and stereotypes of varying social groups and identities. Everyone has implicit bias. The multicultural educator is continuingly examining his/her biases and associations and is intentional in working to remain open and honest about them, and exploring ways they may be transmitted to students, families, and colleagues.

Reflection: Think about beliefs and biases in four ways. First, what are biases and beliefs you learned from your family or caregivers growing up? Second, what groups of individuals did those biases and beliefs target? Third, how do you feel about the social group targeted by those biases today? Finally, how might your beliefs and biases, which you likely learned throughout your life, be transmitted to your students?

CULTURALLY RELEVANT PEDAGOGY AND CULTURALLY RESPONSIVE TEACHING

Culturally relevant pedagogy and CRT are subsets of multicultural education. The term culturally relevant pedagogy was coined by Gloria Ladson-Billings and focused on increasing engagement and academic success of students from diverse cultures who have historically been excluded. In doing so, culturally relevant pedagogy looks to support all students in developing positive cultural and academic identities, as well as call attention to the pervasive inequities and inequalities in education.

CRT, developed by Geneva Gay, focuses more specifically on instructional strategies to meet the same goals. Gay (2010) defines CRT as, "using the cultural knowledge, prior experiences, frames of reference, and performance styles of ethnically diverse students to make learning encounters more relevant to and effective for them" (p. 31).

Geneva Gay sees CRT as teaching that identifies and integrates the cultural backgrounds and experiences of all students, especially students of color who have historically been left out of curriculum, materials, and pedagogy, in an effort to make learning more meaningful and relevant to their lives which, in turn, leads to more academic success. When students' home lives, families, interests, and experiences are integrated into curriculum, classroom instruction, and interactions, it supports students in developing not only stronger academic identities but stronger cultural and personal identities as well.

In this way, a CRT is one that cares about his/her students. Gary Howard (2010) developed what he calls the *Seven Principles of Culturally Responsive Teaching* which demonstrate that his definition of CRT centers on the notion that relationships precede learning (figure 3.1).

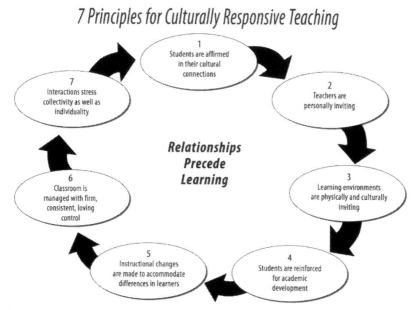

Figure 3.1   Seven Principles of Culturally Responsive Teaching. *Source*: https://www.edu catored.com/CourseResource/course/103993/681656/ce5dbb6a681e4fab90324a915da 8f897_Seven%20Principles%20for%20Culturally%20Responsive%20Teaching.pdf.

Howard points out that the first three principles focus on, "honoring students in their cultural connections, being personally and culturally inviting toward our students, and creating learning environments that are inclusive and welcoming and richly representative of the many diversities our students bring to our schools." He calls those "the front porch" of learning and believes the seven principles to be "profoundly grounded in relationships" (Association of California School Administrators, 2020).

Building relationships with their students is exactly how educators learn about them. It is through these relationships that educators can develop their cultural awareness and cultural competence to be effective and caring, CRTs. It is also how educators can become aware of, and replace, any notions of stereotypes or implicit bias. Once educators build "the front porch" and break down the barriers that implicit bias creates, student engagement and success will follow.

Another way to ensure the building of the "front porch" is by focusing on the four Crucial C's, which was created by Betty Lou Bettner, MSW. The four C's are: connect, courage, capable, and count. Betty Lou Bettner, a family therapist and social worker, took Adler and Dreikurs' theories about and identified the four Crucial C's that work together to help us feel a sense of significance and belonging in a constructive healthy way. Children, and adults, are constantly seeking ways to feel that they connect to others, that they are capable, that they count (are valued), and that they have courage (1990).

Reflection: What strategies do you use to cultivate relationships with your students? In what ways do you demonstrate signs of caring? Think of a time when you struggled to build a relationship with a particular student? What do you perceive were the obstacles? How did you get around them?

In addition to the above aspects of multicultural education, cultural awareness and competence, culturally relevant pedagogy and CRT, it is important to discuss the role cultural capital plays in multicultural education. The Oxford University Press (2021) defines cultural capital as,

> a term introduced by Pierre Bourdieu to refer to the symbols, ideas, tastes, and preferences that can be strategically used as resources in social action. He sees this cultural capital as a "habitus," an embodied socialized tendency or disposition to act, think, or feel in a particular way (para. 1).

Pierre Bourdieu (1986), postulated that cultural capital, which he believed to be generational and passed down within families to students, has a direct impact on students' ability to obtain academic success. Bourdieu believed that students with cultural capital come to school with a road map, intentionally or unintentionally written by their families, which shows them how to successfully navigate their educational experiences.

For instance, students with cultural capital may have heard "the language" of school from their families, their families may be more actively involved in their education, and they may have more social and economic resources to support their academic success. One example that we see in higher education relates to first-generation college students. First-generation students may not have come to college having inherited the "language" of college from their families (i.e., the role of good advising early on, to withdraw from a course if needed to protect your GPA, etc.), and this lack of preparation or prior knowledge, capital, can impact their ability to succeed.

A multicultural educator understands that not all students come to school with the same cultural capital. Instead of treating students with less capital as less capable, educators see that some are simply more privileged and prepped for success. Rather than making implicit associations, the multicultural educator actively works to fill in the gaps and level the playing field. In addition, a multicultural educator works to remain aware of their own cultural capital, and the ways in which it might keep them from seeing, and supporting, all students. Understanding your own privilege is an important step to becoming more consciously aware of your unconscious bias or associations.

Understanding your own privilege will also help guide conversations in the classroom. Recently a sixth-grade student was discussing college choices with one of his teachers. During the conversation the teacher made a statement that included the term "first-generation students." Confused by this statement, the sixth grader asked, "There are some people who would be the first people in their family to go to college?" The teacher, being aware of this student's cultural capital, was able to engage in a conversation of capital, privilege, and awareness.

Reflection: What cultural capital do you have that your students and families do not? What cultural capital may your students not be aware of, such as the example above? How might either of these reflections get in the way of building relationships with your students, and teaching them effectively?

SOCIAL IDENTITY WHEEL

Similarly, to cultural capital, is social capital. People are grouped by social identity primarily based on social, physical, and mental attributes such as race, gender, sex, sexual orientation, ability/disability, and so on. Some of these attributes are highly visible, such as physical abilities or skin tone, and often ascertained by schools and other government organizations, while others can be invisible, such as sexual orientation. There is a tendency to want to organize or categorize people by their identities, and society strongly influences how we do so.

The Social Identity Wheel (Univeristy of Michigan, n.d.) identifies the following social groups: race, ethnicity, gender, sex, sexual orientation, religion, socioeconomic status, physical/emotional/developmental (dis)ability, language and culture, age, and national origin. It provides the impetus for in-depth reflection of our social identities and invites individuals to determine with which group(s) they self-identify or are ascribed to. After exploring and identifying their own identities, participants are asked:

- Which identities do you think about the most in your daily life (it's most salient to you)?
- Which do you think about the least?
- Which of your identities do you think is most salient to students?
- Which of your identities do you think have had the greatest effect on your life?
- Which identities put you in a dominant position, and which put you in a subordinate position?

These prompts for self-examination can be seen on the Social Identity Wheel in figure 3.2.

Reflection: How do you identify/what are your social identities? Explore your identities and then answer the questions above. What do you know about your students' identities? How do you know that? Where/how do your and your students' identities meet, where/how do they miss? (For more activities, visit this website:

Figure 3.2 Social Identity Wheel. *Source*: https://sites.lsa.umich.edu/inclusive-teaching /wp-content/uploads/sites/853/2021/03/Social-Identity-Wheel.pdf.

INTERSECTIONALITY

Many of the identities depicted in the Social Identity Wheel, as well as other identities, intersect to create individuality. It is important for individuals to explore the complex nature of their own identities, or the concept known as intersectionality. The concept of intersectionality was made popular by law professor Kimberlee Crenshaw in 1989. In the article "Mapping the Margins," Crenshaw describes the complex identities individuals juggle throughout their life. Identities that overlap privilege, power, and oppression (Coleman, 2019). Failing to acknowledge the complexity of identities, or the intersection of multiple identities within oneself or students, "is failing to acknowledge reality" (Coleman, 2019, para. 11).

The identities that create our intersectionality can be defined as our pastimes, familiarities, personal experiences, or anything that is in the Social Identity Wheel and beyond as a fact of your self-identity. These are the characteristics that come to mind as we define who we think we are. Our social identities clearly impact our personal identities in numerous ways. For instance, an individual's socioeconomic status has a direct impact on their ability to develop hobbies, go on vacations or excursions, or have access to a high-quality public or private education.

Our social identities can influence the experiences we have in both positive and negative ways. Some identity groups are oppressed, targeted, or marginalized, and others are dominant, privileged, and afforded agencies that members of subordinate groups lack. Dominant groups or identities are socially valued, and as such enjoy social capital. Individuals who identify as a member of a group or groups that are socially marginalized are constantly reminded of how they are not valued, respected, or represented, as they lack social, political, and/or economic power. For example, until recently with the appointment of Rachel Levine, the first openly transgender official to serve in any Senate-confirmed position as the assistant health secretary in Joe Biden's administration, members of the oppressed transgender identity were, and arguably still are, left out of conversations regarding reproductive health, sport team membership, and gender.

Also, important to note is how we make assumptions of ourselves and others based on social identities. Our social identities impact how others perceive and treat us, or if they are even open to getting to know us. How we identify and behave, and how that varies in different contexts. Since people with marginalized identities are often judged by assumptions, and as such are targets of implicit/explicit bias and microaggressions, they may find they need to behave differently in different contexts or settings.

At times this is even done for survival. A tragic, yet pervasive, example is how Black men must be excruciatingly mindful of their behavior when pulled over by a police officer, or one might suggest, in every public setting. This has become even more apparent with the mandate of masks in public places during the Covid-19 pandemic. The masking of Black men has anecdotally increased fear and quick Ladder of Inference judgments that can impact physical, social, and psychological safety for Black men.

An important role of the multicultural educator is to identify ways in which students of marginalized groups experience implicit/explicit bias and microaggressions based on their identities, from both educators and their peers. Once identified, multicultural educators can explicitly and collectively work to dismantle assumptions and biases in effort to minimize associations and aggressions. In this way they are using their cultural and social capital to advocate for students and families who are oppressed. One specific way to do this is to be aware of the hidden curriculum that exists in schools.

THE HIDDEN CURRICULUM

The hidden curriculum is a concept that describes the often unarticulated, unacknowledged, and unconscious concepts students are taught in school through teacher language, school policies, and curriculum, that affect learning and overall self-esteem. The term "hidden curriculum" focuses on how schools create inequitable environments and was popularized, although around prior, in 2018 with the publication *Curriculum Development* by P.P. Bilbao, P.I. Lucido, T.C. Iring, and R.B. Javier (Crossman, 2019).

The hidden curriculum is defined as,

> the unwritten, unofficial, and often unintended lessons, values, and perspectives that students learn in school. While the "formal" curriculum consists of the courses, lessons, and learning activities students participate in, as well as the knowledge and skills educators intentionally teach to students, the hidden curriculum consists of the unspoken or implicit academic, social, and cultural messages that are communicated to students while they are in school (The Glossary of Education Reform, 2015).

The hidden curriculum touches every aspect of education. So much so that The Glossary of Education Reform (2015), prefaced their list of examples with, "While the hidden curriculum in any given school encompasses an enormous variety of potential intellectual, social, cultural, and environmental factors—far too many to extensively catalog here." They go on to identify examples such as cultural expectations (lowering academic expectations for students based on tracking-level, family history, social class, culture, ability, immigration status, etc.), cultural values (school values transmitted in various ways such as cliques, "He's a jock, he won't do well in an AP class," or tolerance of prejudice, "That teacher was right there when you yelled "fagot" at him and she didn't do anything!" etc.).

The Glossary of Education Reform (2015), then goes on to discuss curricular topics (teaching history from a Eurocentric perspective, failing to represent women's contributions when teaching science or the LBGTQ+ population in sex education, etc.), teaching strategies (rewarding only compliant behaviors, always or never asking students to work in groups, giving extra credit for things that are not in reach for some students, etc.), school structures (not making AP classes accessible to all, separating English language learners, placing the special education classrooms in the basement, etc.), and institutional rules (saying some African-American hairstyles don't align with school policy, or having specific dress codes for females so they don't show "too much skin," etc.).

Loaded messages, such as the ones outlined above, are transmitted from educators to students and students to students pervasively in schools, on the bus, in after-school activities or sports, and so on. These messages tell and show students how to perceive and interact with individuals based on their social identities and groups.

This is called the hidden curriculum because individuals may not know they are transmitting these assumptions or beliefs and/or they are doing so to satisfy status quo. As a result, all students may be victims of stereotypes, assumptions, and biases. This is taken to the next level, though, for students of marginalized groups or with oppressed identities as they are more likely to be bullied, ostracized, or exempt from the opportunities necessary to succeed. The hidden curriculum just perpetuates that behavior.

Another aspect of the hidden curriculum is the outright omission of the values and experiences of marginalized groups or identities. What is *not* being taught in schools is also a part of the hidden curriculum. Remember, as we reflected on in the prologue, "Silence is loud." This omission is not limited to the exclusion of historically underrepresented or marginalized groups, but also the exclusion of any discussion or acknowledgment of the privileges or cultural and social capital of those with dominant identities.

In a study focused on the intersection of audism and racism, researchers found that when curriculum is non-diverse Black d/Deaf college students experience highly oppressive learning environments (Stapleton, 2016). Another study that focused on the impact of hidden curriculum, specifically in physical education learning environments. The results of the study show that "hidden curriculum perpetuates positive or negative outcomes in physical education" (Jung, Ressler, & Linder, 2018, p. 262). Furthermore, the hidden curriculum embedded into physical education programs "shapes the values, norms, and attitudes" of students (Jung, Ressler, & Linder, 2018, p. 262).

Through the implementation, conscious or unconscious, of the hidden curriculum, educators perpetuate the status quo results in schools that are breeding grounds for implicit bias, and micro/macro aggressions.

STATUS QUO

According to the National Center for Education Statistics (2020), in the 2015–2016 school year, there were 3.8 million full and part-time public-school teachers. Seventy-seven percent of those teachers were female and,

> 80 percent of public-school teachers were White, 9 percent were Hispanic, 7 percent were Black, 2 percent were Asian, and 1 percent were of two or more races; additionally, those who were American Indian/Alaska Native and those who were Pacific Islander each made up less than 1 percent of public-school teachers.

Further, "average salaries were higher for Asian than for Hispanic teachers and were higher for White teachers than for Black teachers and teachers of Two or more races." Lastly, the percentage of Black teachers went down since the last survey in 1999–2000 from 8 percent to 7 percent (National Center for Education Statistics, 2020).

Bottom line: American public-school teachers, from preschool to high school, are predominately white, middle-class, heterosexual, English-speaking European Americans. The majority of American children go through thirteen years of school without seeing a single teacher that breaks from that demographic. And yet, the incentives or invitations have not increased for college students of color or any marginalized identity to enter the teaching force.

At the same time, findings from a research study conducted by the National Bureau of Economic Research titled, *The Long-Run Impacts of*

Same-Race Teachers, suggest that if Black students have just one Black teacher in their public-school career, they are 13 percent more likely to go to college, and if they had two, the odds go up to 32 percent (2015–2016) (Gershenon, Hart, Hyman, Lindsey, & Papageorge, 2021). Representation matters.

In the same year as the National Bureau of Economic Research findings, 2015–2016, public schools served 49.3 million children. In 99 percent of those schools, there was at least one student with an Individualized Education Plan (IEP), 76 percent of the schools had specific instruction for English language learners, more than 50 percent of the students qualified for free or reduced lunch, 49 percent of the students from preschool to grade 12 were white, 15 percent Black, 26 percent Hispanic, 5 percent Asian/Pacific Islander, 1 percent American Indian/Alaska Native, and 3 percent two or more races (Gershenon, Hart, Hyman, Lindsey, & Papageorge, 2021).

In sum, in 2015, 51 percent of public-school students were non-white and more than 50 percent were living in poverty. For perspective, in fall 2000, 61 percent of students were white, that's a reduction of 15 percent in fifteen years. The projected numbers for 2027 show an even greater disparity between the teaching force and student body, with only 45 percent of students identified as white (Gershenon, Hart, Hyman, Lindsey, & Papageorge, 2021).

In light of this, and in review of this chapter, it is easy to see how the wide majority of teachers have cultural awareness/competencies/capitals and social identities that are drastically different than their students'. It is not far-fetched to surmise that this discrepancy creates schools and classrooms full of misunderstandings, miscommunications, assumptions, implicit bias, and micro/macro aggressions.

Reflection: What is the demographic makeup of your school? What school-wide discussions or practices take place to address the disparity between educators and students and families?

One of the misunderstandings that often occurs under the umbrella of multicultural education is definitions for culture and diversity. It is important to understand what culture is, and what it is not. It is not purely stereotyping that is based on countries. For example, adding artifacts into your room or a language into your room that is "Chinese culture" or "Mexican culture" is not truly understanding all of the experiences, traditions, and knowledge that are embodied in the term "culture." There is individuality within cultures and groups of people.

People may look the same, sound the same, or even share multiple other identities, but their culture could be drastically different. A good graphic to understand culture is located in figure 3.3. This is the culture tree, illustrated by Aliza Maynard in the book *Culturally Responsive Teaching and the Brain,* by Zaretta Hammond (2015). The top part of the tree is the "surface culture" or the "observable patterns (with) low emotional impact on trust" (p. 24). The trunk of the tree is the "shallow culture" or the "unspoken rules (with) high emotional impact on trust" (p. 24). Finally, the roots of the tree are the "deep culture" or the "collective unconscious beliefs and norms (with) intense emotional impact on trust" (p. 24). All of these parts are important to understand and accept.

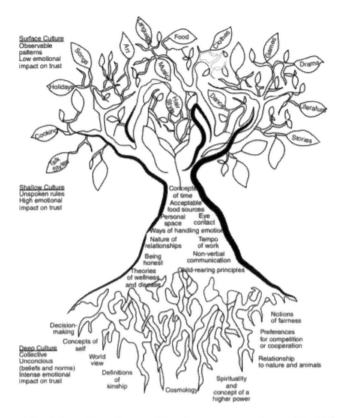

Figure 3.3 The Culture Tree. *Source:* https://resources.corwin.com/sites/default/files/0 3._figure_2.1_culture_tree.pdf.

Diversity is the other term often misunderstood or misrepresented in conversations surrounding multicultural education. Specifically, diversity is "The practice or quality of including or involving people from a range of different social and ethnic backgrounds and of different genders, sexual orientations, etc." (Lexico, 2021, para. 2). In figure 3.4, what diversity is and is not is depicted as a way to truly understand and reflect on your own practices of engaging in conversations and lessons around the term diversity.

CANNOT: [is NOT]	CAN: [IS]
Cannot be taught directly	Can learn about backgrounds (personal)
Is not a curriculum	Similarities and differences between and among people
Not a lesson plan	See themselves, their families, and their communities represented throughout
Not only Cinco de Mayo, Black History Month, or Chinese New Year	Continually exposed activities, materials, experiences to destroy stereotypes
Not people dressing up in costumes, wearing headdresses or eating tortillas	Appreciating and seeking differences
	Many ways to solve a problem or answer a question

Figure 3.4   Diversity Is and Is Not. *Source*: Created by A. Reinking, 2021.

Finally, multicultural education involves having enough cultural awareness and competence to be a culturally responsive teacher—one who cares enough to get to know her/his students and their families and is skilled at using that information to differentiate instruction and interactions to best meet the identities and needs of all students.

Educators must also be aware of social and cultural capitals, and social identities, and the ways in which they impact a student's access to, and experiences in education. With such a great disparity in demographics between public-school teachers and their students it is easy to see how, even in schools with the best intentions, the hidden curriculum is alive and well. Many educators are struggling to support students with marginalized identities, and many are not aware of the ways in which they transmit implicit bias. In the midst of all of this, implicit/explicit bias and micro/macro aggressions are sure to flourish.

As we dive into the language of bias and its impact on students, it is important to reflect on this quote: "Words are containers of power. How are you going to use yours?" (Baldridge, 2015). How are we, as educators, going to use language that creates equitable environments for all students, regardless of their identity?

Reflection: One Word. What is your one word to summarize your thoughts or feelings after reading this chapter? What is your one word?

Examples of one word are provided in this word cloud (figure 3.5), which was created by using the words in this chapter.

Figure 3.5   One Word, Chapter 3. *Source*: Created by Bouley & Reinking, 2021.

Chapter 4

Section 2

In Section 2, we are going to explore individual identities through the lens of microaggressions. Since we strongly believe that becoming an anti-bias, anti-racist educator is a personal journey that demands constant reflection and self-awareness, we have created Section 2 to be interactive and reflective.

Before reading and reflecting on the chapters focused on identity microaggressions, we need to define terms and concepts. Specifically, we will define the terms anti-bias educator and anti-racist (-ism) educator, we will outline the three choices to consider when addressing microaggressions, the concept of calling in or calling out, and finally we encourage you to return to the previous to re-read the sections on intersectionality and clearly understand the concept of intent versus impact.

An anti-bias educator is an educator who focuses on the four domains of the Social Justice Standards: identity, diversity, justice, and action (IDJA), as defined by Learning for Justice (2018) (formerly Teaching Tolerance). Within these standards, anti-bias educators focus on one of two areas:

1. Reduce prejudice: This focuses specifically on minimizing conflict and changing attitudes or behaviors of the dominant group.
2. Advocate for collective action: This focuses specifically on challenging inequality by raising consciousness and focusing on improving conditions for underrepresented groups.

The definition of anti-racist educator is also provided on the Learning for Justice website. An anti-racist educator:

- Believes in love.
- Studies and is committed to deepening their critical consciousness.

- Moves away from checklists and embraces a holistic approach.
- Focuses on healing and love in action.

Overall, "anti-racist educators believe in the intellectual power of teaching. They believe they have to honor the practice and take teaching very seriously because they know and understand how schools have been used either to oppress or to liberate" (Pitts, 2020, para. 11).

Aside from defining anti-bias and anti-racist educator, there are three choices we all have when choosing to address microaggressions (Washington, Birch, & Roberts, 2020). We can let it go, respond immediately, or respond later. The researchers who developed this idea also provide a framework for deciding on which response in best for the situation. Specifically, you:

1. Discern: How much do you want to invest in addressing the microaggression?
2. Disarm: Make known the conversation may be uncomfortable, but invite them to join in the difficult conversation. This is the process of "calling in," which will be discussed further on.
3. Defy: Challenge the perpetrator with a probing question, such as "What do you mean by that?"
4. Decide: Take control of how the microaggression incident will impact your life. Will you let it take from you or will you learn something from the interaction? In this step it is important to remember that "intent does not supersede impact." In other words, your feelings and reactions matter more than the intent of the perpetrator.

The important piece of this framework is the concept of choice. It is important to remember you have a choice to call someone into the conversation, call someone out, or do nothing. What is meant by calling in or calling out?

The importance of calling people into a conversation was re-introduced in March 2019 when "New York congresswomen Alexandria Ocasio-Cortex tweeted a message to her progressive followers about the importance of "calling in" (Austrew, 2021, para. 2). While the definition of "calling in" has changed over the centuries, in current social justice circles "calling in" refers to "the act of checking your peers and getting them to change problematic behavior by explaining their misstep with compassion and patience" (Austrew, 2021, para. 5). In 2013, the activist Ngoc Loan Tran explained the concept of calling in as a useful way to address oppressive behavior among people you trust and want to continue a relationship with, such as a friend.

The concept of "calling out", or in current culture what is known as "speaking truth to power," is possibly more familiar because it is a strategy many individuals use when responding to social media posts or in other public arenas. Calling someone out is a public and direct challenge to something someone has said or done. The purpose is to expose the person's wrongdoing to others (Austrew, 2021). The impact of calling someone out is usually malicious and spreads false information. Calling someone out is in opposition to calling someone in because the process of calling out lacks empathy and patience.

Which one is better for classroom discourse? According to Learning for Justice (@learnforjustice), "When we call students out instead of building a call-in culture in the classroom, we contribute to increasingly toxic and polarized conversations. And we make learning less inviting" @Loretta JRoss. Essentially, "calling in is a tool for reaching others in safe situations, and it can be particularly useful if you are someone from a privileged group who can do the work of calling in others who share your privilege and challenging their problematic beliefs" (Austrew, 2021, para. 16). Whichever route you choose, the important thing is to not be silent.

Reflection: As you prepare to continue your journey through this book, reflect on the following quote: "Silence is loud. Speak up. Act out. Be bold."

We ask that you return to this quote as a way to ground yourself in the transformative work of creating equitable environments for all. And finally, as we move into the chapters focused on identity it is importance to recognize that there is individuality within each group, however we have chosen to develop this book around identities as a way to ground all of our work in becoming aware of our implicit biases.

Chapter 5

Racial Microaggressions

Seemingly innocuous statements, that in the context of racist assumptions and stereotypes, are actually quite harmful (such as):

"When I see you, I don't see color."

"We are all one race, the human race."

"I wish I could change my hair everyday like you do with all the fun hairdos. Is that a wig?"

—Washington, Birch, & Roberts, 2020

Why is understanding racial bias important? In a study by Walter Gilliam and his team at the Yale Child Study Center, implicit bias was measured among preschool teachers. From this study, and recent data from the U.S. Department of Education, it was found that "black children are 3.6 times more likely to be suspended from preschool than white children. Put another way, black children account for roughly 19 percent of all preschoolers, but nearly half of preschoolers who get suspended" (Turner, 2016, para. 13).

Connected to the concept of confirmation bias, Gilliam postulates that teachers are looking for "bad" so they are looking toward the Black boys. This is based on many concepts, one of which is the negative view of "Black" in the American culture. Important to point out from this study is that the teacher's race did not impact the bias against Black or Black boys.

Furthermore, in another study, it was found that preservice teachers graded students who appeared to have a migrant background worse than students who did not appear to have a migrant background (The Graide Network, 2018). Overall, racial bias stems from centuries of a white privileged view in society, which embraces the unconscious, often unrecognized, process of embracing the Ladder of Inference through a biased point of view. The dominance of privilege takes hold and impacts everyday life.

Figure 5.1   Macro, Micro, Impact, ABE. *Source*: Created by Bouley & Reinking, 2021.

When searching, "common racial stereotypes" many are populated. Some include the idea that indigenous peoples are silent and stoic, Arab and Middle Eastern peoples are anti-American terrorists or barbaric, Black peoples are loud, animalistic, or magical, Latinx peoples are maids or gardeners, and Asian Americans peoples excel in science, technology, engineering, and math (Nittle, 2020). Most of these stereotypes are not only prevalent in daily life but are reinforced through the Cycle of Socialization, specifically media such as television shows, movies, and commercials and confirmation bias.

All racial microaggressions are based in the center of the Cycle of Socialization, fear or ignorance of the unknown perpetuated by white privilege and hegemony. Hegemony is the social, cultural, ideological, or economic influence exerted by a dominant group. It is the dominance or leadership of one group over another. White privilege is the societal privilege that benefits white people over non-white people in some societies, particularly if they are otherwise under the same social, political, or economic circumstances.

White privilege, as defined by Schumer (2020), does not "imply that white people haven't struggled, just that our (white) challenges aren't related to the color of our (white) skin" (para. 1). From this definition, the collective "we" understand that the concept of privilege is position not a feeling. However, the way the definition is written is problematic. The definition was written with a hegemonic view of "white as dominant" through the assumption that the readers of the article shared the authors' racial identity, white, through the use of the word "our." Remember, language is powerful.

White privilege infiltrates all parts of society from language, to policies, to "acceptable" and "unacceptable" hairstyles, to interactions with the law. These topics, along with the ones outlined below, all support the hegemonic view of white as dominant in American culture. As stated by Jacob Bennett, education researcher, society has "the power of normal. If public spaces and goods, like, 'acceptable' hairstyles and relegating certain foods to 'ethnic' aisles in the grocery store, cater to one race and segregate the rest into special sections, that's indicative of an unequal society" (Schumer, 2020).

Overall, white privilege does not negate experiences of white people, but recognizes that it is a privilege to not experience or empathize with the racial microaggressions experienced by Black, Indigenous, People of Color (BIPOC) individuals on a daily, hourly, and sometimes a minute-by-second basis. One activity that is often used to understand personal white privilege, if you self-identify as white, is to go through your family history and point out times that privilege assisted in familial gains. This process also helps individuals and groups of people understand the historical contexts of white privilege.

For example, author Reinking's grandfather was educated through the GI Bill, a bill that was only available to white people when it was first introduced. When Reinking was born the umbilical cord was wrapped around her neck. Knowing the high rate of Black infant and mother deaths at birth, the privilege of being white in a hospital in the 1980s could have helped in her and her mother's survival. Finally, Reinking's family had land, farms, and businesses that passed on wealth for generations before she was born. As a white family in America this was a privilege, while many Black families had their wealth taken from them during the same generations Reinking's family was acquiring wealth.

It is imperative to acknowledge white privilege, especially if you are white. This realization that whites privilege exists is essential to growth for all educators toward anti-racist practices. "You can be a target of oppression AND oppress others. IE—you can be black and perpetuate anti-blackness" @LearningToLiberate.

Furthermore, the COVID-19 pandemic has shed light on the macroaggression of educational disparity. According to *Morning Edition* (2021),

> As of January and early February of this year (2021), . . . the survey found large differences by race: 68% of Asian, 58% of Black, and 56% of Hispanic fourth graders were learning entirely remotely, while just 27% of White students were. Conversely, nearly half of white fourth-graders were learning full-time in person, compared with just 15% of Asian, 28% of Black and 33% of Hispanic fourth-graders. The remainder had hybrid schedules.

Reflect on racial macroaggressions. Is your school embedding macroaggressions through actions, policies, and language? If so, what can you do to combat the inclusion of macroaggressions in the learning environment?

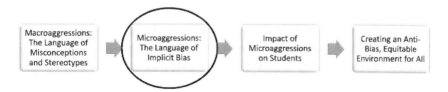

Figure 5.2 Macro, Micro, Impact, ABE. *Source*: Created by Bouley & Reinking, 2021.

Before we begin this section, please take time to reflect on the terminology in the table below, table 5.1. Stop and reflect to fill in the second column.

Table 5.1   Reflection of Terminology

Terminology	Prior to Reading the Section: Reflect: What Is Your Definition of the Term?	After Reading the Section: Reflect: What Is the Definition of the Term in Your Own Words?
Cultural Appropriation		
Colorblind		
BLM		
Acting White		
Colorblind		
Colorism		
Model Minority		
Perpetual Foreigner		
Adultification		
Exoticize/ Fetishize		
Dehumanization		

Racial microaggressions are different from outright acts of bigotry, but their effects are just as insidious. Well-meaning statements . . . subtly reinforce the idea that the target is not a part of the dominant culture. These statements dismiss the target's personal identity and experience. (Marshall, 2018, para. 7).

Unlike race, which is a social construct, racism is very real. Racism is a system of power that restructures an inequitable distribution of resources, opportunities, and benefits and assigns value based on the social interpretation of how one looks, such as skin color.

For generations discussions around race have been ignored or brushed off. This is likely due to feelings of fear, anxiety, or being uncomfortable by both white people and BIPOC. When conversations of race and equity begin, white people may be facing their privilege for the first time, and BIPOC people have the sometimes-difficult decision of calling out everyday microaggressions in the environment (Washington, Birch, & Roberts, 2020) or the burden of calling individuals into a conversation to repair a damaged relationship based in microaggressions.

Racial microaggressions can occur to any racial group. However, it has been found that Black Americans disproportionately experience microaggressions as compared to white, Latinx, and Asian Americans (Lloyd, 2020). "The flashpoints that spark national conversations on racism are often instances of violence, but for many Black Americans, their experiences with mistreatment and discrimination are much subtler and are woven into the routines of their normal, daily lives" (Lloyd, 2020, para. 13). However, with the violence against Asian Americans in 2021 and the destruction of Mexican families at the border, the statistics are constantly evolving.

RACIAL MICROAGGRESSIONS

While there are too many racial microaggressions to outline here, we will outline some. From this brief list, we encourage readers to take this knowledge and continue to research, reflect, and discover the multitude of racial abuses that happen in our society, especially in our school buildings and classrooms.

The small list of racial microaggressions discussed in this chapter will be broken down into six large categories: cultural appropriation, invisibility, second-class citizen, othering from a dominant privilege, dehumanization, perpetual foreigner, and model minority.

Cultural Appropriation

"Cultural appropriation refers to the use of objects or elements of a non-dominant culture in a way that doesn't respect their original meaning, give credit to their course, or reinforces stereotypes or contributes to oppression" (Cuncic, 2020, para. 1). Essentially, cultural appropriation is taking elements of one's culture without permission, a culture that does not belong to "you," usually meaning the dominant group, and using the cultural traditions, language, dress, and so on to exploit or further oppress a historically oppressed group.

How does cultural appropriation occur in schools as a microaggression? The simplest form of cultural appropriation microaggression is Halloween costumes. As stated by Haller (2019), "Halloween is a land mine of cultural appropriation examples for parents because it is easy to see Disney characters and cartoon character animations and imagine those costumes are safe (para. 8)." However, that is not the case because Disney, an organization that has generations of structural and institutionalized racism, is creating costumes for people to "play" in rather than respect the culture of the people the costumes represent.

So, is cultural appropriation ever good? One researcher argues that there can be "good borrowing," such as making a Moroccan soup and talking with your family about it. However, costumes, dressing up as a culture you do not fully embrace or identify as, is not "good borrowing," but rather offensive (Scafidi, 2005). "Cultural appropriation can be offensive when the person doing the borrowing is privileged, while the person who is being borrowed from is oppressed" such as dreadlock costumes, Pocahontas costumes, or Maui (Moana) costumes (Dastagir, 2017).

Invisibility

Invisibility happens when historically marginalized individuals are omitted from conversations. Asian Americans, indigenous peoples, and Latinx are often left out of conversations on race and racism in the United States.

Invisibility also happens through statements of being "colorblind." Most people who state they are "colorblind" when it comes to seeing (or not seeing) race in society are well-intentioned, however, the impact on BIPOC (Black, Indigenous, People of Color) individuals can be dehumanizing by not fully seeing individuals for their true identity, or putting an invisibility cloak over part of who they are and how they function in society Furthermore, it has been argued that colorblindness denies the lived experiences of people. When hearing someone state they are colorblind, questions that could be asked focus on an activity called the "circle of trust."

The circle of trust is an activity where an individual writes down the ten most important people in their lives. Then, for every identity they personally have, such as female, white, Christian, thirty-something, they put a check next to each name that matches that identity. Generally, with this activity it becomes evident that we tend to have people in our close circle of trust who are in our "in group," or the social group with which we identify.

The importance of using this activity as a way to question the concept of being "colorblind" in relation to race is because if race truly doesn't matter than the neighborhood one lives in would be racially integrated, the social institutions (i.e., schools, churches) one attends would be racially integrated, and one's ingroup or trust circle would be racially integrated. Essentially, our society, our ingroup, is not "colorblind" because of the -ism fog we continually breath.

Furthermore, Jon Greenberg (2015), a 15+-year veteran, outlined "7 Reasons Why 'Colorblindness' Contributes to Racism Instead of Solves It." He states that colorblindness invalidates people's identities, as stated above. Anecdotally, when a person of color is asked to self-identify they state their race first, which displays the importance of race in their lives and in the interactions they experience in society.

Another concept Greenberg outlines is the concept that colorblindness equates color with something negative. The microaggressive meaning behind "I don't see color, I see people" arguably states, "I can see who you are despite your race." To support the concept that this is an example of racial abuse is the fact that the term, "I don't see color" is never or almost never used in relation to white people. This concept is also problematic when disciplinarians do not reflect on their implicit biases of race as a way to discipline or punish Black children and youth.

This concept is supported through work by Monica T. Williams, PhD. In her article she discusses colorblind ideology as a form of racism because when someone states, "I am colorblind" it is usually a white person to a BIPOC person and the message is "I don't see that bad 'colored' part of you" (Williams, 2011). Furthermore, stating that you are blind to an issue is stating that you do not want to see the issue clearly and therefore negate any experiences that might be a result of a colorblind ideology (Williams, 2011).

The name-based microaggression is another invisibility racial microaggression Michelle Kim (@mjmichellekim) tweeted, "I hated the shame I felt every new school year when the teacher would butcher my Korean name on the roster. If you went to a school with a lot of Asian kids, you know the drill—Teacher: [mispronounced Asian name]. Asian Student: uh . . . I go by Peter. [Other kids chuckling]."

This experience is unfortunately not unique to Asian American students, but to many students who have "racially and ethnically distinct names" (Perina, 2019). The teacher renaming a student to make the pronunciation "easier" is othering the child, creating an unsafe space for the child, and centering your (educator's) comfort over the identity and well-being of a student. Names provide identity, culture, traditions, meaning, familial connections, and so much more. Learning to correctly say a student's name is one small step that can make or break a relationship in the learning environment.

Second-Class Citizen

The microaggressions of "second-class citizen" are experiences in which BIPOC receive substandard service or interactions as compared with their white counterparts. One institutional second-class-citizen racially based microaggression many students of color experience in the United States is the sub-par educational opportunities and access to resources as compared to their predominantly white counterparts. While this opportunity gap is closing, there is still a wide variance between the funding and opportunities to students at schools with a high population of students of color compared to schools with a high population of white students.

Another second-class citizen microaggression focuses on the discrimination experienced by Asian Americans. Specifically, since the rhetoric around COVID-19 "hate crimes against Asian Americans in major U.S. cities surged by nearly 150 percent in 2020—even as the number of overall hate crimes fell" (Sy & Nagy, 2021). Rhetoric such as "Kung-Flu" or the "Chinese Virus." Furthermore, the group "Stop AAPI Hate has logged nearly 4,000 anti-Asian incidents since the start of the pandemic" (Sy & Nagy, 2021).

In an interview with Public Broadcasting Service (PBS) NewsHour, story after story were relayed to the interviewer about violent acts toward Asian Americans in 2020. The violence in some communities, such as Oakland's Chinatown, has even resulted in day-long patrols to walk with

Asian Americans, specifically elderly Asian Americans, in the community. In Texas, a Burmese family was stabbed inside of a Sam's Club. In 2021, the surge of Asian American hate crimes continued to rise, from an Asian American couple returning from the movies to find slurs spray painted on their car to the murder of Asian Americans in Atlanta as nail salons.

These experiences are not only happening at public places but just as other community microaggressions, these comments, actions, and impact enter the classroom on a daily basis. From students calling their Asian American peers, "coronavirus" to peers asking Asian American students to speak their "native language" to students pulling the sides of their eyes to exaggerate the slanted eyes of some Asian American communities. Each of these experiences has a negative impact on the classroom community creating an unsafe space for all students. Each of these experiences also perpetuates the microaggression of second-class citizens.

Finally, the All Lives Matter and Blue Lives Matter movements to counter the BLM movement can be categorized as a second-class citizen microaggression.

The BLM movement sparked from the substandard interactions Black and Brown individuals experience at the hands of police officers, as compared with their white counterparts. The history of BLM, Inc began as a movement in 2013 as a direct "in response to the acquittal of Trayvon Martin's murder" (www.blacklivesmatter.com). The mission of BLM is to "eradicate white supremacy and build local power to intervene in violence inflicted on Black communities by the state and vigilantes." In addition to the hashtag Black Lives Matter or #BLM, the organization developed thirteen guiding principles. The principles are (blacklivesmatteratschool .com):

1. Restorative Justice
2. Empathy
3. Loving Engagement
4. Diversity
5. Globalism
6. Queen Affirming
7. Trans Affirming
8. Collective Value
9. Intergenerational
10. Black Families
11. Black Villages
12. Unapologetically Black
13. Black Women

These principles are important to understand because of the intersectionality demonstrated throughout the principles. The principles advocate not only for Black lives but for gender, LGBTQQ+, age, and more.

In response to Black Lives Matter there are two movements that are falsely placed in a dichotomous relationship to BLM. Specifically, Blue Lives Matter and All Lives Matter. By stating Blue Lives Matter in response to BLM, a false equivalent is being made. A Black person, who does not have a choice in the color of their skin, is being compared to someone who does have a choice in their occupation. However, this does not mean that people who wear blue as part of their occupation do not matter, but to state the people who have a choice in putting on or off an occupational color, as compared to someone who can never "take off" the color of their skin is based in anti-blackness (Ware, 2016). As stated on a sign held by a Black woman during racial protests around the country, "You're (police officer) only blue '40 hours a week. I'm Black 24/7 365."

Moving onto the slogan of "All Lives Matter," the statement is inherently disingenuous, because it can't be true that all lives matter until BLM too. And in 2021, with the increase of Asian American discrimination since the start of the COVID-19 pandemic in the United States, all lives can't matter until all marginalized groups including Asians and Asian Americans. Law and government professor Joseph Margulies stated in an essay,

> saying that "all lives matter" is a weapon of racism. It's a weapon of advantage. It is easy for those who systematically accumulate advantages to say of course, we are all equal. Yet, it's only black lives that are being systematically depressed, oppressed, and repressed, and historically always have been. The viciousness of attacks on black bodies is reason enough to treat it separately (Bassett, 2020).

Othering from the Dominant Privilege

In relation to race, white, English speaking individuals are seen as dominant and inherently have privilege based on the socialization within our country. "Being articulate" with language or speaking "proper English" is a resulting microaggression under this category.

Being articulate, or well-spoken, is subjective and based on assumptions, stereotypes, and a privileged idea that only people who have formal education and home experiences that are embedded with "proper" or standard English are intelligent. When a statement regarding language, based on the hegemonic view of language or the dominant language being standard English, microaggressions are inevitable.

One example is when someone tells a Black person, "You don't sound Black." This is a microaggression based on the hegemonic assumption of standard English is dominant, and African American Vernacular English

(AAVE; Black English, Ebonics, Black Talk, Blaccent) is subordinate or unintelligent. This statement is offensive because it implies the offender made an initial judgment, based on an intellectual stereotype of Black people. Essentially, in this situation, the offender "complimented" the Black person for surprising them with standard English.

Another example is when people, such as educators, insist students speak standard English as opposed to Spanish or a combination of Spanish and English through a process of codeswitching. While maybe well-intentioned, the impact can be demeaning and detrimental to the academic success and sense of belonging for students. Rather than seeing the codeswitching of language as a deficit, we would encourage you, the reader/educator, to think of codeswitching as an asset the student brings to the learning envronment.

Additionally, it is important for educators to understand the history of language in educational settings. For generations indigenous peoples were taken from their families, sent to boarding schools, and were beaten if they used their family language. The same happened with Spanish-speaking students in school and orphanages for many decades within American history. This harsh history is at the core of "speaking white" or not allowing for codeswitching.

Building from mandating standard English in the classroom is another microaggression known as "acting white." The statement, "you are acting white" is usually said to BIPOC individuals or students as a way to imply the student is betraying or "selling out" their culture by assuming the student is embracing the hegemonic expectations of white society. While educators may not state this microaggression, students may say it to each other. In those situations, it is imperative the educator speaks up and decreases the micro-aggression, which as a result will build a trusting and positive relationship between the educator and student victim.

The impact on student academics of the "acting white" microaggression is detrimental and discourages BIPOC students in school. The research on this phenomenon began in 1986 with John Ogbu and Signithia Fordham. Their study found high-performing Black students in a Washington, D.C. school used strategies from the hegemonic white culture to achieve high academics, but also struggled to maintain a Black identity. In turn, this hegemonic adoption of strategies to achieve high academics, with the cognitive dissonance of maintaining a societal defined "Black identity" birthed the concept of the Acting White Theory.

A final type of "othering from the dominant privilege" is colorism. Colorism is a type of racial abuse and is defined in the Merriam-Webster dictionary as "prejudice or discrimination especially within a racial or ethnic group favoring people with lighter skin over those with darker skin." Another definition is "a practice of discrimination by which those with lighter skin are treated more favorably than those with darker skin" (National Conference for Community and Justice, 2021).

The history of colorism dates back to the time of slavery. "Enslavers typically gave preferential treatment to enslaved people with fairer complexions" (Nittle 2020, para. 5), at times because they were their own kin through rape. While it dates back to the time of slavery, the legacy of colorism still endures today. People with lighter skin are given more roles on the big screen, are seen as what "beauty" means and can increase bullying within school buildings for dark-complected students.

Dehumanization

In schools the hidden curriculum and whitewashing of history stems from or begins the process of dehumanization. Due to the structures of school all stories are not told or included in the classroom and in some instances erased from the history books altogether.

Another type of dehumanization occurring in society and school buildings is the adultification of Black and Brown students.

Adultification is a form of dehumanization, robbing black children of the very essence of what makes childhood distinct from all other developmental periods: innocence. Adultification contributes to a false narrative that black youths' transgressions are intentional and malicious, instead of the result of immature decision making—a key characteristic of childhood (The Annie E. Casey Foundation, 2017).

Below is a blog post from Reinking posted on June 6, 2020 (Crumm, 2020), which introduces the concept of BIPOC children becoming adultified.

Black is darkness. Black is death. Black is scary. Black is bad. Black is feared.

Today, we all have witnessed murders of black persons—especially George Floyd—at the hands of police. The global outpouring is forcing all of us to confront this uncomfortable truth that, in our society and culture, "Black is scary."

Adding to this reality is the concept that in America Black bodies are owned. The concept of owning Black bodies is embedded into the foundation of our country—on the backs of Slaves, on the backs of Black people racially profiled, on the backs of Black people murdered, whose blood is flowing through this land—and those forgotten.

We have a history to fight against, but we are strong and this fight is not over.

This piece of writing came about because of a picture I saw on social media— one that truly spoke to me. It was the picture of a Black boy holding a sign asking why society turns their view of him from cute to scary. This happens in the blink of an eye for Black children.

Black children are "adultified" and miss out on the growing years of adolescence where mistakes can be made and people forgive, rather than kill. Black children, in the eyes of Americans, go from cute to scary in the blink of an eye. But white children? They get the advantage of the learning and growing years where people forgive and dismiss occasional misbehavior as: "Kids will be kids."

Remember, Tamir Rice was 12 years old when he was murdered by police bullets. In the eyes of white Americans, he was "adultified." He was deemed scary because of the color of his skin. He was seen as an adult because of the color of his skin. (Emmett Till, who was murdered by a mob of white men for allegedly whistling at a white woman, was only 14 years old).

Remember—12-year-olds are 5th and 6th graders. Think about 5th and 6th grade students. They are still children. Their brains are still forming. They are still learning about life. And for some Black children, they may be just starting to become aware of a society that is scared of them, especially because one year earlier they were seen as cute.

The adultification of Black children moves them from cute children to scary adults and skips the learning years of adolescence and young adults.

Another form of the dehumanization microaggression is the exoticizing or fetishizing specific racial groups. A common group exoticized or fetishized are Asian American women. For generations, Asian Americans have been discriminated against from the Chinese Exclusion Act (1882), to Japanese Internment Camps (1942–1945), to the "exoticizing" Asian American women. What is exoticization and fetishization? The experiences in which POC dehumanized or tokenized, or in which a person's culture is appropriated or sexualized. Similar to the adultification of Black children, exoticizing Asian American children can begin early.

Perpetual Foreigner

The perpetual foreigner can be summarized with the question: "What are you?" Or "Where are you really from?" Both of these microaggressions essentially state that you, the person I am talking to, does not belong here and therefore I need to investigate on what you are or where you are really from. Essentially, they are "not American enough."

To the question "what are you," a Buzzfeed contributor stated, "Human. Being biracial doesn't make me a 'what.'" When the question "what are you" arises, and it arises often for biracial and multiracial individuals, it is a microaggression that "others" the individual by essentially stating, "You are not white, and I cannot determine what you are, so you must be an 'other.'"

To the question, "Where are you really from? No, where are you really from?," the assumption again is being made that the person does not belong. While the question may seem "small" to outsiders, the question is personal. Anecdotal reports from people who have been asked this question in their lives stated, "I feel like I have to prove my ethnicity," "They question my loyalty to my country," or "They want to chop down my family tree," which really gets at the sense of identity (Zdanowicz, 2017).

Model Minority

The myth of the model minority is a stereotype that is applied to a minority group, usually the identity of Asian Americans, who appears to be more successful academically, economically, or culturally, as compared to other racial groups. On the ISAASE.org blog it was stated,

> the model minority myth is misguided and misleading, and is a false stereotype . . . it hurts Asian American students, whether they are low-achieving or high-achieving, and creates divides between these students and others. It may also lead teachers to provide less support to their Asian American students, as they may believe the students need less support than they actually do.

This perception results in harmful situations for Asian American students, which is displayed through statistics. Specifically, U.S. Department of Health and Humans Services Office of Minority Health (2019) states,

> suicide was the leading cause of death for Asian Americans, ages 15 to 24 in 2017; Asian American females, in grades 9-12, were 20 percent more likely to attempt suicide as compared to non-Hispanic white female students, in 2017; the overall suicide rate for Asian Americans is half that of the non-Hispanic white population.

The myth of the model minority often occurs in academic settings and can be harmful to self-image. For example, Sarah-Soonling Blackburn (2019) wrote about her experience as being seen as a model minority of Asian descent. Instead of receiving differentiation when she struggled with academics, her teacher continued to teach while Sarah-Soonling fell behind. Due to the pressure of the model minority myth, as well as receiving no extra help, she eventually stopped trying in school.

Reflection: Stop and reflect. Using the table 5.1 (Reflection of Terminology) from the beginning of this section, fill in the final column of the table.

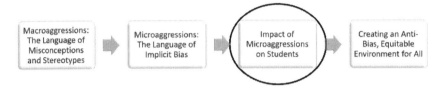

Figure 5.3   Macro, Micro, Impact, ABE. *Source*: Created by Bouley & Reinking, 2021.

As outlined in several of the sections above, racial microaggressions, or as Kendi would state, racial abuse and racist acts, impact students academically and socially. Some researchers even state that "the invisibility of racial microaggressions may be more harmful to people of color than hate crimes or the overt and deliberate acts of white supremacists such as the Klan and Skinheads" (Sue, 2010).

Discussing the mental, physical, and academic health problems racial microaggressions can cause, Sue (2010) outlines seven harmful impacts:

1. Attack the mental health of microaggression recipients,
2. Create a hostile and invaliding work or school climate,
3. Perpetuate stereotype threat (social, mental, and academic),
4. Create physical health problems,
5. Saturate the broader society with cues that signal devaluation of social group identities,
6. Lower academic/work productivity and problem-solving abilities (academic),
7. Partially responsible for creating inequities in education, employment, and health care (circling back to the Cycle of Socialization).

Relating to the impact on brain health, one study, which included 506 participants, found "that higher frequencies of racial microaggressions negatively predicted participants' mental health and that racial microaggressions were significantly correlated with depressive symptoms and negative affect" (Nadal et al., 2014).

Diving further into the concept of stereotype threat as mentioned by Wing Sue, and introduced by Steele and Aronson (1995), research shows the negative academic impact for students. In a study completed by Steele and

Aronson they found that when students were told that the test measured their intelligence, Black students performed significantly worse than their white peers, but when they were told that the test diagnosed their ability to solve problems, the race-based performance gap disappeared. This finding supports the fact that stereotypes and biases, which are the language of macro and microaggressions, impact the academic performance of students based on the socialized and internalized concepts of who is "good" at school and who is "bad" at school or certain subjects.

Figure 5.4   Macro, Micro, Impact, ABE. *Source*: Created by Bouley & Reinking, 2021.

Creating an equitable environment for all students, specifically in reference to this chapter based on race, begins with self-reflection and awareness. As part of the reflection process, it is important to be aware of the historical contexts, be aware of language, be aware of policies and procedures that are not critically analyzed, and be ready. Be ready for what?

Be ready to have difficult discussions regarding zero-tolerance policies in schools that disproportionately impact students of color as compared to their white classmates; be ready to speak up when something is done or said that is a racial microaggression; be ready to address a microaggression you may have stated or engaged in. Remember, silence can be loud and when not addressed the attitude or mindset will perpetuate. Finally, be humble and be open to feedback from others; allow people to call you into the conversation.

Another important concept when discussing racial microaggressions, or any microaggression, is to speak from the I. Speaking from the I was stated at the beginning of the book as part of our community agreements, but what is it? Speaking from the I means you speak or encourage students to speak only from their experiences.

When educators, or individuals begin to use rhetoric such as, "all Asian Americans" or "all African American" or, while talking about personal experiences using the term "we" or "our", the impact is an assumed monolith. The understanding that is communicated is that there is no diversity within groups of people. Obviously, this is not the case, therefore using "I" when discussing experiences is imperative to decreasing racial stereotypes. Every racial identity has diversity within the racial group, therefore expecting a student or teacher to speak for "all" people within their racial group is inappropriate and disingenuous to recognize individuals as individuals.

As part of the reflection process, there are two graphics that provide guidance through the process of self-identifying as a way to grow. The first graphic is the "Racism Scale" (provided in the resources list). By using this scale, you can self-identify where you may fall today, knowing that each day, depending on experiences, your placement on the Racism Scale may differ.

An additional reflection piece is the "Continuum on Becoming an Anti-Racist, Multicultural Institution" (provided in the resources list). This scale can be used to identify where you are as a classroom teacher within your classroom environment, as a whole school system, or as an entire district. This is a way to place yourself on a continuum, which then leads to action planning for growth.

Reflection: What are steps you are going to take to create a more equitable environment for your students and colleagues?

DISCIPLINE

Due to educators' and policymakers' implicit biases, discipline, and discipline policies in school districts, schools, and learning environments can cause harm to the overall sense of self for students of color. It can also cause decreased motivation resulting in lower academic scores and social connections for students of color.

The specific racial discriminatory discipline actions and/or policies that are discussed in this section do not include an exhaustive list, but are a great start for evaluating, reflecting, and analyzing current practices.

Hair Discrimination

The regulation of bodies is evident in school policies, specifically around uniform or clothing rules, which include specifications on how hair can be worn. Examples of discriminatory policies focusing on hairstyles include policies around hairstyles that are deemed "appropriate" and "inappropriate." Inappropriate hairstyles are often stated in a way that does not allow Black students to wear their hair in culturally appropriate ways such as dreadlocks, afros, or beads.

There are multiple news stories regarding students who are suspended due to hairstyles, predominantly Black students. For example, in a news article written by Janelle Griffith on Jan. 24, 2020, it was stated, "A second teenager at a Texas high school was suspended and told he could not return to class until he cut his dreadlocks to be in compliance with the school's dress code."

This was after Kaden Bradford, a Texas teen, made headlines after being suspended for refusing to cut his dreadlocks.

While these policies are not new, in 2019 the CROWN Act was "created as a way to ensure protection against discrimination based on race-based hairstyles by extending statutory protection to hair texture and protective styles such as braids, locs, twists, and knots in the workplace and public schools" (thecrownact.com).

Associated with the biases and microaggressions around hairstyles is the implementation of "crazy hair day" many schools create as part of a spirit week. While this is not a policy, schools and learning environments do partake in this type of "fun" activity on a yearly basis. However, often the "crazy hair" that is styled by well-intentioned white students and families makes fun of or is a type of microaggression toward Black hairstyles that have a history, meaning, and cultural context.

For example, some braided hairstyles were used as maps for slaves to escape from the south to the north, or the concept known as "mapping out freedom." Therefore, creating policies that do not stop crazy hair days is actually supporting the implementation of crazy hair day, a racial abuse. Arguably, silence is loud. (The concept of "crazy hair" day as a microaggression will also be discussed in the chapter based on ability and disability.)

Zero Tolerance

Zero-tolerance policies were adopted in 1994 when federal legislation required states to expel any student for a year who brought a firearm to school. Taking the lead from that legislation, many schools adopted zero-tolerance policies for weapons, drugs, and bullying. However, zero-tolerance policies disproportionality negatively impact students of color due to the subjectivity of what constitutes disciplinary actions (Pitlick, 2015). For example, a student with nail clippers or Ibuprofen could be viewed as holding a weapon or a drug. If the student is white, many students will look past that infraction, however, for students of color, that infarction may not be ignored due to implicit biases.

Furthermore, a task force was tasked with understanding the impact of the zero-tolerance policy. They found that "zero-tolerance policies were unnecessarily preventing children from getting a public education and causing many children to face legal charges for relatively minor offenses" (Morin, 2020). Essentially, the ACLU (2021) found,

> zero tolerance policies criminalize minor infractions of school rules, while cops in schools lead to students being criminalized for behavior that should be handled inside the school. Students of color are especially vulnerable to push-out trends and the discriminatory application of discipline.

Suspension/Expulsion

Suspensions and expulsions have been used in schools for a long time, however, they are found to negatively impact student achievement and motivation, which results in higher dropout rates. Additionally, suspensions and expulsions impact students of color at a higher rate than white students. Specifically, "national data show that black students in K-12 schools are 3.8 times as likely to be suspected, and twice as likely to receive out-of-school suspensions as students without disabilities" (Education Commission of the States, 2018). This disproportionality is arguably due to implicit biases.

As we wrap up this chapter, it is important to remember that race is a socially constructed idea that is not based in science (Gannon, 2016). However, race impacts every part of society.

Reflection: One Word. What is your one word (figure 5.5) to summarize your thoughts or feelings after reading this chapter? What is your one word?

Examples of one word are provided in this word cloud, which was created by using the words in this chapter.

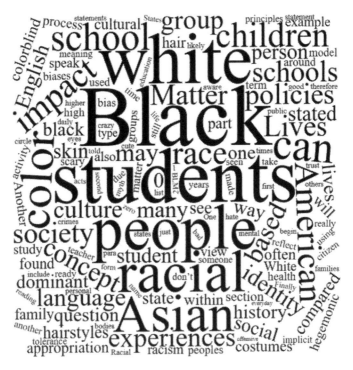

Figure 5.5   One Word, Chapter 5. *Source*: Created by Bouley & Reinking, 2021.

After reading this chapter, what are some ways you will hold yourself accountable through intentional, thoughtful actions?

Table 5.2   Reflections and Intentions

Reflection Question	Your Answer
My interactions with students…	
My interactions with their families…	
Physical classroom environment…	
Classroom materials and materials used for instruction…	
Lesson planning and curriculum…	
Instructional strategies such as grouping…	
Creating an anti-biased anti-racist school climate…	

RESOURCES

Black Lives Matter: www.blacklivesmatteratschool.com

Continuum on Becoming an Anti-Racist, Multicultural Institution: https://racc.org/wp-content/uploads/buildingblocks/foundation/Continuum%20on%20Becoming%20an%20Anti-Racist,%20Multicultural%20Institution.pdf

Learning for Justice (formerly known as Teaching Tolerance): https://www.learningforjustice.org/. *This website provides "free resources to educators—teachers, administrators, counselors and other practitioners—who work with children from kindergarten through high school. Educators use our materials to supplement the curriculum, to inform their practices, and to create inclusive school communities where children and youth are respected, valued and welcome participants."*

Racism Scale (and website): https://racismscale.weebly.com/

Social Media Handle: *@ARENWashington (Antiracist Education Now)*

Chapter 6

Gender, Gender Identity/ Expression, and Sexual Orientation Microaggressions

All young people, regardless of sexual orientation or identity, deserve a safe and supportive environment in which to achieve their full potential.

—Harvey Milk, 1977

In 2017 the *National Geographic* released a special topic issue titled: *Gender Revolution* in conjunction with a two-hour primetime documentary titled, *Gender Revolution: A Journey with Katie Couric*. Susan Goldberg, the magazine's Editor in Chief wrote,

Now that we know XX and XY, and blue and pink, don't tell the full story, it is time to write a new chapter to ensure that we all can thrive in this world no matter what our gender—or decision to not identify a gender. That is why *National Geographic* has set out to tell the story of the gender revolution (Goldberg, 2017, p. 4).

We truly are in the middle of a revolution in gender expression and identity, and the terms used to describe these changes may seem as fluid as the changes themselves. As traditional gender roles and identities are being challenged on an international level and non-binary notions of gender are rapidly evolving, schools are looking to support children and families in new ways.

While acceptance of gay marriage and same-sex families is up nationally, the recent focus on gender identity and expression appears to be seen by some as more radical, and as such, there seems to be even less room for understanding and inclusion. This is highly problematic since, according to

National Geographic (Goldberg, 2017), we are entering what is being called the "Gender Revolution."

As we know from the Cycle of Socialization, from birth we are inundated with messages about how the popular culture defines gender. These messages are presented to us often in the form of what it means to be a boy or girl, and how each should express and identify their gender.

As we discuss microaggressions toward students and families who express their gender and sexual orientation in non-conforming or non-hetero ways, it is important to keep in mind that gender roles, gender identity, and gender expression are socially constructed concepts. In addition, all children and youth are exploring their gender, not just those who may express or identify it in ways that fall outside of the societal norm.

When discussing macro and microaggressions, it is important to have a basic understanding of the many definitions or terms that surround gender, gender identity and expression, and sexual orientation. Having a foundation of definitions provides a place of shared knowledge to have discussions and grow on our journey to creating a more equitable and inclusive classroom/school environment for all.

What are gender roles? Gender roles are defined as, "The expected role determined by an individual's sex and the associated attitudes, behaviors, norms, and values" by the Open Education Sociology Dictionary (2021). As such, gender roles are socially constructed. Every society, culture or ethnic group has varying gender role expectations and while these expectations can change over time, in many ways that progress has been slow. Gender roles are a socially constructed idea.

What is gender expression? Gender expression is how an individual expresses his/her gender. Gender expression can be through clothing, hairstyle, make-up, behavior, voice, and so on. Similar to gender roles, gender expression is socially constructed. Research supports that gender expression is fluid and moves across a spectrum (Killerman, 2015).

Fluidity in gender expression is common with most individuals. At times we express our gender in more feminine or masculine ways than we do at other times. The term non-binary is often used to describe the spectrum of gender. According to the Human Rights Campaign (HRC) (2021b), "Gender does not simply exist in those binary terms; gender is more of a spectrum, with all individuals expressing and identifying with varying degrees of both masculinity and femininity" (para. 3).

A student who expresses her gender similarly to the gender she was assigned at birth, is cisgendered and conforming to society's expected expression for that gender. An example of a student who is expressing his/her gender outside of the norm could be a student who was assigned male at birth, but expresses his gender in more feminine ways. This is called gender non-conforming.

What is gender identity? Gender identity relates to how an individual identifies his/her gender. A student who was assigned male at birth, may identify as female and prefer a female name, female pronouns, and to express in feminine ways; this student perceives/identifies herself to be female. This individual may identify as transgender, which according to the HRC is "an umbrella term for people whose gender identity and/or expression is different from cultural expectations based on the sex they were assigned at birth" (Human Rights Campaign, 2021a, para. 22).

All students identify their gender, some may identify differently than their sex assigned at birth (transgender), while others identify in a way that is consistent with their sex assigned at birth (cisgender). According to the HRC an individual who is cisgender is someone "whose gender identity aligns with those typically associated with the sex assigned to them at birth."

Reflection: How have you noticed your students identifying and expressing their gender? Do you see it as fluid?

Figure 6.1   Macro, Micro, Impact, ABE. *Source:* Created by Bouley & Reinking, 2021.

Research supports that many adults who identify as the gender they were not assigned at birth were aware of this identity in their early childhood years. Gender dysphoria is a term used to describe the experiences of an individual who unequivocally and consistently expresses that their gender identity is not consistent with what they were assigned at birth.

Gender dysphoria is defined as, "An intense and persistent discomfort with the primary and secondary sex characteristics of one's assigned birth sex" (Broady, 2019, para. 14). Children with gender dysphoria are relentless in their pursuit to be, and to be seen as, their non-biological gender.

According to the American Psychological Association (2015), when children with gender dysphoria have their identity affirmed and supported, the dysphoria is decreased significantly. In fact, parent testimonials serve as powerful demonstrations of this (American College of Pediatricians, 2018; Hembree, Cohen-Kettenis, Gooren, Meyer, Murad, Rosenthal, Safer, Tangpricha, & T'Sjoen, 2017; Leibowitz & de Vries, 2016).

Conversely, forcing children with gender dysphoria to identify as the gender they were assigned at birth exacerbates the dysphoria, and often results in negative behaviors, overwhelming sadness, and has even resulted in suicide attempts in young children (American Psychological Association, 2015; Janicka & Forcier, 2016).

An individual could also be gender fluid and not identify with either gender or gender expansive which is a term associated with the notion that gender is non-binary, and an individual may not identify as man or woman, but both or somewhere in between on a spectrum of gender identities. They may see their gender as fluid.

At present we are seeing rapid changes in how children and adults explore, express, and identify their gender. Research consistently maintains that it is in the early years that the majority of individuals become aware of their gender nonconformance.

It is during the foundational years that children look to their families and teachers for affirmation and acceptance of who they are, and who they are not. A supportive school climate can easily make a life-long positive impact not only on children who are gender non-conforming, but on all children's ability to know, feel comfortable with and support diversity in gender expression and identity.

Sexual orientation is defined by HRC as, "an inherent or immutable enduring emotional, romantic or sexual attraction to other people." HRC notes that "an individual's sexual orientation is independent of their gender identity." Individuals who are gay or lesbian have "emotional, romantic, or sexual attraction" to individuals of the same gender, and bisexual individuals experience the same attraction for more than one gender.

The term LGBTQQ+ relates to individuals who identify as lesbian, gay, bisexual, transgender, queer, or questioning+. Often times people use the term queer to "express a spectrum of identities and orientations that are counter to the mainstream" (HRC). Questioning is used to describe people who are exploring their identities and/or orientations.

Regardless of gender identity, expression, or roles, gender bias and microaggressions are based on stereotypes, the language of macroaggressions, and misconceptions. Sexist language and gender role prejudice and stereotyping are pervasive in schools. Sexist language refers to terms that degrade women or exclude women all together. Gender role prejudice or stereotyping relates to when traditional gender roles or stereotypes are not only conveyed but also expected. The Gender Equality Law Center identifies key gender stereotypes by age group from the early years to youth, to adulthood, located in table 6.1.

Table 6.1   The Gender Equality Law Center: Gender Stereotypes. *Source:* Gender Equality Law Center, 2015.

Early Years	Youth	Adulthood
Girls should play with dolls and boys should play with trucks	Girls are better at reading and boys are better at math	Victims of intimate partner violence are weak because they stay in the relationship
Boys should be directed to like blue and green; girls toward red and pink	Girls should be well behaved; boys are expected to act out	There is something wrong with a woman who doesn't want children
Boys should not wear dresses or other clothes typically associated with "girl's clothes"	Girls and are not as interested as boys in STEM subjects;	Assertive women are unfeminine and are "bossy," "bitches" or "whores"
Girls are talkative	Boys should engage in sports and refrain from more creative pursuits	Women are natural nurturers; men are natural leaders
Boys are too energetic and can't sit long enough	Boys and men are expected to use violence and aggression to prove their manliness;	Women don't need equal pay because they are supported by their husbands
	A boy that doesn't use violence or aggression is an understandable target for bullying;	Women who appear less feminine or reject advances from men are lesbians
	Girls should be thin and beautiful to make them appealing to men;	Women with children are less devoted to their jobs
		Men who spend time with family are less masculine and poor breadwinners
		In heterosexual couples, women should take time off to care for children or elders

Finally, heteronormative language in school buildings also creates an unwelcome environment through macroaggressions. For example, students who have same-sex parents, or youth who identify as lesbian, gay, or bisexual, may never see their family or themselves represented in school curricula, materials, and classroom discourse.

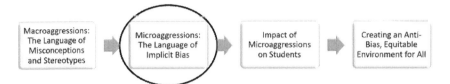

Figure 6.2   Macro, Micro, Impact, ABE. *Source*: Created by Bouley & Reinking, 2021.

Heteronormative behavior is defined by HRC as "The assumption of heterosexuality as the given or default sexual orientation instead of one of many possibilities, and that the preferred or default relationship is between two people of 'opposite' genders." Schools are extremely heteronormative as sexual orientation representation in classroom materials, programs, books, and discourse relates to straight, heterosexual individuals and families.

Reflection: Take a moment to reflect on gender and gender diversity/sexuality in your classroom. Is there a way in which you interact differently with one gender than the other? What have you noticed about your students' gender expression? Have you worked with students who identify as their non-biological gender? What role has sexual orientation played in your classroom?

GENDER ROLE BIAS

Gender role bias and microaggressions are so common in our culture and schools that we tend to not even notice them, nor the impact they have on both girls and boys. They are insidious and may seem small at times, but small moments add up, and students are bombarded with gender microaggressions through their years in school.

When discussing gender role microaggressions we are referring to microaggressions that are based on an individual's sex, male, or female. Students, both male and female, experience numerous gender-related microaggressions, and at all ages. Females may hear they should "man up" or be strong like a boy/man, and males may be told they shouldn't act like a girl, or show their feelings.

GENDER BIAS

Gender bias is prevalent in classrooms and can go both ways—against boys and against girls. Boys are expelled from preschool almost five times more than girls. Further, boys are more likely to drop out of school, less likely to do homework, and make up an increasingly low number of college graduates (Reichert, Hawley, & Tyre, 2010).

On the other hand, girls get interrupted by teachers more, are less likely to get called to demonstrate their work for the class, and less likely to be engaged in open-ended questions during a lesson (Chemaly, 2015), all of which decreases their academic engagement. Gender bias also impacts how teachers grade assignments. It has often been found that teachers unconsciously treat female students unfairly when grading math and science, which feeds on the view in society that girls are not part of STEM education/careers.

Reflection: What role does gender play in your daily interactions with students? Do you feel you approach students differently based on their gender? How so?

When discussing gender stereotypes and bias, it is important to also look at the intersectionality of gender and race and the data on school discipline. An analysis of the data gathered by the U.S. Department of Education Office for Civil Rights found, in almost all categories, that "girls of color were over disciplined compared to their white counterparts at even higher rates than boys of color compared to white boys" (Georgetown Law Center on Poverty and Inequality, 2020).

This data is perhaps the most egregious example of gender stereotyping and bias. Excessive discipline is a form of microaggression. Compared to white girls, Black girls were four times more likely to receive out-of-school suspension, expulsion, and arrest at school. All girls of color had a higher rate of discipline compared to white girls, and the disparity was greater for girls of color/white girls than their boy counterparts (Codeswitch, 2014).

Numerous studies in early childhood education have found that preschool teachers track boys more than girls, and they also track boys of color at significantly higher rates than white boys, or girls of color (Miller, 2018). The Civil Rights Data Collection (CRDC) data show that while boys only account for a little over half (54 percent) of preschool enrollment, 84 percent of the preschool suspensions are boys, with Black boys suspended from preschool at twice the rate as white boys (U.S. Department of Education, 2016).

Further, they found that while males and females each make up approximately 50 percent of the student population, around two-thirds of the students expelled are boys, and boys are suspended at more than twice the rate of girls (U.S. Department of Education, 2016). African American boys and girls have higher suspension rates than any of their peers (University of Michigan, 2018).

The gender and racial bias in discipline is even more disturbing when you examine the reasons for discipline, as demonstrated in data out of Seattle Public Schools. When considering extreme behavior such as assault, the data show more equitable discipline with the percent of Black vs. white students near exact. However, when you look at more ambiguous reasons for discipline such as rule breaking (African American 50 percent, white 17 percent) and interfering with school authority (African American 56 percent, white 6 percent), or intimidation of school authority (African American 55 percent, white 18 percent), African American students were close to three times more likely to be suspended than their white peers (Rowe, 2015).

Another concept of bias is something known as the "teacher's pet effect." If a student has positive interactions with a teacher, the teacher can become biased in favor of that student and grades of more subjective assignments may be skewed. This also occurs in the reverse with a student who has negative interactions with a teacher and the teacher grades a paper or subjective piece of work prior to fully reading it. Since the wide majority of educators are female and white, gender and race may play a significant role in the "teacher pet effect."

GENDER IDENTITY AND GENDER EXPRESSION

Gender identity and gender expression microaggressions are often straightforward and transparent. While they tend to be more explicit than gender role microaggressions, they are equally common and have a cumulative impact. When discussing gender identity and gender expression microaggressions we are referring to how an individual presents their gender (gender expression) and how they identify their gender (gender identity).

A student who identifies as a male but wears stereotypically feminine or female clothing is expressing their gender in a non-conforming way and may hear microaggressions such as "why are you dressed like a girl?" or "you are so gay." A student who identifies differently from the gender they were assigned at birth may be consistently called "he or him" when her preferred pronouns are "she or hers."

SEXUAL ORIENTATION BIAS

Similarly, sexual orientation microaggressions are palpable and unmistakable. A student who identifies as lesbian, gay, or bisexual or who has a gay or same-sex parent(s) might hear the term "that's so gay" or receive the direction "give this to your mom and dad" numerous times over any school year.

All microaggressions toward individuals based on their gender, gender identity, expression and/or sexual orientation are extremely harmful to a person's sense of self and individual identity, not to mention academic achievement. Students who identify as LGBTQQ+ are inundated with microaggressions throughout their school career and as such, are identified as a high-risk group.

This is in part due to the predominant heteronormativity found in schools, which can serve as blinders to the importance of addressing gender identity/ expression and LGBTQQ+ diversity in young children and youth. Hetero cisgender teachers from hetero cisgender families may not realize the importance of including and affirming the experiences of LGBTQQ+ students and families, nor are they necessarily aware of how they transmit and validate hetero cisgender behavior in their classrooms.

Without knowledge or experience they may feel students are too young to know how they identify. Even well-intentioned teachers end up transmitting traditional views of gender. Seeing gender as dichotomous is what they know, and even though they may want to convey to students that they have autonomy in the way they express their gender and need not conform to stereotypes or cisgendered behavior, that is what they consistently exhibit.

Not only are students hearing pervasive language that stereotypes and dichotomizes gender, diversity in gender identity and expression and sexual orientation is noticeably absent in classroom discourse. This silencing or systematic exclusion is a common microaggression.

Microaggressions toward students and families who are non-conforming in how they express or identify their gender or non-heteronormative in their sexual orientation are pervasive in schools. Some common examples are in table 6.2.

Table 6.2 Sexist, Gender Expression/Identity, Sexual Orientation Examples. *Source*: Created by Bouley, 2021

Gender	Gender Expression/Identity	Sexual Orientation
Using male pronouns exclusively "he"	Commenting on hair or clothing (i.e., you look like a girl with your long hair)	Asking students to bring something home to "mom and dad"
Lining students up by boys/girls	Not using the correct pronoun	Assuming a single lesbian mom parent is divorced
Having to choose between male and female	Using a student's legal name instead of their gender preferred name (Joanna, instead of Joe)	Asking a student if they have a boyfriend/girlfriend that is of the opposite gender (only)
Using comments that are often used to defend sexual harassment ("Boys will be boys" or "you'll have to fight boys off with a stick if you wear that.")	Telling a student expressing his non-conforming gender to "tone it down" or that their expression is "over the top"	Outing a student in front of their peers
Telling girls who are teased by boys, "he just likes you"	Not calling out or staying silent when a student experiences a microaggression or microassault from a peer	Telling a student to not "act so gay" or to "tone it down"
Using sexist language: "Act like a lady"	Using only binary pronouns	Not calling out or staying silent when a student experiences a microaggression or microassault from a peer
"Man up." "Don't cry like a girl." "You throw like a girl."	Silencing: Using materials, books, etc. that only include gender conforming characters	Using heteronormative language only

(*Continued*)

Table 6.2   Sexist, Gender Expression/Identity, Sexual Orientation Examples (*Continued*)

Gender	*Gender Expression/Identity*	*Sexual Orientation*
Asking students to do tasks based on their gender: "Can a few strong men help me with this."	Refusing to allow students who are transgender to receive health services	Silencing: Using materials, books, etc. that only include heterosexual characters
Differentiating language based on gender (i.e., calling girls bossy instead of leaders or boys overly sensitive if they express feelings)	Not having gender-neutral restrooms	Using the term "gay" to describe something you don't like or not calling out use of that term
Using gender stereotypical language (i.e., "you look like a pretty princess" to girls and/or "you're so strong you can pick it up" to boys)	Assuming or anticipating a student's, emotional response based on their gender expression or identity	Using only heteronormative examples, metaphors, etc.
Using materials, books, etc. that only depict characters in gender stereotypical roles	Assuming a student's gender	Creating classroom rules, projects, classrooms that are heterosexist
Girls against boys in debates, etc.	Creating classroom rules, projects, classrooms that are heterosexist	Consistently endorse heteronormative behaviors and culture
Creating classroom rules, projects, classrooms that are sexist	Expressing your belief that gender non-conforming is "going too far" or when you were a kid it was simpler because "there were just boys and girls"	Assuming behaviors based on sexual orientation such as gay men are promiscuous or a gay student must have AIDS or a lesbian must have "problems with men"
	Asking private questions about a transgender person's body	

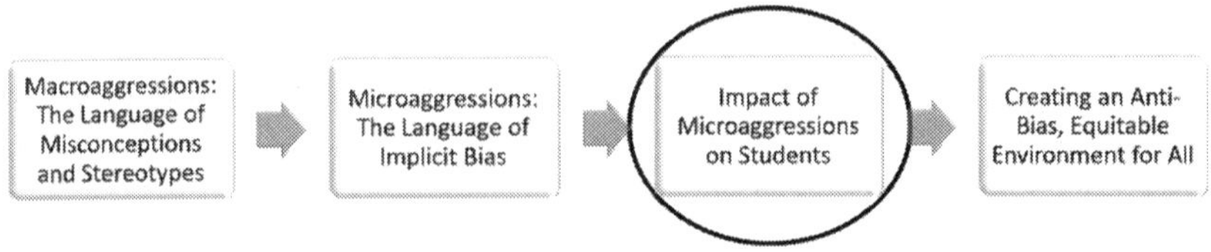

Figure 6.3   Macro, Micro, Impact, ABE. *Source*: Created by Bouley & Reinking, 2021.

Overall, it is clear that children and families who express or identify in the non-binary are often silenced in public elementary schools, exactly at the age that accepting and affirming their existence can make the most powerful impact on their overall health and happiness.

The majority of the research and discussion on LGBTQQ+ populations and schools are focused on middle and high school youth. According to the NAME, LGBTQQ+ populations and rural poverty were deemed to be the two areas of multicultural education most lacking in the research, "Recent findings reveal and confirm the invisibility of LGBTQ and how little attention is paid to sexual orientation, heterosexism, homophobia, heteronormativity, queer theory, and other related concepts" (Baptiste, Ryan, & Duhon-Sells, 2015, p. 176).

Responding to this call to action is especially important since according to the Gay, Lesbian, Straight Education Network's (GLSEN) "2017 National School Climate Survey" LGBTQ+ middle/high school youth are the most likely group to experience bullying, harassment, and death threats and is the group with the highest rates in school dropouts, suicide, homelessness, and other high-risk behaviors (Kosciw, Greytak, Zongrone, Clark, & Truong, 2018).

Reflection: What is your school's policy around bullying? How do you address bullying in your classroom?

Similar to all microaggressions, gender, gender identity, and expression and sexual orientation microaggressions reinforce stereotypes and often go overlooked. Yet, they have a tremendous impact on a student's sense of self and self-worth. Having the opportunity to openly discuss gender, gender identity/expression, and sexual orientation with colleagues, administrators, and family members is an important starting place to identifying and eliminating bias and microaggressions.

Although there has been an increase in intolerance and bullying in schools and on a national level (Todres, 2018), polls show that more Americans than ever support lesbian and gay rights. The Pew Research Center (May 2019) reports 61 percent of Americans believe in legalizing same-sex marriage.

The battle for gay marriage started nearly fifty years ago in 1970 when two men applied for a marriage license in the state of Minnesota. The movement picked up strength during the early 1990s and gay marriage became legal in the United States in 2015, at a time when it remained outlawed in only thirteen states.

While acceptance rates of same-sex families have increased, many schools are still not systematically including or even discussing the presence and needs of LGBTQQ+ children and families and, as a result, many children and families are not seeing themselves represented in school curricula, materials, and policies (Baptiste et al., 2015; Bouley, 2007, 2011, 2018; Kosciw et al., 2018; Woolley, 2019), and this silencing can have a devastating impact (Kosciw et al., 2018; Perry, Pauletti, & Cooper, 2019; Woolley, 2019).

While it appears that public schools are far behind public opinion, there has been some progress. Polls would indicate that the majority of teachers are more accepting of same-sex families and support equal rights and, as a result, some same-sex families are more comfortable being open in their child's school. In some areas, teachers are slowly becoming more inclusive (e.g., reading a children's book on families that includes a same-sex family) and some teachers are more mindful to establish safe climates (e.g., addressing a child's parents correctly "bring this home to your moms").

Yet few schools have offered professional development, established LGBTQQ+-inclusive policies or curricula, or even started to discuss the issue. Today it is gender identity and expression that has entered into national discourse and at a time when schools are still struggling to find ways to openly discuss and include same-sex families.

As visibility (i.e., helped by celebrities like Caitlyn Jenner) and support (i.e., boycotting North Carolina) increases, there has been a surge in parents coming forward with their experiences and advocating for schools to meet their child's needs. Children as young as two or three are outwardly identifying as their non-biological gender, while many others are more openly expressing their gender in non-conforming ways.

This speaks to the power of open discourse, or in this case, coming out. Of course, these students have always existed, but since gender expression and identity have entered societal discourse, students and their families are more likely to be making these discoveries, and early on. As a result, parents of pre-kindergarteners who are non-gender conforming are making a variety of difficult decisions from allowing their child to dress outside of gender norms, to choosing what gender their child should start his/her school career.

Schools are being asked to support families in this process, yet journal publications in the United States in the area of gender variant children and schools are mostly recent and limited (Bouley, 2018; Sherouse, 2015; Perry et al., 2019; Woolley, 2019). Without knowledge of diversity in gender roles/expression/identity and sexual orientation, educator implicit bias may go unknown and unchallenged and as a result, students with varying gender identities may be inundated with microaggressions throughout the school day.

Figure 6.4   Macro, Micro, Impact, ABE. *Source*: Created by Bouley & Reinking, 2021.

Teachers and administrators need to develop knowledge of gender roles and diversity in gender identity, expression, and sexuality as well as resources, policies, and child/parental rights that support their ability to effectively create safe and inclusive classrooms, and confidently support students and families.

This knowledge and awareness are also important to minimize bias and microaggressions that students and families may experience when working with teachers who predominantly identify as cisgender female, heterosexual women.

As established, it is important that teachers are aware of ways to include and support the growing number of students who identify as LGBTQQ+ and/or with diverse gender identity/expression. Professional development in multicultural education should always start with teacher self-reflection and awareness. Heightening self-awareness and increasing basic knowledge are important starting places when developing a teacher's competence and confidence in creating classroom and school climates that are inclusive and safe for LGBTQQ+ students and families.

Reflection: How have you included same-sex families and/or LGBTQQ+ youth in your classroom materials and discussions?

Taking time to stop and think about beliefs and biases is an important first step. Do you believe children can identify as their non-biological gender? Do you believe gender is non-binary? How are your biases and beliefs transmitted in your classroom? One important area to explore is teacher-student interaction. Do you call on girls more than boys during math? Do you identify and use student preferred pronouns? Do you refer to a student's family as "mom and dad" when unsure if they could have same-sex parents?

How often do you express binary, traditional beliefs on gender and how often do you explicitly integrate the non-binary or non-conforming into classroom discourse? Are you open and willing to learn more and analyze your classroom practices to become more inclusive of gender variance and sexual orientation? These are all important questions to explore.

A systemic approach to the inclusion of diversity in gender expression/identity and sexual orientation in schools is critical to creating safe and affirming school/classroom environments, and should start in early childhood/elementary settings. Many microaggressions happen in school hallways or outside at recess, and all school personnel should be involved in discussions and professional development on gender-related diversity.

It is well established in the research that the early childhood years are an opportune time for multicultural and empathy education. Young children are open, accepting, and empathetic. Further, since even cisgendered children are exploring their gender at this age, it is important that early childhood/

elementary teachers model acceptance of diversity in gender expression/ identity and allow for open and on-going dialog.

Equally established in research is how positive support and acceptance for students who are gender non-conforming has an extremely positive impact on their overall development. When family members accept their child's gender diversity it decreases suicide and other high-risk behaviors, and increases happiness, school success, and overall health.

The role of the teacher should always be to nurture and support the child-parent/caregiver relationship. To do this effectively teachers need to have the cultural awareness and cultural competence necessary.

There are an abundance of resources available for educators to utilize in supporting LGBTQQ+ students and families. Administrators, teachers, and all school personnel such as nurses and social workers should be aware of and knowledgeable in the resources available to be a part of a school-wide plan to support children and families.

Reflection: Have you and your colleagues discussed bullying toward LGBTQQ+ children and families? Do you feel your school climate is safe and inclusive?

Open, on-going, school-wide dialog is a must first step to support LGBTQQ+ students and families. None of the above can occur without school-wide discussions around diversity in gender identity and expression. Teachers need to have the opportunity to safely explore how they are, or are not, addressing gender variance in their classrooms and how they can better support children and families.

Because policies and terms are changing quickly, a point person who stays current and acts as a resource for administrators, teachers, and families (school nurse, psychologist, etc.) could be designated in each school.

Generally, educators are ready and willing to learn more and develop the knowledge and skills to support students and their families. They are also likely concerned about how gender variant children may be treated by other children, and unsure if their school is a safe climate.

It is clear that we are in a "Gender Revolution" and will not be reverting back to the binary notion of gender. The number of individuals who identify as LGBTQ+ is on the rise and how we define gender is expanding widely, and rapidly. Yet, transgender people continue to be bullied, dehumanized, and battered at alarming rates. School administrators need to make time for this important professional development.

Reflection: One Word. What is your one word (figure 6.5) to summarize your thoughts or feelings after reading this chapter? What is your one word?

Examples of one word are provided in this word cloud, which was created by using the words in this chapter.

Figure 6.5   One Word, Chapter 6. *Source:* Created by Bouley & Reinking, 2021.

After reading this chapter, what are some ways you will hold yourself accountable through intentional, thoughtful actions?

Table 6.3 Reflections and Intentions

Reflection Question	Your Answer
My interactions with students…	
My interactions with their families…	
Physical classroom environment…	
Classroom materials and materials used for instruction…	
Lesson planning and curriculum…	
Instructional strategies such as grouping…	
Creating an anti-biased anti-racist school climate…	

RESOURCES

Educator Resources: https://www.glsen.org/educator-resources

Explore Transgender Children and Youth: https://www.hrc.org/explore/topic/transg ender-children-youth

Families Acceptance Project: Supportive Families, Healthy Children: http://familypr oject.sfsu.edu/sites/default/files/FAP_English%20Booklet_pst.pdf; http://family-project.sfsu.edu

GenderBread Person: https://www.genderbread.org/wp-content/uploads/2017/02/ Breaking-through-the-Binary-by-Sam-Killermann.pdf

GLSEN Elementary School Toolkit- https://www.glsen.org/sites/default/files/GLS EN%20Ready%20Set%20Respect.pdf

It Gets Better Project: https://itgetsbetter.org/stories/

Loaded Language: Changing How We Talk About Gender:https://drive.google.com/ file/d/1KSlK1uxghsiLqITV-LIKAuvErEBJbnMB/view

National "I am Jazz" Day of Reading: https://www.hrc.org/videos/national-i-am-jazz -day-of-reading

Schools in Transition: A Guide for Supporting Transgender Students in K-12 Schools: https://www.hrc.org/resources/schools-in-transition-a-guide-for-suppor ting-transgender-students-in-k-12-s

The Safe Zone Project: https://thesafezoneproject.com/activities/

Welcoming Schools: https://www.hrc.org/blog/filter/topic/25221

Chapter 7

Religious, Spirituality, and Non-Religious Microaggressions

*I am not an atheist; I believe in God. But my religion ends there. I
have my own personal belief system that is so strong it allows me to do
what I do. I don't have to worry about going to Hell because of Slayer,
you know? Everyone has a personal belief system and believes in life
somehow.*

—Tom Araya, Chilean-American musician,
best known as the vocalist and bassist of
American thrash metal band Slayer

Arguably, religion is used as a way to cope or explain difficult topics or
events in our lives. When someone passes away, many people respond in
prayer or stating "you are in my prayers." When there is a national tragedy
politician often state, "thoughts and prayers are with the families." When we
are fired from a job, go through a divorce or separation, or are physically or
emotionally hurt, many people respond in prayer or stating "you are in my
prayers." Assuming that everyone has a religious or spiritual belief in and
of itself is a microaggression. While this chapter is primarily about religion
and spirituality, it is also important to note that not everyone has the coping
system of religion or spirituality, but rather rely on coping systems unique to
their family background, which can be described through investigation of the
Culture Tree.

That being said, in America it is often assumed that "everyone" is Christian
and therefore celebrates Christian holidays such as Christmas, Easter, and
arguably Halloween. However, that is not the case, as the statistics show, 70
percent of Americans report they are Christians, which include Catholicism,
5.9 percent report a non-Christian faith, which include Judaism, Muslim,

Buddhist, Hindu, and 17.3 percent report an "other" or "don't know" (Pew Research Center, 2021). Arguably, the Christian hegemony is even shown in the reporting of statistics by basing data in "Christian" verses "Non-Christian." This displays the dominant culture of assuming that everything is based on the idea of Christianity, the often assumed "norm" in the United States.

What is Christian hegemony? It is defined as "the everyday, pervasive, and systematic set of Christian values and beliefs, individuals and institutions that dominate all aspects of our society through the social, political, economic, and cultural power they wield. Nothing is unaffected by Christian hegemony (whether we are Christian or not) including our personal beliefs and values, our relationships to other people and to the natural environment, and our economic, political, education, health care, criminal/legal, housing, and other social systems" (Challenging Christian Hegemony, 2009). For example, schools have breaks around Christian holidays such as Christmas and Easter. While these breaks impact everyone, taking into consideration additional religious holidays that are non-Christian are often ignored.

This hegemony impacts not only our society but also our schools through microaggressive language and actions. This is also explained through Christian Privilege, which "refers to the idea that in our society (and in many others), Christian people receive various social benefits purely because of their religion. Everyone else is denied those benefits and experiences various oppressions instead." One oppression that non-Christian or non-religious students often face from peers is bullying or physical violence due to "othering" or "being different" (Mogilevsky, 2016).

Figure 7.1   Macro, Micro, Impact, ABE. *Source*: Created by Bouley & Reinking, 2021.

When searching, "common religious stereotypes" the first entry on the curated google search page was titled "Common Christian Stereotypes," again placing the power in Christianity. However, after scrolling through the results, many are populated around stereotypes for religions spanning from the Jewish religion to the Mormon religion to the Muslim religion or the practice of Islam. Some of the stereotypes include the concept of polygamy in the Mormon religion, the idea that all Christians are judgmental, and that all individuals who practice Islam are terrorists. As with all stereotypes, most of these stereotypes are not only prevalent in daily life but are reinforced through media such as television shows, movies, and commercials, which is supported by the process we completed while reflecting on the Cycle of Socialization.

In relation to religious microaggressions and students, it is important to note that Title VI of the Civil Rights Act of 1964 (Title VI) protects students of any religion from discrimination, including harassment, based on a student's actual or perceived: shared ancestry or ethnic characteristics, or citizenship or residency in a country with a dominant religion or distinct religious identity.

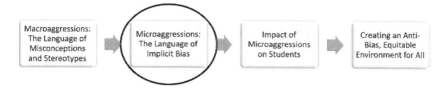

Figure 7.2   Macro, Micro, Impact, ABE. *Source*: Created by Bouley & Reinking, 2021.

Religious and non-religious microaggressions are divided into six specific categories. Arguably, all types of religious microaggressions can be placed into one of these six categories. The categories, as stated by Nadal, Griffin, Hamit, Leon, Tobio, and Rivera in 2012, are:

1. *Endorsing Religious Stereotypes*: statements or behaviors that communicate false, presumptuous, or incorrect perceptions of certain religious groups.
2. *Exoticization*: instances where people view other religions as trendy or foreign and therefore create an atmosphere of seeing another's religion as "bizarre" or "foreign."
3. *Pathology of Different Religious Groups*: Statements and behaviors in which individuals equate certain religious practices or traditions as being abnormal, sinful, or deviant.
4. *Assumption of One's Own Religious Identity as the Norm*: Comments or behaviors that convey people's presumption that their religion is the standard and behaves accordingly (e.g., greeting someone "Merry Christmas" or saying "God bless you" after someone sneezes conveys one's perception that everyone is Christian or believes in God).
5. *Assumption of Religious Homogeneity*: Statements in which individuals assume that every believer of a religion practices the same customs or has the same beliefs as the entire group.
6. *Denial of Religious Prejudice*: Incidents in which individuals claim that they are not religiously biased, even if their words or behaviors may indicate otherwise.

The six categories will be used as a way to discuss and provide examples of common religious microaggressions.

ENDORSING RELIGIOUS STEREOTYPES

This category of religious microaggressions communicate false or incorrect perceptions of specific religious groups. Examples of endorsing religious stereotypes would include stating or believing all Muslims are terrorists or that Jewish people are cheap in regards to spending money. Other examples could include the belief or perception that all Mormon men are polygamous or that all Catholics are homophobic. These microaggressions can enter classrooms or other environments through conversations, interactions, and nonverbal communication.

Conversations, interactions, and nonverbal communication were one way that endorsing religious stereotypes entered schools after the terrorist attacks on 9/11 in the United States. After the events of 9/11 there was widespread anti-Muslimism sentiment. Such terms as "towel head," "camel jockey," and "terrorist" were used toward and about Muslim students creating an unsafe learning environment. While this happened in 2001, this sentiment and microaggressive behavior is still present today.

In a study conducted with New York students, 69 percent of Muslim students felt that mainstream society was suspicious of them, nearly all of the students surveyed felt that discrimination had increased since 9/11, and 66 percent of the students felt that wearing "traditional" Muslim attire would risk facing discrimination in the workplace or in school (Cristillo & Louis, 2008) Furthermore, in a lesson plan focused on the impact of 9/11 it is stated that "while the number of hate crimes committed against Muslims after 9/11 has decreased, it has never returned to the pre-9/11 levels" (9/11 Memorial & Museum, 2021, para. 14).

EXOTICIZATION

Exoticizing religion is similar to racial exoticizing and cultural appropriation, both of which were discussed in the chapter focused on racial microaggressions. As a reminder, "cultural appropriation refers to the use of objects or elements of a non-dominant culture in a way that doesn't respect their original meaning, give credit to their course, or reinforces stereotypes or contributes to oppression" (Cuncic, 2020).

Overall, exoticizing, as a religious microaggression, is the act of focusing on viewing "other" religions as trendy or foreign and therefore create an atmosphere of seeing another's religion as "bizarre." Some examples of this may be individuals who dress in religious garb to be "fashionable," however, not truly believing in the meaning behind the practice, such as men and women covering their head as a form of identity, modesty, and reduction of sexual objectification. Another type of exoticizing microaggression is asking questions about why a person wears a kippah or hijab (Kaplin, 2017). A way this question may be heard in a learning environment is someone stating, "It is so hot. Why are you all covered up?" While the intent may be curiosity, the impact can be perceived as bullying, questioning, or othering.

PATHOLOGY OF DIFFERENT RELIGIOUS GROUPS

Pathologizing various religious groups, specifically religious groups or beliefs that may be different than your own, occurs through behaviors and actions that indicate the "other" (as compared to you) is abnormal, sinful, or deviant. This can occur by telling someone they are the "wrong" religion.

One example that anecdotally occurred in a teacher's lounge several years ago was a conversation around death. In this specific instance, someone close to many people on staff had passed away. The teachers and staff were discussing "life after death" of the individual who passed, who was Jewish. One of the teachers stated, "I just wish she would have taken Jesus as her savior before she died so she could be in heaven now." While this statement and microaggressive comment could fall under several religion microaggression categories, this specific comment sent the message of Judaism as "wrong" compared to her religion, which was self-identified as "conversative Christian." This same experience could play out in learning environments when talk of death and religion is brought up by students. Ensuring that the educator in the classroom is welcoming of all viewpoints, while not dismissing any viewpoint, is essential to creating an inclusive learning environment.

Another example could be conversations around God or Gods/Deities, as well as understanding that not all individuals or families are religious or spiritual. Therefore, one way to create a transformational environment is to acknowledge, and not assume, that everyone is not religious. As a classroom teacher I (Reinking) often had students bring up God, Jesus, or other aspects of Christianity during discussions or lessons. When these discussions would occur a statement, I often used to say, "We all have different beliefs, no one's belief is right and no one's belief is wrong. It is a belief that we hold with our family and that is what makes us all unique."

A final example is the "worry," which is arguably based on ignorance or fear, and has a negative impact, occurs during Ramadan. During the month of Ramadan, Muslims fast from sun up to sun down.

Ramadan is important, not only because it is a religious requirement but because it teaches patience, selflessness, and improves one's character. A Muslim is not going to sacrifice all of that just for a quick snack. . . . There shouldn't be an expectation or praise for breaking the rules during a religious holy month (Igusti, 2017).

During this time, individuals observing Ramadan often are bombarded with the microaggression of questioning. The specific question often revolves around "sneaking" food during the day or pressure to break fast before the sun goes down. Fear and ignorance grounding the insensitive questions around breaking fast also impact learning environments. This microaggression often occurs in lunchrooms around the country when Muslim children, who are safely engaging in the process of fasting, are questioned at lunchtime, made to eat, or are made the center of attention for not eating.

ASSUMPTION OF ONE'S OWN RELIGIOUS IDENTITY AS THE NORM

It is normal for humans to place personal beliefs and experiences at the center of our "normal"; however, it becomes problematic when we engage in microaggressive behaviors and comments due to our personal perceptions of "normal." When we assume that our own religious identity is the norm, we are excluding the unique beliefs and views of everyone in our environment.

Since the dominant religion in the United States is Christianity, many of the interactions and microaggressions revolve around Christian norms. Examples of category of microaggression occur when someone sneezes and we say "god bless you" or require everyone to stand up and say the Pledge of Allegiance, which includes the line "one nation under God, indivisible, with liberty and justice for all." As a side note, in 1943 the Supreme Court of the United States ruled that no one can be forced to say the Pledge of Allegiance after a group of Jehovah's Witness parents brought a suit when their students were expelled due to their refusal to participate in the pledge (FindLaw.com, 2017). Both of these examples assume that everyone is a Christian and/or believes in God.

The assumption that everyone is Christian and celebrates Christian beliefs occurs yearly in schools around the United States. How? It occurs through the decisions and actions of the school calendar that schedules breaks around Christian holidays. It occurs when schools decide which holidays to celebrate, which are primarily Christian based. Our society and public-school system are based on the history of Christianity, therefore, Christian holidays are and have been celebrated in schools for generations. However, when holidays are celebrated in classrooms, whether the "Christian" part of them is discussed or not, there is a message that is being sent to students and families. The holidays that are religiously based and are often celebrated in schools are Halloween (All Hallow's Eve), Christmas (the birth of Jesus), Valentine's Day (St. Valentine), Lent (serving fish on Fridays), and Easter (the resurrection of Jesus). See table 7.1 for an example.

Table 7.1 Microaggression Messages

Marginalized Group based on Identity	Microaggression	Intended/Unintended Message
Religion	Scheduling a major test on a religious holiday. Or Decorating the school/ classroom for a Christian holiday (ex. Christmas, Easter)	Historically only Christian holidays have been provided a day off from school. Therefore, scheduling a test on holidays not celebrated by Christians, portrays the message that Christianity is the only important and worthy holiday for schools to follow

Furthermore, even if a student or teacher is not Christian and is "okay" with celebrating Christian holidays in school, Jehovah's Witnesses, Orthodox Jews, and Seventh-Day Adventists, to name a few, cannot and do not celebrate all or some holidays. Overall, the practice of celebrating Christian holidays, and more widely celebrations in school buildings overall, is an exclusionary practice. A clear movement in schools, to create a more inclusive environment, is to truly separate religion from school and remove the holiday celebrations. While this is a hard concept for many people, it is a way to create a more inclusive, safe, and welcoming environment for all.

Reflection: How does your school create an inclusive environment around the concept and celebrations of holidays? What are areas that you may change or brainstorm replacement traditions?

ASSUMPTION OF RELIGIOUS HOMOGENEITY

The assumption of religious homogeneity is very similar to endorsing religious stereotypes. When we make assumptions about a group of people, we then begin and/or strengthen our stereotype of that group. We associate customs and beliefs to the group as a monolith. For example, when we assume that due to someone's ethnic identity, they "must" have the religious identity that goes along with the former. Such as, assuming all Muslims practice Islam or all Jewish people practice Judaism. Similar to language diversity of dialects (ex. American-English Southern accent, American-English Northern accent), ethnically Jewish or Muslim individuals have diversity within their religion or sect.

DENIAL OF RELIGIOUS PREJUDICE

The denial of Religious Prejudice is often in the form of implicit (unconscious) biases. Essentially, it includes incidents where individuals claim that they are not religiously biased, even when their words or behaviors may indicate otherwise. A common example of this is in airports. "Airport screening disproportionately targets religious minorities and reinforces harmful racial stereotypes" (Kaplin, 2017). This religious targeting increased after the attacks on 9/11, and then again after President Trump's "Muslim Ban." Both of these incidents entered classroom and learning environments through conversations, media, and actions.

ASSUMPTION OF RELIGION

One microaggression that is not added into the list of religious microaggressions is the microaggression of assuming everyone has a religious or spiritual belief. This denies the views of both atheists and agnostics, and for individuals who do not self-identify as any category on the religious slice of the social identity wheel. For grounding purposes, atheists refers to someone who does not believe in the existence of a god or any gods and an agnostic refers to someone who does not know whether there is a god, or if such a thing is even knowable.

Additionally, there are religions, such as Wicca or witchcraft, which is categorized as a modern-day Pagan religion, that were not mentioned. For background knowledge, Wicca is a modern, Earth-centered religion with roots in the ancient practices of our shamanic ancestors.

Therefore, the concept of being open to all types of religious, spiritual, or non-religious concept is part of creating an inclusive and transformative learning environment. Assuming that everyone has a religious or spiritual belief is a microaggression that is even evident in this chapter. When conversations occur in educational settings that often are explained or reasoned out through one's religious beliefs, such as death or classroom holidays, it is also important to understand that everyone does not have the coping system of religion or spirituality, but rather rely on coping systems unique to their family background.

Figure 7.3 Macro, Micro, Impact, ABE. *Source*: Created by Bouley & Reinking, 2021.

Regardless of the religious stereotype, actions and thoughts impact the way individuals in educational settings interact with each other. Specifically, in the classroom, a macroaggression, which also becomes a microaggression as described earlier, is the infusion of Christian holidays in the school setting. In association to this concept, students who celebrate non-Christian, yet religious, holidays are punished for missing school. For example, Jewish children celebrate High Holidays, which are not recognized by most school districts as an excused absence or a holiday to have "off," such as Christmas break or Easter break.

Furthermore, during the Trump presidency, Muslim students were discriminated against at a societal macro-level, which ultimately impacted school engagement. For example, a Muslim student was told by their teacher, "I can't wait until Trump is elected. He's going to deport all you Muslims" (Ochieng, 2017). This language created an unsafe and unwelcoming environment for that student and for students who heard that comment. Additionally, the publicly displayed executive order toward Muslim immigration into the United States heightened anti-Muslimism rhetoric and behavior in schools, which was discussed earlier.

Finally, a macroaggression already discussed is the assumption that everyone has a coping strategy for large events in life based in a religious or spiritual understanding of the world. Telling a student, "everything happens for a reason" when someone passes away, or assuming a child will be celebrating a holiday by asking questions regarding their costume, or presents, or experiences. Creating an equitable environment is consciously changing your language, especially during times in our lives when humans traditionally lead on coping strategies such as prayer and spirituality.

Reflection: As we transition to the next step in this chapter, let us reflect on our morals and values, which are often associated with our religious and non-religious beliefs. How are your morals acted upon in the learning environment? How do your values impact your interactions in the learning environment?

Figure 7.4   Macro, Micro, Impact, ABE. *Source*: Created by Bouley & Reinking, 2021.

Creating an equitable environment for all students, specifically in reference to this chapter based on religion and spirituality, begins with self-reflection and awareness. As part of the reflection process, it is important to be aware of your personal values based on your religious or non-religious morals.

As you were reflecting on the reflection questions posed above, you might ask yourself, "what is the difference between values and morals?" Values are taught through our Cycle of Socialization and are often based on lessons and

experiences we have in childhood. Values are belief systems that an individual builds as they grow and interact in the world and they tell us what is
right and wrong or what is just and fair. Morals, on the other hand, are often
associated with religion based on what is sinful and what is not sinful. Morals
are viewed as mandatory and all individuals should follow them. In general,

> morals are codes of conduct that tell us what is right and what is wrong, and they
> mostly come from religion and society. Values are internal belief systems held
> by individuals that guide their behavior . . . are personal and subjective while
> morals are universal and objective. Values can change while morals remain the
> same (differencebetween.com, 2012).

*Reflection: Additional questions to ask yourself, specifically around the
concepts of the dominant Christian religion as it plays out in learning environments include questions outlined in "Leading Anti-Bias Early Childhood
Programs" by Louise Derman-Sparks, Debbie LeeKeenan, and John Nimmo:*

- *What assumptions are you making about the children and families, specifi-
  cally their traditions and cultures?*
- *How are you reinforcing a religious hierarchy?*
- *Which holidays are centered in your classroom's décor and activities?*
- *How are you centering your own traditions and values?*
- *How do you address holidays outside of December?*
- *What are you taking for granted as "non-religious" (such as elves, rein-
  deer, Santa, etc.) that are really based in Christian traditions?*
- *How are you tokenizing December-based holidays? (If your classroom
  decked out for Christmas but you have one Menorah or Kinara in a
  corner?)*

Finally, through this process of reflecting on how your values and morals
impact your teaching and learning environment, reflect on the three choices
in addressing microaggressions as outlined by Washing, Birth, and Roberts'
(2020): Let it Go, Respond Immediately, or Respond Later. These three choices
are a great way to create an anti-bias learning environment thinking about all
identities, including religious/spiritual or non-religious/spiritual identity.

DISCIPLINE

Punishment, embarrassment, and questioning are three ways that students
who do not fit into the "mold" of the dominant Christian beliefs in a public-
school setting are reprimanded or disciplined. For example, children who are
excluded from holiday celebrations due to religious or non-religious beliefs

may be questioned through the microaggressions already discussed or feel embarrassed for being excluded. Children who need to miss portions of the school year for religious holidays that do not fall in line with already established Christian holiday breaks are disciplined through the addition of work, which is not the case for students when schools are out around the dominant Christian holidays. And, as already discussed, students who do not feel that saying the Pledge of Allegiance in school is part of their identity, yet are made to stand or be punished for not standing.

A final example focuses on the religious practice of praying five times a day. When students are not afforded the space, time, or inconspicuous release from class, this is a type of punishment through refusal or being ridiculed or questioned by peers and teachers alike. As with all microaggressions, and as we reflect on the Cycle of Socialization, ignorance and fear are often guiding our thoughts, actions, and emotions. It is also important to create an environment focused on the four Crucial C's.

Reflection: One Word. What is your one word (figure 7.5) to summarize your thoughts or feelings after reading this chapter? What is your one word?

Examples of one word are provided in this word cloud, which was created by using the words in this chapter.

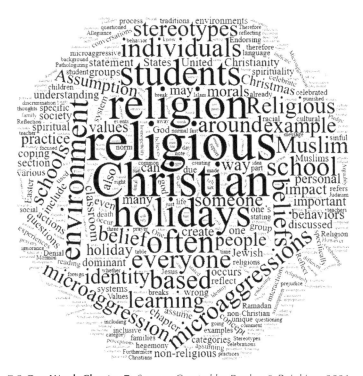

Figure 7.5 One Word, Chapter 7. *Source*: Created by Bouley & Reinking, 2021.

After reading this chapter, what are some ways you will hold yourself accountable through intentional, thoughtful actions?

Table 7.2 Reflections and Intentions

Reflection Question	Your Answer
My interactions with students...	
My interactions with their families...	
Physical classroom environment...	
Classroom materials and materials used for instruction...	
Lesson planning and curriculum...	
Instructional strategies such as grouping...	
Creating an anti-biased anti-racist school climate...	

RESOURCES

Celebrating Holidays: https://www.naeyc.org/resources/blog/anti-bias-and-holi days

Holidays and Anti-Bias Education: http://www.antibiasleadersece.com/wp-content/ uploads/2016/09/Holidays-and-ABE-Bisson-Derman-Sparks.pdf

Learning for Justice: Religious Diversity in the Classroom https://www.learningforju stice.org/professional-development/religious-diversity-in-the-classroom

Lesson Plan Focused on 9/11 and Muslims in America: https://www.911memorial.o rg/learn/students-and-teachers/lesson-plans/muslims-america-after-911-part-ii

Religious Diversity through Children's Literature (article): https://files.eric.ed.gov/ fulltext/EJ1104911.pdf

Chapter 8

Economic Microaggressions

The problem is the problem; the person is not the problem. (Michael White and David Epston) We know what we do, we think we know what we think, but do we know what what we do does?

—Michael Foucault

For students living in poverty, school is often a safe haven; it may be the one place in their lives where they feel they can let their guard down, where life makes sense. Schools offer refuge from violence and inconsistencies and are a place where students can feel a sense of security and assurance. For many students school is where they are nourished, emotionally, intellectually, and physically. It is a place where they might get their most sound sleep, as they feel their welfare is of utmost concern. For students living in poverty, school can be a sanctuary.

Due to the many challenges impoverished communities face, such as a lack of health care, poor nutrition, stress and trauma, students living in poverty are some of our most at risk. Jensen (2009) exposes the many risk factors of poverty and the impact they have on academic and behavioral performance. He states that children living in poverty are "faced daily with overwhelming challenges that affluent children never have to confront, and their brains have adapted to suboptimal conditions in ways that undermine good school performance" (Jensen, 2009, p. 14).

Jensen (2009), uses EACH as a mnemonic to identify the pervasive risk factors children raised in poverty experience, Emotional and Social Challenges (E), Acute and Chronic Stressors (A), Cognitive Lags (C), Health and Safety Issues (H). As a consequence, students raised in poverty are more likely to act out in schools or behave in undesirable ways. These behaviors may be misinterpreted by teachers and, as a result, children living in poverty are more likely to receive discipline in schools.

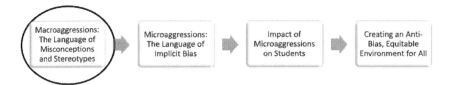

Figure 8.1   Macro, Micro, Impact, ABE. *Source*: Created by Bouley & Reinking, 2021.

Barnum (2017), states studies consistently demonstrate that "black and poor students have substantially higher suspension rates than white and more affluent peers." He then states, "Figuring out why is tricky. Is it because certain groups of students behave differently, or because teachers and administrators respond differently to the same behavior?" (para. 1).

As a result, students raised in poverty are recipients of some of the most egregious implicit bias, and are often devalued and shamed by the microaggressions they experience daily. Consequently, in a space where it is most viable for students living in poverty to develop a bond with adults outside of their family, the educator-student relationship is strained, damaged, and/or laden with mistrust and low expectations. Students living in poverty experience deficit-based thinking and microaggressions more often than their more affluent peers.

While poverty-based bias has received less attention than race and gender bias, it is pervasive in schools. Gibson and Barr (2017) state that students living in poverty,

> often face additional obstacles of bullying, class prejudice, racial prejudice, low teacher expectations, weak curriculum, and having the least experienced/ least capable teachers (Barr & Gibson, 2013; Gorski, 2013; Jensen, 2009). The effects of these experiences are further amplified or exacerbated by unconscious, implicit biases about poverty (Flannery, 2015, p. 39).

It is difficult to discuss poverty bias without considering the role of race. Children of color, in particular Black, Latinx, and Native American, are three times more likely to be living in poverty. As discussed earlier in this book, Kimberly Crenshaw coined the term intersectionality in 1989 to describe the intersected experience of subordination from being Black and being a woman. The Webster dictionary defines intersectionality as, "the complex, cumulative way in which the effects of multiple forms of discrimination (such as racism, sexism, and classism) combine, overlap, or intersect especially in the experiences of marginalized individuals or groups."

It is important then to consider racial stereotypes and poverty stereotypes simultaneously.

When considering intersectionalities and poverty, it is also important to consider gender. More women than men live in poverty in the United States and those numbers have only risen during the COVID-19 pandemic. The 2018 U.S. Census Bureau data shows that 56 percent of the 38.1 million people living in poverty are women, and that women have higher rates of poverty than men across all races and ethnicities.

Furthermore, one in every four single-parent mothers' lives in poverty, and women between 25 and 34, childbearing ages, are 69 percent more likely to live in poverty than men of the same age group. Since the COVID-19 pandemic, the wide majority of workers to leave the workforce are women (nearly 70 percent) and instead of the expected decrease in the gender gap of 2.7 percent, it rose 9.1 percent (U.S. Bureau of Labor Statistics, 2021).

Reflection: How do you know if your students live in poverty?

Fergus (2019) discusses "poverty-disciplining belief" as a way of seeing poverty as its own culture, and one that is "characterized by dysfunctional behaviors that prevent success in school" (para. 3). He describes this belief as a form of pathology, and one that does not focus on race explicitly but, "is often used as a proxy for race and to justify racial disparities in disciplinary referrals, achievement, and enrollment in gifted, AP, and honors courses, as well as to justify harsh punishments for 'disobedience' or 'disorderly conduct' or 'disrespect.'"

When discussing the many international studies focused on the concept of a poverty culture, Gorski (2008) states,

> These studies raise a variety of questions and come to a variety of conclusions about poverty. But on this they all agree: *There is no such thing as a culture of poverty.* Differences in values and behaviors among poor people are just as great as those between poor and wealthy people (p. 32).

Yet, there are common misconceptions and stereotypes for people living in poverty. Most of the misconceptions relate to motivation, determination, and making poor choices. Generally, polls over the past twenty years have found anywhere from one-third to one-half of Americans believe that people living in poverty are not doing enough to get themselves out (Population Reference Bureau, 2021). The majority of the studies on poverty culture find the most pervasive myths or stereotypes of poor people are that they

- lack motivation, are lazy, and have poor work ethic,
- don't work hard enough to achieve social mobility,
- are linguistically challenged or deficient,

- make bad choices like abusing drugs and alcohol,
- are looking for handouts and to "milk the system,"
- if they go on welfare, they never go off,
- don't value education and are not involved in their child's learning.

However, as Jervis (2006) explains, "Given the complexity and ambiguity of our world, it is unfortunately true that beliefs for which a good deal of evidence can be mustered often turn out to be mistaken" (p. 643).

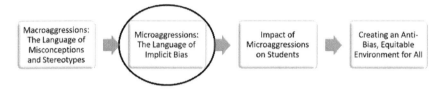

Figure 8.2   Macro, Micro, Impact, ABE. *Source*: Created by Bouley & Reinking, 2021.

As we begin this section, please take a moment to read each statement and then write the first thing that comes to mind in the table below. You will be asked to complete this reflection at the end of this section also.

Table 8.1   Reflection Table. *Source:* Created by Bouley & Reinking, 2021.

Statement	Reflect: What First Comes to Mind?
School transience/mobility	
Frequent absenteeism	
Family/parent misses teacher conferences	
Little to no family/parent communication	
Free lunch and no snacks	
Incomplete homework	
Behavioral outbursts or sleeping in class	
Apparent apathy/not caring about schoolwork	
Lack of openness to building relationships	
No coat, boots, physical education clothes	

Students and families living in poverty experience numerous microaggressions in schools, and most stem from common stereotypes or macroaggressions, which you just reflected on in the table above. As mentioned, the vast majority of studies focused on people living in poverty have found more affluent Americans believe they are not interested or involved in their child's education and that they don't value education in general.

The assumption here is if people in poverty worked harder at their own or their child's education, they would be able to get themselves out of poverty.

Or, as the common saying goes, "pull themselves up by their bootstraps." But, what boot straps? No all boots have straps. No all students or families have the same opportunities.

Reflection: As you have gotten to know your students' families in the past, what assumptions have you made? What assumptions have you made when you are working with families who live in poverty or single-mom families? Have you ever assumed that a family member/parent who could not make a conference or work in the classroom, etc., just didn't care? What did you do with or about your assumptions? How were they transmitted to your students and their families?

SCHOOL TRANSIENCE/MOBILITY

Students and families living in poverty have to overcome many daily obstacles. Living in poverty comes with extreme consequences. Due to lack of affordable housing and unemployment, evictions and moving are common for people living in poverty, not to mention the 60,000 families who are homeless (National Alliance to End Homelessness, 2018). One in every thirty American children experiences homelessness each year (White, 2014). In the United States, there are more homeless families than any other industrialized nation, and single mothers with two children make up the majority of those families.

Think about the consequences of frequent moving and/or homelessness on students and families. Then think about what kinds of assumptions based on implicit bias educators might make toward these students. How might these students and their families experience microaggressions?

FREQUENT ABSENTEEISM

The relationship between absenteeism and student success has been well documented (Goodman, 2014; Gottfried, 2015; Romero & Lee, 2007). Chronic absenteeism has been shown to negatively impact both academic achievement and social-emotional development. Likewise, so do transient students, defined as those "who change schools 6 or more times in their K-12 careers, or for some, those who change schools 3 times through 3rd grade" by the National Institute for Urban School Improvement.

Students who are chronically absent or who are transient, also fail to develop positive social interactions and relationships. Schafft (2009), was quoted in Jensen's (2009) book, pointing out that

whereas middle class families usually move for social or economic improvement, the moves of low-income households are typically not voluntary. In
addition to increasing children's uncertainty about the future, these moves
compound their stress load by disrupting their social interactions both within
the community and in academic environments (para. 46).

In these circumstances teachers might make assumptions as to why students are absent, and potentially assume the parents/family members do not
value education or care appropriately for their child. Other assumptions about
students living in houses, and having resources like computers or supplies,
may be made.

In more egregious cases students may be disciplined or punished for their
absenteeism/transience, and made to feel responsibility and shame for their
situation. Each of these assumptions that teachers may make about the student or family is the Ladder of Inference in action. It is human nature to make
judgments and assumptions, but we need to be aware of these inferences in
order to work against our human instinct of judgment.

Garcia and Weiss (2018), found that "Students who were diagnosed with
a disability, students who were eligible for free lunch, Hispanic English
language learners, and Native American students were the most likely
to have missed school, while Asian students were rarely absent" (p. 1).
Assumptions may be made that certain groups of students care less about
student school attendance, as opposed to examining the conditions that are
responsible.

Garcia and Weiss (2018) report,

> Poor health, parents' nonstandard work schedules, low socioeconomic status
> (SES), changes in adult household composition (e.g., adults moving into or out
> of the household), residential mobility, and extensive family responsibilities
> (e.g., children looking after siblings)—along with inadequate supports for stu-
> dents within the educational system (e.g., lack of adequate transportation, unsafe
> conditions, lack of medical services, harsh disciplinary measures, etc.)—are all
> associated with a greater likelihood of being absent, and particularly with being
> chronically absent (Ready, 2010; U.S. Department of Education, 2016, p. 5).

LITTLE TO NO FAMILY/PARENT COMMUNICATION

While research supports that family/parent engagement positively impacts
student outcomes, there are many reasons why poor families may not be able
to be as involved in their child's school. Family members living in poverty
may work multiple jobs with early morning and night shifts, impacting their

ability to support the completion of assigned homework or get their children off to school on-time.

They may not have transportation or gas money to bring their children to school when they miss the bus or to attend school events. Further, they might avoid going into school themselves because of their own past experiences in school or for fear that they will be judged as a parent or receive bad news about their child, and so on.

Reflection: What are some ways that you support students living in poverty, and their families?

Regardless of the reason, families living in poverty may be less involved or engaged in school which may perpetuate the stereotype that they don't value education or care. Jensen (2009) refers to the U.S. Department of Health and Human Services (2000) which showed that "only 36 percent of low-income parents were involved in three or more school activities on a regular basis, compared with 59 percent of parents above the poverty line" (para. 12). The potential for bias is compounded by the fact that educators have less opportunities to build relationships with these families, leaving assumptions and stereotypes unchallenged.

CULTURAL CAPITAL

Another opportunity for bias and microaggressions relates to the opportunity gap and cultural capital. Students coming from more affluent families have many more opportunities to develop the type of prior knowledge most utilized in academic settings. More affluent students are more likely to attend preschool, summer camps, museums, travel, and so on. They are also more likely to have parents/family members who have cultural capital for education, they know how school works, have had success in school and instill that knowledge and confidence in their children.

Yet, all students come to school with experiences and background knowledge. A common bias stems from the failure to see that while students living in poverty may not have the same prior knowledge of their more affluent peers, they have backgrounds that can be tapped into to best support their learning. The assumption that students living in poverty lack prior knowledge or experiences is a common microaggression.

Expressing that a student seems smart for a person living in poverty is a microaggression. Since a common stereotype of people living in poverty is that they are linguistically challenged or deficient, students who are articulate or linguistically talented may be seen as an exception, and may be told they speak well for a student who is poor.

ECONOMIC SHAMING

Perhaps one of the most common microaggressions students living in poverty experience relates to economic shaming. When students come to school wearing old or dirty clothing, without snacks or receiving free or reduced lunch, without winter or physical education clothing or without field trips or extracurricular money, and so on, they often experience microaggressions by both educators and their peers.

Asking students and families to contribute money for school activities is a microaggression. Taking away lunch choices for students who receive free or reduced lunch is a microaggression, as is handing out free/reduced lunch tickets or asking them to stand in a separate line. Not allowing students to have hot lunch because their family member owes lunch money or asking students to come to the school office to discuss outstanding money is a microaggression.

Sending students to the nurse's office for a "clean shirt" or making students sit on the wall for recess or physical education because they don't have the proper clothing are microaggressions. Students living in poverty are bullied and teased by their peers and shamed for the ways in which their low SES impacts their daily appearance and activities.

Reflections: Sometimes we do things for students living in poverty that could result in shaming (a great example of intent vs. impact). How might you change your or your school's policies and practices to minimize economic shaming?

Students are also often teased and ashamed by their bus stop. Students who live in low-income housing, run down houses or who are homeless, experience microaggressions and shaming on the bus. Ignoring student-to-student microaggressions is a microaggression in and of itself.

LACK OF OPENNESS TO BUILDING RELATIONSHIPS

Students living in poverty are also recipients of bias and microaggressions due to their lack of interpersonal skills or ability to develop relationships. In response to the U.S. Census Bureau data (2000), showing that children in poverty spend more time home alone watching TV with their siblings and less time playing outdoors or in after school activities, Jensen (2009) states,

> Unfortunately, children won't get the model for how to develop proper emotions or respond appropriately to others from watching cartoons; they need warm, person-to-person interactions. The failure to form positive relationships with peers inflicts long-term socioemotional consequences (Szewczyk-Sokolowski, Bost, & Wainwright, 2005, para. 13).

Reflection: Stop and reflect. Using the same table from the beginning of this section, fill in the second column with what first comes to mind. Have your thoughts changed? How so?

Figure 8.3   Macro, Micro, Impact, ABE. *Source*: Created by Bouley & Reinking, 2021.

The opportunities for students living in poverty to experience microaggressions are great, and so are the consequences. Perhaps the most common and most impactful consequence or impact is shame.

The social scientist and research professor Brené Brown has spent over twenty years researching shame and vulnerability. On her website she defines shame as, "the intensely painful feeling or experience of believing that we are flawed and therefore unworthy of love and belonging—something we've experienced, done, or failed to do makes us unworthy of connection." She then goes on to say,

> I don't believe shame is helpful or productive. In fact, I think shame is much more likely to be the source of destructive, hurtful behavior than the solution or cure. I think the fear of disconnection can make us dangerous (https://brenebrown.com).

Children and families living in poverty face the challenges of shame on a daily basis simply because of their socioeconomic status (SES). Yet, many educational philosophies have been based entirely on humanistic theory. Maslow theorized that there is a hierarchy of our basic human needs, and the needs at the bottom of that hierarchy (air, water, sleep, food, shelter, clothing, safety, love) must be met before we can learn and before we can reach becoming self-actualized beings.

Maria Montessori based her philosophy of teaching and learning from grades pre-K to grade 12 on humanistic beliefs. Her original research was on children living in extreme poverty and while no one else at the time believed the children were capable of learning, Montessori proved that if their basic human needs were met, they could learn.

As Brené Brown (2013) points out, not only does shame create an intense lack of the very things children and families living in poverty need the most from their school community, safety, love and belonging, but it also perpetuates the belief that many children and families living in poverty have, that they are flawed and unworthy. Shame may prevent people living in poverty from seeing that they are not the problem, but the problem is poverty.

It would be difficult for anyone to achieve academic success under these conditions. Without their basic human needs being met, there is far from a level playing field between children living in poverty, and their more affluent peers. As a result, students who live in poverty are, in a way, set up to fail academically, which just perpetuates the cycle of shame.

Often children and families living in poverty feel disconnected from the school community. If the behavior is seen to be a problem within the child, and not the circumstance, family members are also blamed and seen as responsible for their child's challenging behavior. The bias or macroaggression here may be "Your child wouldn't be behaving this way if you made sure he/she got more sleep, or was more respectful of adults, or you disciplined him/her better at home, etc."

Family members may receive phone calls with negative feedback about their child, be called in to school for conferences with a whole team of school personnel or be told their child may receive a suspension or even be expelled. In other words, families may be blamed and shamed. When we blame the student and family it creates a cyclical pattern of negative behaviors that is close to impossible to reverse.

An educator's job is to nurture our students' relationships with their family, to help them to feel pride in their family/parents and know that they love and care for them whenever we can. Instead, an educator's implicit bias may cause students who experience shame about their economic status to feel ashamed of their family. Students living in poverty may not want their peers to see the car their caregiver drives up in, or the clothing they are wearing, or the house they live in as the bus pulls up.

There are many ways in which children living in poverty may experience the feeling of shame about their family members. This is extremely difficult as it perpetuates even more shame because they may feel badly that they were ashamed of the people they love. Marc Brackett (2019) in his book *Permission to Feel* would call this a meta-emotion, having feelings about our feelings. As Brown (2013), reminds us educators need to do everything we can to prevent our students and families from experiencing shame, "I don't believe shame is helpful or productive. In fact, I think shame is much more likely to be the source of destructive, hurtful behavior than the solution or cure" (para. 3).

In discussing the school engagement disparities that exist between students and families living in poverty and their more affluent peers, Gorski (2016) believes people fall on a continuum of two ideological positions. He states,

> On one end of the continuum are people, including educators and policy-makers, who see people experiencing poverty as the agents of their own economic conditions. They adhere to deficit ideology (Gorski, 2008a; Sleeter, 2004), believing

that poverty itself is a symptom of ethical, dispositional, and even spiritual deficiencies in the individuals and communities experiencing poverty (p. 380).

He sees this as the dominant belief.
Then, Gorski (2016) continues,

On the other end of the continuum are people who tend to understand poverty and issues such as the family involvement disparity as logical, if unjust, outcomes of economic injustice, exploitation, and inequity. adherents to a structural ideology (Gorski, 2016b), they are likely to define gaps in in-school family involvement as interrelated with the inequities with which people experiencing poverty contend. So, recognizing people experiencing poverty as targets, rather than causes, of these unjust conditions, they might understand lower rates of in-school involvement as a symptom of in-school and out-of-school conditions that limit their abilities to participate at the same rates as their wealthier peers (p.380).

In order to create an anti-bias, equitable environment for all, and to minimize implicit bias and microaggressions toward students and families living in poverty, we must first consider the sociopolitical contexts and extreme conditions those living in poverty experience.

Figure 8.4   Macro, Micro, Impact, ABE. *Source*: Created by Bouley & Reinking, 2021.

In doing so, think about the term "the achievement gap" and consider how much word choice matters. When we use the term "the achievement gap" we are essentially blaming students for their lack of achievement rather than seeing the role out-of-school factors and lack of opportunity plays.

When we are on the side of Gorski's (2016) continuum that understands "poverty and issues such as the family involvement disparity as logical, if unjust, outcomes of economic injustice, exploitation, and inequity" we see that there isn't an achievement gap, but an opportunity gap. Believing in an achievement gap is a microaggression against students and families living in poverty.

To minimize microaggressions toward students and families living in poverty, educators must be careful to use the right terms in all of their interactions. Telling a student who is homeless to "bring this home" may feel like a microaggression as would asking a student to use his computer to do his homework when he doesn't have one at home.

To support students' prior knowledge and help them to make connections, we need to learn about their past experiences and what they are interested in. We can then use that information to direct our instruction and support their academic success, this is the beginning of student-centered learning.

We can also survey students and their families, use questionnaires, writing journals, and more to ascertain their background experiences, interests, and learning styles. The Cognitive Psychologist Piaget believed all learning is a connection between the known and the new. When we start with students' prior knowledge and connect the learning objectives to what they know, they can better understand the material.

Finding out about students' learning styles and intelligences allows us to differentiate our instruction and give choices about how students engage in lessons. Some students may have strong verbal intelligence but not have much success with writing and struggle. We can find ways to utilize their strength to support their weakness. Other students may be kinesthetic learners and need to engage with materials and move their bodies to learn the content of the lesson.

When we start with student background knowledge and interests and differentiate our instruction to accommodate learning styles and intelligences, the learning will be greater. Perhaps most important, when we diversify our instruction like this it is highly motivating and can easily start a positive cycle of student engagement.

In *The Economic and Opportunity Gap: How Poverty Impacts the Lives of Students* Reinking and Bouley (2021), discuss the importance of using literature-based lessons to support students living in poverty. The authors share literature-based lesson plans focused on social and racial justice for grades preschool to high school and remind us to focus critical discussions on how "poverty is a great injustice that happens within sociopolitical contexts, not on charity" (p. 120). Focusing on empathy building, feeling sorry for individuals, or raising money for "poor people" are experienced as microaggressions.

Reflection: What are some ways that you work to identify and integrate student background knowledge?

Equally important is using consistent data-based assessments to ensure students living in poverty are being challenged. Teachers must be aware of the downfalls of ability grouping or tracking based on labeling students or having low expectations. Measuring progress frequently, communicating that progress frequently, and involving students in progress monitoring and goal setting keeps us all accountable for providing challenging learning. Further, when teachers have high expectations for all students, students can begin to recognize that failure is part of, or rather the path to, learning and they will take more risks in the process.

Besides incorporating student learning styles and intelligences, instruction should be fluid or change often, especially when it is clear that it is not working. When instructional strategies vary from working collaboratively, to working alone, are student centered with active meaningful engagement, we are setting the stage for more productive and positive learning. Yet, we also need to consider how we assess learning and apply the same ideas.

In order for any assessment to have validity, it must assess what we actually want it to assess. For instance, if I am assessing whether or not a student understands a math concept by using a worksheet that the student cannot read, I am not assessing what I set out to. This example is especially important since students living in poverty may not be reading on grade level but can certainly understand concepts that are often assessed via reading (e.g., science, social studies, etc.).

Varying and differentiating how we assess students allows us to get a more accurate assessment of what they understand. Overall, being flexible and giving students choices of instructional strategies and assessments would allow us to both deepen learning and better evaluate what students understand.

Bandura's theory of perceived self-efficacy is an important concept especially when working with students living in poverty since they often come to school without the same experiences and background knowledge as their more affluent peers. Bandura (1994), saw self-efficacy as one's belief about their abilities to achieve at a task.

He believed that when students were self-efficacious toward the presented learning, they were more motivated and more persistent in their learning. There has been a plethora of studies since Bandura's that validate the critical role of confidence in learning. When a student perceives that he/she can accomplish a task, they will engage, and work harder. Students living in poverty may not have experienced a high level of academic success in the past and bring a lack of confidence into new learning.

Bandura (1994), believed there are four main ways to increase a student's perceived self-efficacy. He believed students develop increased self-efficacy by having "mastery experiences" (success increases our beliefs that we can succeed), by having "vicarious experiences through social models" (witnessing others like us succeed increases our beliefs about our own abilities), by "social persuasion" (when others model high beliefs and expectations that we can learn we begin to believe it, too), and by "reducing people's stress reactions and alter their negative emotional proclivities and misinterpretations of their physical states" (being aware of the role our emotional state plays in our ability to succeed—being nervous on a test, being a positive mood, etc.) (p.3).

An educator who believes the challenges students and families living in poverty experience in school are the fault of the conditions of poverty, not the individuals, believe all students can achieve academic and personal success. Rather than leading with judgments and assumptions based in implicit bias, these educators will work tirelessly to support that success!

DISCIPLINE

Leading with asset-based thinking (focusing on the good) and a wider view of poverty, educators can also take a closer look at the discipline practices that negatively impact students experiencing poverty. After reading and reflecting on the many microaggressions and the impact of those microaggressions on students, it might make sense that students living in poverty might find it difficult to focus in school, follow directions, and behave according to expectations.

Implicit bias causes educators to fail to look deeply into the causes, and discipline or punish students instead. As mentioned earlier, studies show students of color and those living in poverty are suspended more often, and for longer periods of time. Further, Petrilli (2017), notes, "high-poverty, high-minority schools suspend a lot more students than lower-poverty, lower-minority ones" (para. 11).

In fact, many studies show discipline-related issues are the responsibility of the school, and better approaches to disciplining students are needed. In *Discipline Reform through the Eyes of Teachers*, coauthored by Fordham Institute researchers David Griffith and Adam Tyner (2019), teachers reported school-wide discipline approaches to be "inconsistent or inadequate." Welsh and Little (2018) state, "The disparities in disciplinary outcomes may be better explained by the behavior of teachers and principals in schools rather than student characteristics such as misbehavior, poverty, or race. Recent evidence suggests that school-level variables are the strongest predictors of disciplinary outcomes" (Skiba, Chung et al., 2014, p. 758).

Conversely, when challenging behaviors are seen as a problem with the child, they may be subjected to numerous isolating, embarrassing and near abusive classroom practices, or microaggressions. For example, the child's desk may be moved away from a group and isolated somewhere since he is "unable to behave in a group."

Maybe a behavior modification program is set up for that child and as a consequence she misses recess often. Or even worse, a whole class behavior modification program is put in place and the child is responsible for the whole class losing a marble, resulting in a loss of recess time for everyone.

Blaming the student for behavior issues without assessing and addressing the potential context or cause is a microaggression. Looking at a student's SES as the explanation for behaviors more often for students living in poverty than their more affluent peers is a microaggression. Likewise, having low expectations for students living in poverty and overlooking their lack of discipline or unacceptable behavior is also a microaggression and indicates a deficit, as opposed to an asset-based approach.

Reflection: One Word. What is your one word (figure 8.5) to summarize your thoughts or feelings after reading this chapter? What is your one word?

Examples of one word are provided in this word cloud, which was created by using the words in this chapter.

Figure 8.5   One Word, Chapter 8. *Source*: Created by Bouley & Reinking, 2021.

After reading this chapter, what are some ways you will hold yourself accountable through intentional, thoughtful actions?

Table 8.2   Reflections and Intention

Reflection Question	Your Answer
My interactions with students…	
My interactions with their families…	
Physical classroom environment…	
Classroom materials and materials used for instruction…	
Lesson planning and curriculum…	
Instructional strategies such as grouping…	
Creating an anti-biased anti-racist school climate…	

RESOURCES

Association for Middle Level Education: *Leading Learning for Children from Poverty:* https://www.amle.org/leading-learning-for-children-from-poverty/

Book: *The Economic and Opportunity Gap: How Poverty Impacts the Lives of Students (Reinking & Bouley, 2021).*

Doing Good Together (book list): https://www.doinggoodtogether.org/bhf-book-lists/picture-books-hunger-poverty-homelessness

Documentary: *"Frontline PBS: Growing Up Poor:* https://www.youtube.com/watch?v=qAxQltlGodA and *"Frontline PBS: Poor Kids":* https://www.youtube.com/watch?v=HQvetA1P4Yg

Edutopia: *5 Ways to Help Students Affected Generational Poverty:* https://www.edutopia.org/discussion/5-ways-help-students-affected-generational-poverty

Teaching Children from Poverty and Trauma: https://www.nea.org/sites/default/files/2020-07/NEAPovertyTraumaHandbook.pdf

Chapter 9

Ability, Disability, and Ableism Microaggressions

There is a persistent belief amongst abled people that a cure is what disabled people should want. To abandon our disabled selves and bodies and assimilate into a perhaps unachievable abled skin. Pushback to this idea often comes in the form of the social model of disability, which states that we are disabled by society and lack of access rather than by our bodies. For many, the social model can be liberating: by locating the cause of our problems outside our bodies, we can begin to love ourselves again. Tackling systemic ableism may feel like tilting at windmills, but it is still easier to address than some kind of failing within ourselves. There is a criticism of the social model of disability, located in the idea that some disabled people may want a cure.

—Alice Wong, *Disability Visibility: First-Person Stories from the Twenty-first Century*

Even before the time of Shakespeare's play called *Richard III*, society had viewed individuals with disabilities as evil and morally suspect. In the play, Richard III's disabled body, the hunchback, was an "invitation to degenerate behavior" and view a body, a person, as grotesque (Solomon, 2019). In the play, Richard the III is referred to as crippled, hunchback, evil, and was written as the villain.

While the rhetoric might have changed since the time of Shakespeare, the mindsets regarding individuals with disabilities remains. That being said, "the group 'people with disabilities' (PWD) has always been the largest 'minority' group in America" (americanhistory.si.edu).

As with the other historically marginalized identities, individuals seen as "disabled" have been ostracized, demoralized, and deemed as "less than" for generations. In 1999, the Olmstead v. LC Supreme Court decision, which was based on the Americans with Disabilities Act (ADA), was the most important civil rights decision for PWD in United States history. The decision held that "people with disabilities have a qualified right to receive state funded supports and services in the community rather than institutions when the following three-part test is met" (olmsteadrights.org):

1. The person's treatment professionals determine that community supports are appropriate;
2. The person does not object to living in the community;
3. The provision of services in the community would be a reasonable accommodation when balanced with other similarly situated individuals with disabilities.

Prior to this decision, PWD were institutionalized and "erased" from society. Children and adults with disabilities were hidden or sent away. They were sent to mental health facilities that were often substandard or secluded in their homes without the needed services to foster independence.

Historically, the concept of disability was not discussed prior to the nineteenth century because there was no discourse or explanation in the variations of human functioning (Stanford Encyclopedia of Philosophy, 2016). Once a term and philosophical genre was created, discrimination and oppression based on a socially constructed concept, specifically disability classifications, was established.

As with other identities discussed in this book, disability has a wide-range of diversity. A disability can be anything from one of the fourteen categories of disabilities outlined in the Individuals with Disabilities Education Act (IDEA). These include autism, deaf-blindness, deafness, developmental delay, emotional disturbance, hearing impairment, intellectual disability, multiple disabilities, orthopedic impairment, other health impairment, and specific learning disability. A specific learning disability is defined as "a physical or mental condition that limits a person's movements, senses, or activities" (dictionary.com).

Figure 9.1   Macro, Micro, Impact, ABE. *Source*: Created by: Bouley & Reinking, 2021.

Creating environments around able-bodied individuals, or engaging in ableism actions and language, is embedding stereotypes into society. Stereotypes which are the language of macroaggressions. Ableism is the discrimination in favor of able-bodied people, which is defined as "fit, strong, and healthy; not physically disabled" (Oxford Dictionary). Furthermore, "ableism is to disabilities what racism is to people of color . . . (it is) the expression of a discriminatory preference for someone without a disability" (Byrne-Haber, 2019, para. 4).

"Historically, people with disabilities have been stereotyped in many different ways . . . Incomplete information, mistaken perceptions, isolation, and segregation have perpetrated many of these stereotypes" held by people in society (Momene, 2015, para. 2). The stereotypes placed on individuals with disabilities have influenced their inclusion, or exclusion, into society, educational trajectory, and negative influences throughout other parts of their lives. Many of the stereotypes include imagery around the idea that people with special needs are pitiful, pathetic, evil, burdens, and not a contributing member of the workforce or society.

Throughout history the term "disability" has had various definitions or has been replaced with more inclusive terms such as disabled, special needs, individuals with exceptionalities, neurodiversity, differently abled, PWD, and developmental differences. Each of the terms that have been used throughout history have placed the "norm" comparison to able-bodied individuals. This has perpetuated the implicit biases and stereotypes in society.

As we discuss common microaggressions, it is important to note that the term individuals with disabilities will be used, however, common language and thought on this term is constantly changing. Additionally, it is noted that the term "disability" is in and of itself a macro/microaggression. However, it is not sugarcoating reality by placing "special" into an identity, such as "special needs".

Sugar-coating the term "special." What does that mean? It has been argued that using the language of "special needs" sugar-coats "society's deep discomfort with disability" (Zulman, 2018, para. 1). Additionally, blogger Zulman argues that using the term "special needs" has the impact of "smugness that implies the speaker's supposed allyship" (para 3).

Supporting the idea that the term "special needs" is demeaning, a mother with a child who has Pfeiffer syndrome reflected on her experiences. She stated that using the term "special needs" limits children. "If our children are hearing this label (special needs) used to describe them, we are teaching our children that they are not equal and that they are 'different'" (Patient Worthy, 2017, para 3).

Finally, special needs are not associated with every disability, but rather have historically been associated with differences in physical appearances or social or behavioral struggles. It is a disingenuous way to identify a child who is more than a label and more than a set of tests and paperwork.

The socially constructed negative concepts associated with individuals with disabilities can be seen, heard, and felt in everyday life through microaggressions. As we discuss the various microaggressions individuals with disabilities experience, continue to reflect on your own inclusive and transformational practices in learning environments.

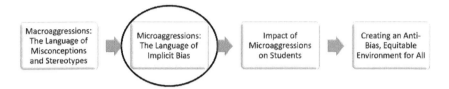

Figure 9.2   Macro, Micro, Impact, ABE. *Source*: Created by Bouley & Reinking, 2021.

OTHERING

One common microaggression is the language of "othering" or otherization. Othering, as defined in an earlier chapter, is the phenomenon in which individuals or groups are labeled as not fitting within the norms of society; they are the "other." We have discussed othering in relation to identities, such as race and religion. However, what makes the identity of disability unique is that "anyone can become disabled at any point in time in their lives" (Lu, 2016, para. 11).

For PWD the process of othering means that society or people in society treat them as "abnormal, an oddity or nonhuman." These statements can lead to conversations and beliefs that individuals with disabilities should not have children, should not have equal access to education, or should not have access to everyday life experiences. One PWD, Cassidy, reported to *The Mighty* that she is often referred to as someone who is "abnormal" or an "oddity" because she has a service dog. She often hears the statement, "What's wrong with you?" (Migdol, 2019).

One way society often "others" individuals with disabilities is through the assumption that the term "disability" is equivalent to "inability." This often takes the form of the unconscious mindset focused on the assumption that someone with a disability has the inability to be a "full person" or is invisible to society. Additionally, there is the assumption that individuals with disabilities have the inability to have loving relationships, eat food independently, or become athletes. Disability is not equivalent to inability.

Often this microaggression results in people treating individuals with disabilities like children, not taking them seriously, or only seeing the person for their disability alone. If a person is in a wheelchair, the person pushing the wheelchair will often be addressed in a store, while the store clerk ignores the person in the wheelchair. This is an example of the microaggression of inability, incompetence, and denial of personhood.

As a way to combat this microaggression, there is a campaign of people-first language. While the people-first language is not fully supported by the diversity of individuals with disabilities, people-first language is a way to see the person and not the disability. Examples of this would be a person with autism or an individual in a wheelchair.

Treating individuals with disabilities like children plays into another type of "othering" microaggression known as helplessness. Helplessness is similar to the assumption of inability or incompetence. Helplessness specifically refers to "treating people with disabilities as if they are incapable, useless, broken and unable to do any tasks without help" (Migdol, 2019, para. 5). This often results in exclusionary actions and language from friends, family, and other community members.

MINIMIZATION/BELITTLING

Another common microaggression experienced by individuals with disabilities is the action or language of minimization and belittling. Specifically, this occurs when people suggest that someone is "overstating" their needs and could be able-bodied if they "wanted to be." These statements have the impact message of a disability being a choice. This then downplays or discredits the discriminatory realities individuals with disabilities experience.

One example of the minimization and belittling was documented by Sheri Byrne-Haber as she reported on the hashtag #AmbulatoryWheelchairUsersExist. This hashtag was created because of the discriminatory understanding and language around individuals who use wheelchairs. In her piece, Byrne-Haber discusses the microaggression of individuals assuming a wheelchair is used for sympathy, especially if the person is ambulatory at times.

Many people believe that wheelchairs are only used for paralysis and if someone is not paralyzed the wheelchair is being used for people to "feel sorry for you." However, the United States has increased the availability of accessible environments; therefore, wheelchairs are a more viable option for individuals who may have heart conditions, balance disorders, osteoporosis, multiple sclerosis, cystic fibrosis, cancer, fibromyalgia, plus other various reasons.

Another way PWD are belittled through microaggressions is by turning disabilities into a minor everyday effect or the punchline of a joke. For example, when a peer, teacher, or barista nonchalantly states, "I'm really OCD about getting this right," or "I can't read this, I am totally dyslexic today" (Lu, 2016). Both of these statements belittle the reality of individuals who experience OCD or dyslexia.

FIXING OR PRAYING FOR YOU

"Can I pray for you?" is a microaggression experienced by individuals with disabilities, often because they are seen as broken, injured, sick, or overall, not well. While this may come from a place of good intentions, the impact can be discriminatory and create an unsafe environment. A person with a disability, hearing this comment, may think, "Why do I need to be fixed? What makes this person think we have the same God, or that I am even religious?"

Along with the assumption that "prayer will fix you" is the microaggression of suggesting a cure. As Byrne-Haber (2019) discusses in her article, she has Type 1 diabetes. People in her orbit will often send her links to unproven medications, treatments, or even diets for Type 2 diabetes. Again, well maybe well-intentioned, the message is that I, the non-disabled individual, has "done my part" to help the "less fortunate."

Going along with this idea of "fixing" someone with a disability is the microaggression of assuming the disability is a negative trait or something that needs to be "fixed." By adding the word "suffer" in front of a disability the negative trait is given power and is transfixed into something needing cured. An example would be, "he suffers from autism." This statement sends that message that autism is bad and needs to be fixed with medication, counseling, or other interventions to make the individual "normal."

PLACING ON A PEDESTAL

"I couldn't do that" or "You are so strong/brave" is an ableist way of saying how you live your life must be unbearable but you do it every day. Placing the daily life of a person with a disability on a pedestal correlates to the standard definition of inspiration porn.

Inspiration porn is when PWD are seen as an inspiration solely, or maybe in part, due to their disability (Ellis & Kent, 2016). What is the difference between inspiration porn and a media clip focusing on the act of inspiring people? Inspiration porn is written to make able-bodied people feel good about themselves, such as a news segment focusing on a "hero" who helped a disabled person. In these news articles, that are inspiration porn, the PWD's voice is completely left out of the segment (Lu, 2016). Inspiration porn has various levels, but cheering for someone completing an everyday task, such as hopping across the road when not wearing their prosthetic leg, is demeaning.

Reflection: How is your current learning environment creating a safe space for individuals with disabilities? Reflect on the microaggressions above, specifically combatting ableist learning environments.

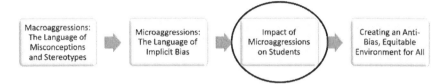

Figure 9.3   Macro, Micro, Impact, ABE. *Source*: Created by Bouley & Reinking, 2021.

Ableist microaggressions impact a multitude of realities in the life of a person with a disability. In figure 9.4, which was designed by Kattari (2017), the four most impacted areas are outlined. They are depression, anxiety, decreased behavior control, and decreased positive affect. The impact of ableist microaggressions has consequences that can be seen in educational settings, therapeutic settings, as well as the individual's brain health. Specifically, decreased resilience and increased suicidal ideation.

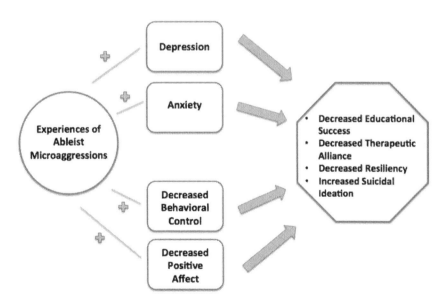

Figure 9.4   *Source*: Kattari (2017).

Kattari (2017) found that "experiencing ableist microaggressions are negatively correlated with positive mental health outcomes and that visibility of disabilities/impairments are correlated with experiencing ableist microaggressions" (p. iii). In her study, it was found that the increase in ableist microaggressions directly correlated to the decrease in one's mental health, which then impacts many parts of a person's life, including in a learning setting.

Understanding the impact of ableist microaggressions also relates back to intent versus impact discussion. "If we tell students with a disability that the perpetrator has good intent, it absolves the perpetrator from any responsibility and silences the student by dismissing their pain" (Inclusive School Communities, 2021, para. 6). Overall, this minimizes the impact and accentuates the intent.

DISCIPLINE

Students with disabilities are disproportionately disciplined in schools around the United States. It has been found that "over 80 percent of students with disabilities suspended out of school multiple times are boys, and over 80 percent of those expelled are boys" (IDEA Data Center, 2021). However, discipline of students with disabilities does not always result in out-of-school suspensions. Discipline also happens in the classroom by separating students with disabilities from the larger group of students who are usually typically developing peers. While educators may not intend to discipline in this way, the impact is separation, withdrawal, and peer bullying based purely on ability.

Compounding these data is the fact that disability and race are a common discriminatory intersectionality students experience in learning settings. Specifically, "Black students with disabilities are 3x as likely as White students with disabilities to be suspended and 2.5x as likely to be expelled" (IDEA Data Center, 2021, para. 2).

While there are laws and mandates in place to ensure that special education students are not being disciplined based on their identified disability, the practices are arguably subjective based on the knowledge the team has at that moment, and students with disabilities are still disproportionately disciplined.

How can we ensure our discipline practices are equitable and safe, while also creating an inclusive environment? The Inclusive School Communities (2021) has collaboratively designed a resource that includes common microaggressions, the message being sent, and an additional column of strategies for educators to create a more inclusive environment. The link is provided in the resources section at the end of this chapter.

In the "Summary of Disability Microaggressions in Schools," which is a handout located on the Inclusive School Communities (2021) website, many of the microaggressions outlined have already been discussed in previous chapters. Microaggressions, such as, the ascription of intelligence, assuming homogeneity, marginalization, second-class citizen, and the myth of meritocracy. However, in the case of this specific table, the microaggressions are described through the lens of a PWD. An edited version of the table is located in table 9.1.

Reflection: After reading through the table, reflect on the last column. What are strategies you currently do or one's you plan to do in the near future?

Figure 9.5   Macro, Micro, Impact, ABE. *Source*: Created by Bouley & Reinking, 2021.

Aside from the information outlined above, there are three important strategies to consider and constantly reflect upon while you transform a learning environment to create an equitable space for all students, specifically students with disabilities.

First, it is important to be perceptively aware of pejorative, derogatory, or abusive language commonly used in schools. Pejorative language is defined as words and phrases that hurt, insult, or disparage someone or something. This can be problematic because it creates an unsafe, unwelcoming environment (Internet Encyclopedia of Philosophy, n.d.). Specifically, the term "special" is often thought of a synonym to segregation and exclusion based on the historical practice of schools having a "special education wing" or "special education hallway."

In addition to the common phrasing used in many schools around the United States, we also need to reconsider other languages often used in rhetoric. Language that often is used without thinking about the impact—such words as insane, psycho, bonkers, crippled, lame, moronic, or crazy. Each of these words is a part of the ableist pejorative language.

This relates to the discussion of spirit days in the chapter on race. When schools have "crazy hair," as already discussed, students often wear hairstyles that are offensive to the history of Black hairstyles, which have meaning and context. In addition, using the word crazy for crazy hair day or crazy sock day is a microaggression based on ableist language. Taking this concept of spirit days one step further, is the intersectionality that often occurs with students

Table 9.1 Edited Summary of Disability Microaggressions in Schools Based on School Communities, 2021

Microaggression Category	Example	Underlying Message	Strategies
Assuming inherent abilities or qualities based on disability. Such as generalizations overlook the individual and lead to inappropriate expectations.	Assuming a student with autism are savants who like trains and lack empathy. Assuming a student with Down Syndrome is happy and compliant.	The individuality of the student with a disability does not matter as their needs are based on diagnostic stereotypes.	Avoid stereotypes by learning about students and their individuality. Used a strengths-based practice where you focus on what the students can do, rather than what they cannot do.
Using ableist language. Such as, language that is derogatory, abusive, or negative about disability, often without the intention of doing harm, expecting students with disability to educate others about the disability, or tone policing by reading subtext that does not exist.	Using disability as an insult or euphemism (ex: "You're so OCD about being on time.") Not allowing students to choose their own self-identify language (ex. Person first or disability first language). Choosing books that contain ableist language.	Disability is seen as a deficit, dysfunction, or limitation, which needs to be fixed.	Listen to the preferred language of the disability community. Be aware of pejorative language and that some terminology commonly used in schools can be problematic in the move to inclusion. Attend professional development facilitated by people with disability.
Assuming the normality and superiority of being without a disability. Such as, children with disability should not look visibility different from their peers, students with disability must conform to the dominant cultural norms, and judging the behavior of students with disability on non-disabled terms.	Insisting that students behave in neurotypical ways such as making eye contact, not stimming, using oral forms of communication over sign language. Being offended when students with disability attempt to address breaches of human rights. Institutions that students with disability be controlled and polite at all times, despite neurological differences that make this challenging.	People from the dominant cultural norm feel uncomfortable when spending time with those who are different from them.	Create an environment where students with disability are valued for who they are. Teach students with disabilities to be proud of who they are. Expose students to positive role models with disability. Support employment of teachers/ assistants with disability.

Refusing to acknowledge lived experience. Such as, questioning the credibility and validity of the personal experiences of students with disability, unwillingness to learn from students with disability or the disability community, preferring non-disabled experts in the field of disability, and claiming reverse ableism exists.	Choosing to learn about disability from non-disabled people. Saying "Why is it always about disability?" Saying "In my opinion I don't think you are correct…" when a student informs you about their personal experience of disability.	Students with disabilities do not have insight into their own disabilities.	Listen to students with disability and those in the disability community. Include literature by disabled writers in your classroom. Provide students with disability leadership positions if possible. Be aware of non-disabled privilege. Attend professional development run by disabled people.

of color and the mislabeling of "disabled" due to cultural misunderstandings based on dominant concepts.

More examples include, let's all walk over there, blind spots, falling on deaf ears, or paralyzed. Instead of using these terms that have become part of everyday jargon, consider using more inclusive and precise language to say what you mean, without slang. Instead of saying "let's all move over there" you could rather say, "let's all transition over there." Instead of saying, "that is crazy" you could be more precise and say, "that just doesn't make sense."

Reflect: Take a moment to reflect on the examples provided above. What are more precise ways of saying the idea you mean? What may be other words or sayings that are said in learning environments that might create an unsafe environment for PWD?

Second, reflect on biases that stem from social conditioning. This relates directly back to the Cycle of Socialization reflection we completed earlier in the book. Often, when the Cycle of Socialization is introduced or provided as a reflection piece, it is primarily based on racial differences in our society. Ableist ideas or disability rhetoric is often not thought of or discussed in relation to the Cycle of Socialization. So, now is your time. Go back and reflect specifically on the Cycle of Socialization through the eyes of ableism, which is continuously reinforced in our society.

Reflection: Go back to the Cycle of Socialization and specifically reflect on your own cycle through the eyes of an ableist society.

Third, the importance of including mirrors, windows, and sliding glass doors in learning environments through the eyes of an individual with a disability. Metaphorical mirrors in classrooms allow students to see themselves in learning materials, metaphorical windows in classrooms allow students to see various identities and realities, and finally, there is the concept of sliding glass doors. The concept of sliding glass doors is not only relevant to students with disabilities, but can be implemented in a classroom for any type of representation.

Sliding glass doors are a way for readers to "walk through" a book or other piece of media using their imagination to become part of whatever world has been created in the story or learning environment. When you implement the concepts of windows, mirrors, and sliding glass doors into your learning environment, these strategies become a means of self-affirmation for students.

Reflection: One Word. What is your one word (figure 9.6) to summarize your thoughts or feelings after reading this chapter? What is your one word?

Examples of one word are provided in this word cloud, which was created by using the words in this chapter.

Figure 9.6 One Word, Chapter 9. *Source:* Created by Bouley & Reinking, 2021.

After reading this chapter, what are some ways you will hold yourself accountable through intentional, thoughtful actions?

Table 9.2 Reflections and Intentions

Reflection Question	Your Answer
My interactions with students…	
My interactions with their families…	
Physical classroom environment…	
Classroom materials and materials used for instruction…	
Lesson planning and curriculum…	
Instructional strategies such as grouping…	
Creating an anti-biased anti-racist school climate…	

RESOURCES

Ableist Language and the Impact: https://pwd.org.au/resources/disability-info/langu
age-guide/ableist-language/
Inclusive School Communities: https://inclusiveschoolcommunities.org.au/resources/
toolkit/disability-microaggressionseducation
National Center on Learning Disabilities: https://www.ncld.org/wp-content/uploads/2020/
10/2020-NCLD-Disproportionality_Trends-and-Actions-for-Impact_FINAL-1.pdf

Chapter 10

Linguistic Diversity and Microaggressions

If you talk to a man in a language he understands, that goes to his head. If you talk to him in his language, that goes to his heart.

—Nelson Mandela

Title VI of the Civil Rights Act of 1964, was designed to protect the rights of individual taxpayers who do not speak fluent English. Due to that addition, states receiving federal funds must provide all vital documents in every language spoken by people receiving the subsidized benefits of the Federal Government. Supporting this mandate, the U.S. Government has never declared any language as an "official" language, despite attempts by numerous politicians since the early 1800s. Essentially, the United States is recognized as a multilingual nation with no official federal language. Important to note though, some states have declared English as their official language with nearly 80 percent of the United States population identifying as monolingual.

Research supports the recognition that the United States is a multilingual nation. Specifically, Hispanic students had the biggest population increase in schools, moving from 16 percent to 27 percent (school year 2000 to 2017), with an anticipated rise to 28 percent of the national student body K-12 by 2029. During the same time period, the number of Asian American/Pacific Islander (AAPI) students increased from 4 percent of the total student body nationwide to 6 percent and is projected to be 7 percent by 2029 (National Center for Education Statistics, 2020a).

With these increases in racial and ethnic diversity, a direct result is an increase in linguistic diversity and English language learners (ELLs) in schools. Specifically, "the percentage of public-school students in the United States who were ELLs was higher in fall 2017 (10.1% or 5.0 million students) than in fall 2000 (8.1% or 3.8 million students)" (National Center for Education Statistics, 2020a, para.1). This rise is estimated to continue from year to year.

Linguistic diversity in homes has also been researched. Specifically, home languages that dominate in the United States, in order, are Spanish, Arabic, Chinese, English, Vietnamese, Somali, Russian, Portuguese, Haitian, and Hmong. That being said, it is evident that many educators will be working with students who are ELLs or bilingual in their teaching careers. However, linguistic bias, or unconscious biases based on language diversity, often impedes the work of educators because a focus is placed on student deficits rather than focusing on the assets of linguistic diversity.

As with other statistics we have reported throughout this book, there is a clear dichotomy or cultural gap between English-speaking teachers and their ELL students, which serves to perpetuate myths, stereotypes, and overall discomfort in learning environments.

One author, Sahra Ahmed (2018) stated, "During my own teaching career, most of the teachers I encountered viewed ELL students mainly in deficit terms. They emphasized what ELL students *cannot* do, rather than what they *can* do, and equated their ELL status with a disability" (para., 1).

There are many misconceptions and stereotypes about linguistically diverse students and families. Whether discussing ELLs, English language proficiency (ELP), bilingualism, dialect and/or discourse style, students and families whose linguistic style falls outside of what is seen as "standard English" are often subjected to macro and microaggressions in schools.

Reflection: What are your thoughts around learning or knowing a language other than English? Do you feel it is valuable to be bi or multilingual?

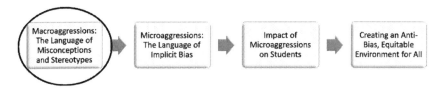

Figure 10.1   Macro, Micro, Impact, ABE. *Source*: Created by Bouley & Reinking, 2021.

Robin DiAngelo (2018), in her book *White Fragility*, discusses the fragile state many white Americans are in when it comes to racial and linguistic diversity as "a state in which even a minimum amount of racial stress becomes intolerable, triggering a range of defensive moves. These moves include the outward display of emotions such as anger, fear, and guilt" (p. 54). While the fear and guilt are displayed through actions of implicit biases, they are based in widely held stereotypes, which are taught through hidden curriculum, interactions, and media.

The PBS outlines three specific stereotypes, which are misconceptions, about Spanish spoken in the United States (2005). Specifically,

1. "Spanish in the United States is purely a function of immigration in the 20th and 21st centuries.
2. Spanish in the United States is a monolithic entity and is not characterized by the same amount of variation as American English.
3. Spanish language use in the United States presents a threat to the use of English."

Yet, the reality is that Spanish either pre-dates English in the United States or has been spoken for as long as English, is highly diverse with many variations, and "poses no threat to the dominance of English in the United States. Spanish and English have coexisted in this country for nearly 400 years" (PBS, 2005).

The myths, stereotypes, and overall fear of losing English is perpetuated through media, widely held assumptions, and the reality that citizens in the United States are "-ism breathers." The -ism being breathed, which perpetuates the bias against linguistic diversity, is called linguicism or languagism.

Supporting the concept of "bias breathers," findings from a Pew Research Center stated that nine of ten people in the United States "voice the view that to be truly American it is very or somewhat important that a person speak English" (Stokes, 2017, para. 1). According to the study, 81 percent of people over fifty believe speaking English is *very* important to being an American, but that number drops to 58 percent for the 18–34 age group (Stokes, 2017).

Anecdotal experiences of language diversity being threatened are reported through news and media almost daily. For example, the *New York Times* reports that in Boston, Massachusetts in 2020 a mother and daughter were physically assaulted walking home while speaking Spanish. The attacker told the women, "This is America! Speak English!"

Another example is from Jose Fermoso (2018), who wrote:

Last January, a woman was kicked out of a Florida UPS for speaking Spanish, the month prior an adult physically attacked legal South American immigrants—including a child—at a Canadian mall, and a few days ago a border agent in Montana arrested two women for the same thing, leaving them shaking with anger and crying at the unfairness of it all. Then there's the case of the rich Manhattan lawyer who berated young workers at a deli for daring to communicate in the second most spoken language in the world (Spanish) in his presence (para. 7).

As a result, stereotypes regarding ELLs and linguistic diversity are pervasive not only in society but also in schools. Whether discussing ELLs, ELP, dialect, or discourse style, students who are linguistically diverse experience microaggressions in school.

Reflection: What stereotypes or beliefs do you have around students/families who are linguistically diverse? Do you feel comfortable when students are speaking near you in a language that you don't understand?

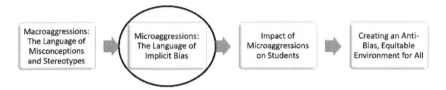

Figure 10.2   Macro, Micro, Impact, ABE. *Source*: Created by Bouley & Reinking, 2021.

These stereotypes or macroaggressions often lead to microaggressions, which is the case with linguistic diversity and linguistic bias in schools. However, linguistic bias is not simply about ELL and bilingual students, but it is rather linguistic discrimination or unfair treatment based on the use of language and characteristics of speech, including first language, accent, size of vocabulary, modality, and syntax. Other terms used to describe linguistic bias are glottophobia, linguicism, and languagism.

"STANDARD" ENGLISH

One of the most prevalent microaggressions is the assumed understanding that there is a "purest" form of English, also known as "accentless." This is also the form of English often heard spoken by newscasters. For a long while during the twentieth century, linguistics believed the language in Northeastern Ohio was the "purest."

This was later refuted when linguistics discovered multiple distinct accents and dialects in that region. Regardless of the continued research, the sentiment of "pure," "accentless," "standard," or even "normal" English had its roots in society (Nosowitz, 2016). This concept, in and of itself, is both a macro- and a microaggression that infiltrate schools on a daily basis.

So, how does linguistic bias enter school buildings? When educators expect students to speak in the same language, dialect and discourse style as the mainstream, they are exhibiting language bias. If undetected and not addressed, this will result in intentional or unintentional microaggressions in the classroom.

Students who are linguistically diverse, who speak a language or dialect or with a discourse style outside of what has been deemed by the dominant culture as "mainstream" or "standard," experience microaggressions regularly at the hands of educators, administrators, other school personnel, and their peers.

Furthermore, in table 10.1, you will see a list of the most common microaggressions, outside of "standard English," that students who are linguistically diverse experience.

Table 10.1   Common Linguistic Microaggressions Created by Bouley, 2021

Theme	Microaggression
Race/ethnicity and language	"You speak well for a (person of that race/ethnicity)"
	"You speak well for just learning English."
	"You're Asian, can you teach us some of your language?"
	"Why are you speaking so loud?"
	"Why are you so quiet? We want to know what you think. Be more verbal." "Speak up more." (To an Asian, Latino, or Native American.)
	"Why do you have to be so loud/animated? Just calm down." (To a Black student.)
	"We speak English here." (To two friends talking in Spanish.)
	"Stop going back and forth from Spanish to English."
	Setting low expectations for English language learners.
	Assuming a student speaks a language based on their last name.
	Sending homework home in English only when the home language is different.
	Asking a student to use a nickname because their real name is too hard to pronounce.
Accent/Dialect	"Where are you from?"
	"Where were you born?"
	"You can talk like that at home but in school you..."
	"That's playground language, use correct English here."
	"You're talking ghetto now."
	"Say that again with good grammar."
	Seeing the dialect as a deficiency.
Ability	Raising your voice or speaking slowly when addressing a student who speaks multiple languages or is not a native English speaker.
	Asking a student with a hearing impairment to speak up or talk more quietly.
	Assuming a student with Autism or Elective Mutism doesn't understand you.
	Assuming people, such as students or families, who do not speak English are less intelligent.
Discourse style	"You talk too quickly. I can't understand you."
	"Look at me when I am talking to you."
	"Come closer when I am talking with you."
	"Don't ramble or talk in circles. Tell me exactly what you mean."
	"Please don't interject when I am talking."
	Seeing the dialect as a deficiency.
	Making assumptions of the student's ability.

ABILITY

Linguistic bias goes beyond ELLs and ELP; there are also stereotypes and misconceptions toward students' dialect and discourse styles. While the research in linguistics clearly demonstrates that diversity in language use does not correlate with academic achievement or intelligence, this notion remains a common stereotype in the United States, which results in everyday microaggressions.

In classrooms, this often plays out through teacher actions based on teacher beliefs, specifically negative attitudes toward and about linguistic diversity. Author and researcher So Lim Kim (2021) found that "teachers do not value linguistic diversity and generally hold beliefs that diversity is a burden or an extra challenge for teachers" (p. 2). He also found teachers' attitudes toward ELLs to be overwhelmingly negative.

At the end of his research, Kim (2021), summarized his findings by saying, "In general, teachers hold negative beliefs toward ELLs; yet, the beliefs differ based on ELLs' race and English fluency. Cultural discrepancies between teachers and ELLs negatively affect teachers' beliefs, attitudes, and understandings of ELLs. Teachers' unpreparedness and limited knowledge to teach ELLs can lead to misunderstandings and negative attitudes towards ELLs" (p. 5).

Additionally, Shim (2017) explored whether or not teachers' negative attitudes toward ELLs were reflective of their general beliefs outside of school. In her study pre-service teachers "demonstrated that they viewed their attitudes as personal" and the most common reason for harboring negative attitudes toward ELLs was "the sense of discomfort around people who spoke languages other than English" (p. 12).

Furthermore, researchers Umansky and Dumont (2019), compared teachers' perceptions of the academic abilities of ELL students who were classified as ELL as incoming kindergartners, to those who were classified as non-ELL over their first three years of schooling. The authors found that teachers did in fact have lower expectations for the academic abilities of ELL students in kindergarten and across content areas (reading, writing, math, etc.), and teacher expectations lessened even more as students progressed through grades one and two.

Supporting the believe that ELL students lack ability in acquiring new academic material, Lippert (2017) found "that although most teachers like the idea of ELL inclusion, they do not necessarily want it in their classroom until the English Language Learner has some level of proficiency" (p. 16).

Rudat (2020), found that many teachers hold the popular myth that "Students can't access grade-level materials unless they are proficient in English" (para.5). This goes along with the common myth that people who do not speak English or who speak "standard English" poorly, are less intelligent. This is often associated with BIPOC individuals and people living in rural parts of the United States. Furthermore, this myth postulates that language diversity deems some dialects "better" than others.

Reflection: What are your experiences working with students who are linguistically diverse? Do you feel adequately trained to support their academic learning? What might help you to do so?

RACE/ETHNICITY AND LANGUAGE (INTERSECTIONALITY)

Adding to the linguistic bias phenomenon is the intersectionality of race and ethnicity. Some studies have found teachers' perceptions, stereotypes, and expectations vary depending on the race or ethnicity of the student. According to Umansky and Dumont (2019),

> Perceptions of EL-classified students, the vast majority of whom are Latinx or Asian, are likely also tied to students' race and ethnicity, with research demonstrating that teachers often hold stereotypes of Asian students as "model minorities" while holding stereotypes of Latinx students as "under- achieving" (Lee & Zhou, 2015; López, 2003; Ochoa, 2013, p. 8).

DIALECT/ACCENT

While dialectical stereotypes are pervasive throughout the United States, it is frequently associated with the dialect often spoken in Black communities. AAVE (African American Vernacular English), which was once referred to as Ebonics, is a form of speech that has a long history and is tied closely to African American culture. Yet, there is an equally long history of bias against AAVE that has had a negative impact on African Americans in many ways from employment opportunities to social mobility to education.

AAVE is addressed in a position statement written by the National Council of Teachers of English (NCTE, 2016), which states "Given continuing myths and misconceptions in the media and in the nation's schools about the language many African American students use, the public deserves a statement reflective of the viewpoints of language and literacy scholars on Ebonics" (para.1).

NCTE (2016) goes on to explain that AAVE,

> Like every other linguistic system, . . . is systematic and rule-governed, and it is not an obstacle to learning. The obstacle lies in negative attitudes toward the language, lack of information about the language, inefficient techniques for teaching language and literacy skills, and an unwillingness to adapt teaching styles to the needs of Ebonics speakers (para. 3).

DISCOURSE STYLES

In addition to dialect, there are many stereotypes or misconceptions on varying discourse styles. All cultures have different ways of communicating with others. Differences in various discourse styles could show up in gestures and body language, participation styles that are active or passive, using soft or loud voice, the speed or cadence of talking, or the content of what is actually spoken orally.

When individuals or educators expect all speakers to follow the same dominant discourse style, misconceptions and stereotypes are likely to occur. Teachers who do not learn the different styles of communication in their classroom may be more likely to identify students (or their family members) as rude, or disorderly and engage in disciplinary actions.

Common misconceptions around discourse styles in education might include labeling a student who does not look in the teacher's eyes as rude, criticizing a student's communication style as not linear or direct, confusing, too loud or fast, and so on. Further, expecting a student to share certain information, participate often in class, not talk over other students, or interrupt when someone is talking can all result in misunderstandings, misconceptions, and microaggressions.

Being classified as an ELL is not static, and once students reach ELP they are no longer classified as ELL. Regardless if a student is currently classified as an ELL student or previously classified as ELL, the impacts of the language microaggressions are long-lasting, especially with the intertwined nature of language, race, and ethnicity.

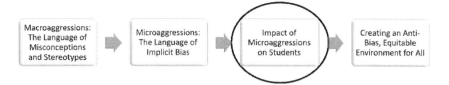

Figure 10.3   Macro, Micro, Impact, ABE. *Source*: Created by Bouley & Reinking, 2021.

LOSS OF NATIVE LANGUAGE

Perhaps one of the most concerning impacts of language discrimination is the loss of one's native language. In a topic brief published by the New York State Education Department, Billings and Walqui (n.d.) state, "Very often, societal pressures to add the dominant language, coupled with the low prestige of the native language (L1), leads to marginalization or even total loss of the native language in favor of English" (para. 3).

Due to fear of discrimination, violence, or deportation, many families refuse to speak their native language outside of their house, and sometimes even in their house. When families stop using their native language for political and safety reasons or due to the many misconceptions around second language learning, their children lose their ability to communicate with their ancestors and continue cultural traditions. Billings and Waqui (n.d.) state,

> Because language is tightly tied to identity and family, the subordination of home languages to English often causes students personal, cultural, and familial tensions. It also can lead to a phenomenon known as "subtractive bilingualism" where the ability to communicate in the home language is severely diminished or forgotten, resulting in the loss of a valuable resource to the individual as well as to our society (Ruiz, 1984, p. 1).

As students lose their native language and culture, they also lose their identity and sense of pride. Students may feel shame for speaking another language, dialect or discourse style, and they may begin to feel ashamed of their family and heritage. Feeling a strong sense of self and one's family is critical for not only positive social-emotional development but also to be successful academically.

Finally, Kaiser and Rasminksy (2019) state,

To form positive self concepts, children must honor and respect their own families and cultures and have others honor and respect these key facets of their identities too. If the classroom doesn't reflect and validate their families and cultures, children may feel invisible, unimportant, incompetent, and ashamed of who they are (p. 1).

DEFICIT FOCUS

Another impact of language bias focuses on the perpetuation of what has been known as the achievement gap, yet is clearly an opportunity gap. The gap between ELLs and non-ELLS gets a great deal of attention, but usually the focus is on what's "wrong" with ELLs or their deficits, not how educational programs, pedagogy and assessment may be disadvantageous to ELL students.

According to Umansky and Dumont (2019),

In the last few years, several studies have emerged documenting that simply being classified as an EL student in school can have a direct, negative impact on students' test scores, graduation, and college-going. Possible explanations for these negative effects include that EL-classified students are often linguistically isolated with other EL students, tracked into low-level classes, and placed into classes with inexperienced teachers, all of which can harm a student's outcomes (p. 19).

It is easy to see how the stereotypes and misconceptions around ELLs and language diversity have impacted school policies and pedagogy, and the negative impact this has had on students. Researchers Samson and Collins (2012), reflected that there is solid evidence that U.S. policies result in school practices that have serious consequences for ELLs. Due to inaccurate and culturally insensitive assessment data gathering practices, ELL students are often unable to pass key assessments due to language barriers, not academic barriers. As a result, these students then end up in remedial programs, which results in an alarmingly high rate of dropping out of school (Samson & Collins, 2012). This supports the idea that assessments are biased toward native English speakers, which creates a lack of validity for assessment results. Overall, these biased assessments can have a negative impact on students' academic success, mental and social-emotional development.

Supporting the idea that assessments are negatively biased against linguistically diverse students, Gok (2020) writes when using, "standardized tests or classroom assessment tools, ESL students might be placed in special education programs even when they may not belong there" (para. 4). This is due to the fact that ELLs may have lower test scores based on language diversity and not academic achievement. Kyung Hee and Zabelina (2015, p. 134), stated that "unjustifiable reliance on IQ and other evaluation tools have been cited as one of the factors contributing to the over-representation of minority children in special education classes."

Placing ELLs in special education programs solely based on their test results or barriers with the English language might seem like an easy solution, but the negative impact for the student's future is impenetrable.

One's language is a big part of their personal and familial identity. When students experience linguistic microaggressions they begin to devalue their native language, dialect, or discourse style. As a result, students may be quick to let go of their heritage out of a desire to fit in. They may learn to see their bilingualism or bidialectism as a negative aspect of themselves, as opposed to a valuable and beneficial skill.

Reflection: How might you help students feel pride in their heritage and native language?

However, when educators value linguistic diversity and see cultural and linguistic differences as resources, as opposed to a deficit, students' home languages, dialects, and discourse styles are affirmed and integrated into classrooms and school buildings. As a result, this creates an anti-bias and equitable environment for students and families who are linguistically diverse. The transformation of the learning environment to include linguistically diverse families and students is imperative for students' academic success and social-emotional well-being, and more importantly to preserve their heritage.

Figure 10.4   Macro, Micro, Impact, ABE. *Source*: Created by Bouley & Reinking, 2021.

So how do we create a more equitable, anti-bias experience for students with linguistic diversities?

In, *Holding High, Not Hurried, Expectations for ELLs*, Gottschalk (2019) discusses the importance of having high expectations for ELLs, not hurried ones. She highlights the NAEP reading and math scores as evidence that ELL students are progressing, and even at faster rates than non-ELL students. Her plea to take a slower, more individualized approach to supporting ELLs is an important one.

Table 10.2 demonstrates the difference between hurried and high expectations.

Table 10.2   Examples of Hurried Expectations vs. High Expectations Source: Gottschalk (2019)

Hurried Expectations	High Expectations
1. Why doesn't this student entering kindergarten know her letters and sounds?	1. Is this student comfortable and happy coming to school?
2. Why aren't all of my kindergarten students reading at the end of the year?	2. Why aren't all of my developmentally ready students reading by the end of kindergarten?
3. Rafi didn't make as much progress this year as last year.	3. Rafi didn't make as much progress this year as he did last year, but students rarely progress on an even upward trend.
4. Let's start the high school day early so that students have time for work or extracurricular activities after school.	4. Let's make the start of the school day later for teenagers. Research says they perform better with later high school start times (Owens, 2014).
5. We're going to get students ready for middle school/high school/college.	5. The best way to help students get ready for next year is to help them reach this year's age-appropriate, grade-level standards.
6. Feedback to a parent: "He's not reading at grade level."	6. Feedback to a parent: "He's not reading at grade level, but he came to the United States just two years ago. He's been making steady progress since then and is on track to catch up completely in a few more years."
7. High school ELLs with limited or interrupted formal schooling should graduate in four years with their cohorts.	7. Four years isn't enough. High school ELLs with limited or interrupted formal schooling should have the time and supports they need to graduate. High schools shouldn't be penalized for giving them the time to do so.
8. ELLs should be reading at grade level by third grade.	8. ELLs in third grade have had just four years of ELL instruction, still not long enough, since it takes five to seven years, on average, to reach proficiency. Third grade reading laws should allow retention exemptions for all ELLs.

Based on this work, educators and schools need to understand the importance of developing environments that focus on what linguistically diverse students can do, rather than focus on the speed at which students can learn the English language. This is especially true since research states that to become proficient in a language it takes between seven and ten years of learning engagement. Professional development and preparation in engaging with linguistically diverse students is important to help educators move away from this deficit mindset.

Educators report a lack of professional development in teaching English to speakers of other languages (TESOL), which creates a lack of confidence that they have the skills needed to support students' academic learning. While urban schools may have twice as many students who are ELL than suburban or rural settings, linguistic diversity is on the rise nationally. All educators need specific training in how to support ELL and linguistically diverse students.

Reflection: Does your school provide professional development in TESOL?

According to Ahmed (2018), professional development efforts ought to be comprehensive and continuous for all teachers, not only teachers directly working with ELLs or "assigned" an ELL position. The rapid increase in the number of ELLs in the United States requires that all teachers be prepared to address ELL needs in general education classrooms, not simply ELL classrooms. By adopting new beliefs for successful inclusion, all teachers will have the tools to successfully teach ELLs in their own classrooms.

Building on that research, Umansky and Dumont (2019a), make three suggestions for creating equitable and inclusive classrooms for ELLs and discuss the need for teacher professional development focused specifically on the examination of implicit bias:

> First, high-stakes decisions for EL students that depend on teacher judgement—such as decisions about when to exit students from EL classification or in what classes to place students—are likely vulnerable to teacher bias. These types of decisions may best be made using established, objective criteria. Standardized assessments (that accurately assess EL students' skills) and clear policies (that are fair and implemented in a standard way for all students) are good alternatives. Second, interventions that attempt to decrease teacher bias may help teachers better understand and accurately assess their EL students' skills and assets. Professional development such as that centered around increasing educators' understanding of implicit bias and empathy toward marginalized students have been shown to decrease bias. Likewise, there is evidence that home visits can help teachers develop more positive perspectives about their families. Finally, expanding bilingual instructional programs can allow more students to be in settings that minimize negative teacher bias. As noted earlier, bilingual education is academically and linguistically beneficial for EL students (para. 8).

Another author, Berg (2013), discusses ways she actively addresses common stereotypes. Specifically the assumption that English proficiency equates to signs of intelligence and a lack of English proficiency equates to signs of unintelligence. She states, "In addition to helping my students look beyond stereotypes about their ELL identity, I explain to them that my class is designed to teach them the academic language they need to communicate their knowledge accurately and creatively" (p. 67). This is an example of open and honest conversations with students.

In addition to having these open and honest discussions with her students, Berg (2013) demonstrates high expectations for her students, and takes an asset-based approach. She stated,

> I also teach them that, because of their unique ELL identities (most of my students have lived and attended school in other countries), they are not only intelligent but have many interesting things to teach us. We talk about school culture in other places around the world, and I look for opportunities to highlight students' unique knowledge and to thank them for teaching me new things every day (p. 67).

Building from the work that is happening in classrooms, as well as research, NCTE (2017) released their definition of what a true anti-racist educator is and encompasses. Specifically, an anti-racist educator:

- Opposes English-only policies.
- Recognizes the importance of adequate materials in students' first language.
- Seeks and leads training in language diversity.
- Works against negative attitudes toward multiple Englishes.
- Is informed on multiple Englishes and ways of communicating as a means of celebrating cultures.
- Includes culturally relevant and sustaining materials in all learning environments.
- Celebrates and respects the power of communities reading in their heritage language and in their own custom.
- Advocates for every student to receive equitable educational opportunities.
- Adopts teaching stances that are culturally sustaining.

* Adapted from Anti-Racist ELA Educators' Actions Infographic based on the NCTE position statement.

Furthermore, in the NCTE (2020) *Position Paper on the Role of English Teachers in Educating ELL*, the importance of scaffolding students to use their home language and prior knowledge in learning is emphasized. NCTE recommends teachers can best prepare learning materials by:

- "Determining students' home languages. Some do not speak the national language of the country they come from (for example, many Latin American–origin students speak indigenous languages at home and Spanish as a second language); they may not be literate in the national language.
- Assessing students' home language literacy. While translations of materials can be helpful for some learners, it's important to check whether students can actually read and write in the language of the translation.
- Building background for content lessons. Multilingual students arrive with different experiences and may not have the same background knowledge as mainstream students" (para. 15).

Michael-Luna (2015), discussed the importance of learning about students' home language from families and integrating that knowledge into the classroom. She states, "Many early childhood educators have questions about DLLs' language development and the home language's role in their learning English at school. Yet, teachers often do not consult with the very people who can answer these questions—the families" (para. 2).

Reflection: How do you gather information from families to learn about their home language?

Michael-Luna (2015), believes learning from families about their home language is critical for the differentiation of language instruction in the classroom, "Each family presents a distinct language environment that calls for different types of supportive pedagogies, curriculums, assessments, and home-school connections" (para. 4). To gain this information she suggests that educators utilize parent focus groups, home language surveys, individual informal interviews, parent workshops and home-school projects.

Another important aspect of developing equitable classrooms has to do with supporting families in preserving their home language. Reminding families of the importance of talking, singing, rhyming, reading, and writing in their native language helps them to see you not only affirm and support their language but understand the importance of using it to maintain familial and cultural connections.

It is important to help families to see that when they support their child in developing skills in their native language, those skills can be transferred to English. Sharing your high expectations that their child will learn English in time, and your concern that they don't lose their native language along the way, gives families the confidence and support they need to continue using their native language at home.

In addition to supporting academic learning and social-emotional development, when educators create anti-bias, equitable classrooms and schools for linguistically diverse students they are also creating opportunities for students and families to embrace their culture, and feel pride in their identity.

Finally, throughout most of this chapter and discourse regarding ELLs, the assumption is that teachers are working with Spanish speaking students, however as stated earlier in this chapter, and in the chapter focused on racial microaggressions, AAVE is a recognized language. Arguably students who speak AAVE and "standard" English can and should be identified as bilingual.

NCTE (2016) released a position statement in support of recognizing AAVE within educational discourse. The NCTE position statement stated:

Teachers, administrators, counselors, supervisors, and curriculum developers must undergo training to provide them with adequate knowledge about Ebonics and help them overcome the prevailing stereotypes about the language and learning potential of African American students (and others) who

speak Ebonics. CCCC thus strongly advocates new research and teaching that
will build on existing knowledge about Ebonics to help students value their
linguistic-cultural heritage, maintain Black identity, enhance their command of
the Language of Wider Communication (Mainstream/Standardized English),
and master essential reading, writing, and speaking skills. Ebonics reflects the
Black experience and conveys Black traditions and socially real truths. Black
Languages are crucial to Black identity. Black Language sayings, such as "What
goes around comes around," are crucial to Black ways of being in the world.
Black Languages, like Black lives, matter (para. 12).

*Reflection: One Word. What is your one word (figure 10.5) to summarize
your thoughts or feelings after reading this chapter? What is your one word?*
   *Examples of one word are provided in this word cloud, which was created
by using the words in this chapter.*

Figure 10.5   One Word, Chapter 10. *Source*: Created by Bouley & Reinking, 2021.

After reading this chapter, what are some ways you will hold yourself accountable through intentional, thoughtful actions?

Table 10.3 Reflections and Intentions

Reflection Question	Your Answer
My interactions with students…	
My interactions with their families…	
Physical classroom environment…	
Classroom materials and materials used for instruction…	
Lesson planning and curriculum…	
Instructional strategies such as grouping…	
Creating an anti-biased anti-racist school climate…	

RESOURCES

50 Incredible Useful Links for Learning and Teaching the English Language: https://www.teachthought.com/pedagogy/50-incredibly-useful-links-for-ell-educators/

Deep Dive: English Language Learners: https://learn.teachingchannel.com/ells

EL Resources by Grade: https://www.colorincolorado.org/ell-basics/ell-resources-grade

English Language Learners: https://www.readingrockets.org/reading-topics/english-language-learners

ESL/ELL Interaction Websites: https://researchguides.library.wisc.edu/c.php?g=177873&p=1169756

ESL/ELL Resources to Succeed in School: https://www.accreditedschoolsonline.org/resources/esl-ell-resources-for-teachers-parents-and-students/

Resources for Teaching English-Language Learners: https://www.edutopia.org/article/resources-for-teaching-english-language-learners-ashley-cronin

Sheltered Instruction Observation Protocol (SIOP): https://cal.org/siop/

Top 5 Dos and Don'ts for an English Language Teacher: https://www.scholastic.co.uk/blog/Top-5-dos-and-donts-for-an-English-Language-Teacher-34582

WIDA: https://wida.wisc.edu/

Chapter 11

Family Diversity and Microaggressions

There is no such thing as a single-issue struggle because we do not live single-issue lives.

—Audre Lorde

Families come in all shapes, sizes, colors, backgrounds, and make-ups. While historically two-parent households were considered to be the norm in America, two-parent households are on the decline as divorce, remarriage, and cohabitation are becoming more socially acceptable. Statistically there is no longer a majority "normal family" or nuclear family foundation in America. However, it is important to look back at past generations to understand mindsets.

In the 1960s, most babies were born within a marriage. Conversely, as of 2015, four-in-ten births occurred to single or cohabitate parents. With these changes, along with other societal and structural family dynamic changes, there is no longer a "norm" or dominant family form.

While the nuclear family, or a family with a married man and wife, were the majority at one point in our history, in 2015 two-parent households were at an all-time low (Pew Research Center, 2015). Educators who understand and acknowledge there is no longer a "normal" family dynamic can create more welcoming environments for all family types.

Researchers also looked at what the Census Bureau defined as "blended families," which included families with stepparents, step siblings, or half-siblings. Blended families have stayed constant around 15 percent since the 1990s in the United States. Furthermore, researchers who study family diversity found that mothers are more in the workforce today than in generations past, although this number has seen a dramatic decrease during the COVID-19 pandemic.

Additionally, "multi-partner fertility" or the situation where people have biological children with more than one partner has also increased. The structural diversity of families has also been disaggregated according to race. According to Pew Research Center (2015),

> The majority of white, Hispanic and Asian children are living in two-parent households, while less than half of black children are living in this type of arrangement. Furthermore, at least half of Asian and white children are living with two parents both in their first marriage. The shares of Hispanic and black children living with two parents in their first marriage are much lower (para. 10).

Further, multigenerational homes, defined by Pew Research Center as "two or more adult generations, or including grandparents and grandchildren under 25" have grown a great deal over the past few decades. According to Cohen and Passel (2018), in a Pew Research Center study, it was found that 20 percent of Americans, 64 million, live in multigenerational homes. Asian-Americans (29 percent) and Hispanic-Americans (27 percent) make up the largest percentage of multigenerational living.

With knowledge of varying family structures, educators can begin to understand that all families are different and that society as a whole is constantly evolving.

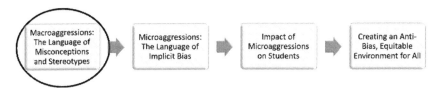

Figure 11.1   Macro, Micro, Impact, ABE. *Source*: Created by Bouley & Reinking, 2021.

The stereotypes of a "normal" American family are historically based on the concepts of two heterosexual adults, a mother and father, and their offspring. This can be seen in media from movies, to television shows, to books. For generations, this type of family, a family with a mom, dad, and kids, has been defined as the "nuclear family." However, as mentioned earlier, this "nuclear" family has become much less common and has been replaced by a plethora of non-traditional family structures.

While it is fair to say that there is no longer a stereotypical family in 2021, stereotypes and misconceptions remain common. The macroaggressions that infiltrate our communities are based on the stereotypes focused on getting married, getting divorced, the multiplicity of family dynamics, single-parent families, and families of color.

Reflection: Who are your families? What types of family structures do your students represent?

GETTING MARRIED

One common stereotype centers on the idea that marriages have declined over the past few decades. The Statista Research Department (2021), reports that in 2021 there are 62.34 million marriages in the United States, a significant rise from 40.2 million in 1960. This increase may certainly be influenced by the overall population increase.

As statistics continue to be noted, it is also important to note marriages that are identified around the country and those that aren't. Specifically, gay marriage is still not legal in thirteen of the fifty United States, therefore, is not documented in marriage statistics.

Interracial marriages have continued to rise in the United States. According to the Pew Research Center (Livingston & Brown, 2017), 17 percent of all marriages in 2015 were of interracial couples which is a stark increase from the 3 percent in 1967. In 2015, one-in-ten married people had a spouse whose race or ethnicity was different from their own. During this same time period Black individuals who entered interracial marriages tripled from 5 to 18 percent, yet Asian (29 percent) and Hispanic (27 percent) Americans are much more likely to be in interracial marriages.

While American's acceptance of interracial marriages has increased, according to Pew Research Center (Livington & Brown, 2017) only 39 percent of Americans believe interracial marriage is good for society with 9 percent believing it is bad for society. The wide majority of Americans who do not support interracial marriage are older, while the majority of Americans ages 18–29 (54 percent) are supportive.

GETTING DIVORCED

Another common misconception is that the heterosexual divorce rate has been steadily rising. However, it has seen a significant decline since 1981. The divorce rate in 1981 was 1.21 and has decreased significantly to 0.75 in 2019 which according to the Statista Research Department translates to 2.7 divorces per 1,000 marriages.

Furthermore, same-sex married couples divorce at a much smaller rate than opposite-sex couples. A traditional stereotype may be that same-sex couples divorce more often, yet according to Pride Legal Law (2021), heterosexual couples have a higher divorce rate than same-sex couples.

Based on the stereotype that gay men may be less interested in commitment than lesbian women, one might believe that married gay men would have a higher divorce rate yet the opposite is true. In fact, according to Pride Legal Law, lesbian married couples account for at least two-thirds of all same-sex divorces.

In terms of divorce, studies have shown that interracial marriages have higher divorce rates. According to Pew (2012), there is a 41 percent chance that interracial couples separate or divorce, compared to a 31 percent chance for same-race couples.

FAMILY DYNAMIC MULTIPLICITY

Another common family dynamic stereotype relates to multigenerational families. According to the Pew Research Center's Census data analysis (Livingston & Brown, 2017), in 2016 there was a record number of Americans living in multigenerational homes, 64 million—near 20 percent of the American population. As mentioned, Asian (29 percent) and Hispanic (27 percent) individuals are more likely to live in multigenerational homes and the increase in diversity in the United States accounts for the overall increase in numbers.

A common misconception or stereotype of families living in multigenerational homes may be that they are unemployed or too lazy to work hard enough for their own home. The stereotype is that they are only living together with extended family because of their finances. While this may be true for many multigenerational families, many families live together for relational reasons, not monetary.

In their 2021 report, *Family Matters: Multigenerational Living is on the Rise and Here to Stay,* Generations United found that seven out of ten (72 percent) of individuals living in multigenerational houses plan to continue doing so in the future. It is important to also note that 57 percent of these families surveyed in 2021 stated that the COVID-19 pandemic was their reason for moving in together.

In the same report, Generations United (2021) stated many reasons why multigenerational living is here to stay and a wise choice for many families including a means to provide child and elderly care, a more environmentally friendly housing option, allows for more flexible work schedules and the possibility of continuing school or a job training program, enhancing mental/physical health of individuals and the bond between family members. In many cultures families have historically lived together purely for relationship reasons, maintaining a long tradition of keeping loved ones together in the same home.

Skip-generation families are families where the grandparent(s) may be taking care of their grandchildren without the assistance of the children's parents. The terms grandparents raising grandchildren (GRGs) or grandparents as parents (GAPs) or parenting grandparents have been used to describe skip-generation families. The Census Bureau (2014), found the number of grandchildren raised by their grandparents doubled from 3 percent in 1970 to 6 percent in 2012, which is 10 percent of all grandparents.

The same report found that 39 percent of those grandparents have been raising their grandchildren for at least five years and women comprise 64.2 percent of the grandparents who live with their grandchildren. The increase in grandparent, skip-generation families can lead to stereotypes, assumptions, or misconceptions as to why these children are being raised by their grandparent and/or if their grandparent is capable of raising them (United States Census Bureau, 2014).

In addition, these grandparents may meet assumptions or stereotypes about their level of involvement in their grandchild's schooling. Skip-generation families struggle through many challenges that could limit their involvement such as health and financial issues, mental stress, and social isolation.

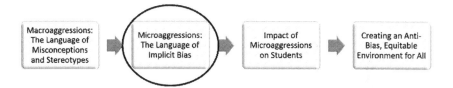

Figure 11.2 **Macro, Micro, Impact, ABE.** *Source*: Created by Bouley & Reinking, 2021.

Reflection: Do you find yourself making assumptions about your students based on their family background or dynamic? How so?

SINGLE-PARENT FAMILIES

Single-mom families have also grown substantially from 11.26 million in 1990 to 14.84 million in 2019. In fact, The Pew Research Center (Kramer, 2019) reports that the United States has the highest number of children living in single-parent families in the world. Twenty-three percent of U.S. children live in single-parent homes compared to the average rate of 7 percent of children from 130 countries around the world. Yet, the report also found that less U.S. children (8 percent) live with extended family compared to children globally (38 percent). In the United States and globally, women are almost five times more likely than men to be living as a single parent.

Single-parent families face numerous stereotypes as they are seen to have "broken families" or less than ideal homes for raising children. Historically, church records back to the 1600s have documented children born to single parents as "bastards" and today, single parents still suffer a great deal of stigma.

Since the majority of single parents are women, they suffer from gender inequalities and sexist ideas such as they chose to become mothers at a young age, or could have prevented their pregnancies. The one-income household of single parents also leads to the "lower-class, single parent" or "welfare queen" stereotyping.

Further, single-parent families experience many other misconceptions such as boys desperately needing a father or children needing two parents to be healthy, that single parents chose to be single or could choose to be coupled, are unhappy about being a single parent, and that children in single-parent homes will grow up to have problems that children in two-parent homes won't.

WOMEN "DO IT ALL"

Building from the data that shows the majority of single-parent households are led by women, it is also important to note that even in two-parent households women do a large portion of the housework and child rearing. This is based on a common microaggression where women are charged with housework and childcare, along with a full-time career outside of the house. This phenomenon has become even more apparent during the COVID-19 pandemic.

As reported in February 2021, 2.5 million women have left the workforce since the beginning of the pandemic. In just the month of September 2020 alone, 865,000 women left the workforce, which was four times more than the number of men. Why? As reported on NPR, "the uncomfortable truth is that in their homes, women are still fitting into stereotypical roles of doing the bulk of cooking, cleaning and parenting. It's another form of systemic inequality within a 21st century home that the pandemic is laying bare" (Gogoi, 2020, para. 5).

The gender pay gap plays a big role in what appears to be a return to the 1980s in terms of household chores or duties. In 2021, women still only make 82 cents for every dollar a man earns. So, when a decision needs to be made on who stays home to take over the parenting, cleaning, cooking, and frankly the remote teaching duties, the obvious choice in many households is the woman.

Derald Wing Sue (2010) provides a view into how microaggressions influence the standard of living and quality of life for women, as well as BIPOC.

"Statistics state that white American men constitute 33 percent of the total population." However, they occupy approximately:

- 80% of tenured positions in higher education
- 80% of the House of Representatives
- 80–85% of the U. S. Senate
- 92% of Forbes 400 executive CEO-level positions
- 90% of public school superintendents
- 99.9% of athletic team owners
- 97.7% of U. S. presidents" (Sue, 2010).

This is a clear depiction of sexist microaggressions impacting women's career trajectories, quality of life, and standard of living.

FAMILIES OF COLOR

Yull et al. (2018), in *Reversing the Dehumanization of Families of Color in Schools: Community-Based Research in a Race-Conscious Parent Engagement Program* discusses the stereotypes of families of color. The authors point out how school-parent engagement expectations are often consistent with white, Eurocentric parenting norms, and not families of color, a blatant macroaggression impacting learning environments. Yull et al. (2018) state,

> School districts across the U.S. often maintain a stance of disengagement with families of color because deficit-model thinking has led to assumptions by school personnel that parents of color are unable to make meaningful contributions to their children's education (Baquedano-López et al., 2013; Noguera, 2001). This perception of parents of color, coupled with the fact that a disproportionate number of students of color live in economically disenfranchised households, often with parents who have limited education, creates an environment where parents may feel less competent and sometimes intimidated when attempting to engage with school professionals (Castro, Bryant, Peisner-Feinberg, & Skinner, 2004, p. 322).

There have been many studies examining the stereotypical and negative portrayal in the media of Black families or families of color. One study, *A Dangerous Distortion of Our Families: Representations of Families by Race in News and Opinion Media* conducted by Travis L. Dixon (2017), was based on content analysis of two years of cable and network news shows and found,

> News and opinion media do, in fact, perpetuate inaccurate representations of Black families across several different areas of coverage. Overall, the findings show that news and opinion media outlets routinely and inaccurately portray Black families as sources of social *instability* in society and portray white families as sources of social *stability* in society, irrespective of facts to the contrary (p. 3).

More specifically, the study found that the media portrayed families living in poverty as overwhelmingly Black over white, the proportion of Black families receiving welfare was exaggerated, perpetuating the stereotype that Black families are lazy and dependent on the government systems, Black fathers were consistently portrayed as uninvolved or abandoning their children, Black mothers were portrayed as making bad decisions about family structures, and lastly, the study found the connection between Black families and criminality to be extremely overrepresented, while white families association with criminality was equally underrepresented (Dixon, 2017).

All of these portrayals are contrary to fact and center on the main stereotypes children and families of color experience in our education system. Incidentally, this report directly relates to Bobbie Harro's (2000) Cycle of Socialization discussed in an earlier chapter.

As established, we have consistently moved away from the two opposite-sex parent family structure, yet those that identify outside of that traditional family are often faced with misconceptions and stereotypes. Implicit bias is when assumptions are made off of these stereotypes, and students and family members from non-traditional families and families of color may experience these biases in the form of microaggressions.

As we begin this section, please take time to reflect on the terminology in the table below. *Stop and reflect to fill in the second column.*

Table 11.1   Reflection on Terminology

Terminology	*Reflect: What Is Your Definition of the Term?*
Broken family bias	
Extended Family bias	
Nuclear family bias	
Traditional family bias	
Diverse family bias	
Multigenerational family bias	

Students and family members living in families that are perceived by society as non-traditional often experience microaggressions in schools. One primary microaggression is through exclusion.

Reflection: Are you intentional in bringing various family structures and backgrounds into your class materials and discourse? If yes, how so? If not, what adjustments might you make to be more inclusive?

EXCLUSION

Whether a student has parents that are divorced, are same-sex parents, are living in multigenerational homes, or are being raised by a single parent or extended family member, students who do not have a mom and dad at home often feel their family is silenced or excluded from classroom curriculum, books, and discourse.

Even though approximately one-third of children in the United States live with an unmarried parent, the majority of them rarely, if ever, see their family represented in school materials. According to Scholastic, 63 percent of parents of children ages 6–17 want more children's books with "Various settings and living situations" (Warkentin, 2019).

Furthermore, in 2018 only 23 percent of children's books depicted characters of color. The percent depicting various family structures is even less. The wide majority of children's books depict straight (81 percent), cisgendered (74 percent) characters or parents (Reach Out & Read Minnesota, 2020). Overall, very few children's books are published that explicitly feature children with divorced, same-sex, grandparent or single-parent families.

As Katie Waters (2017), points out in *Children's Books Featuring Diverse Family Structures and Living Arrangements: Recommendations for Elementary Teachers*,

> Teachers may make assumptions about children based on their family's composition and may expect less of children from certain types of families. Teachers may be influenced by negative stereotypes and may not want to include certain family types in the curriculum; however, it is important for all children to see their families represented in children's literature (p. 127).

Reflection: Examine your classroom materials, books, curricula for the inclusion of varying family structures. Which family structures are represented? Who is excluded?

The exclusion of diverse family structures goes well beyond children's books. Curricula, programs, classroom materials, assessments and classroom discourse are all centered on heteronormative, two-parent families. A common daily microaggression students of varying family structures experience comes through classroom/school discourse, in particular, the words educators use to describe families.

Often educators say "mom and dad" or "parents" or even "real parents" when talking with students who live with a grandparent or other relative. More inclusive language could include "grown-ups" "adults" "family members" or "birth parents."

One strategy early childhood program's embrace to address this diversity is to refer to all adults in the life of a child as their "big person." Sometimes the "big person," who gets them off the bus when they arrive home, are their older brother or sister, aunt, uncle, grandparent, babysitter, and so on. Using inclusive language is one way to create a safe environment.

In addition to exclusive language, students with divorced parents experience microaggressions based on the stereotype that families with divorced adults are "broken." Students may be asked inappropriate questions about which parent they are staying with or say things regarding the parent's custodial plan that show judgment such as, "It must be *so hard* to go back and forth between homes this often."

Further, school administrators and educators might only communicate with one parent, and fail to engage both parents in the student's education. Assumptions might be made about why the parents are divorcing, which impact interactions with both the student and the parents.

ASSUMED DISADVANTAGE

Besides regularly hearing "bring this home to *mom and dad*," students from single-parent families may be met with lower expectations from their teachers, or be addressed with language that is based on the assumption that the child is disadvantaged or from a dysfunctional home, both of which are based in a deficit mindset from the observer.

Students may be disciplined for not getting their homework complete or bringing in a permission slip, when the issue is around the challenges of running a family as a single individual. Students might hear judgment or assumption in their teacher's voice as they ask why their parent wasn't making sure their homework was done or coming to school events.

Students living in multigenerational homes may be asked, "How many people *do* live in your house anyway?" or be questioned on their sleeping arrangements. They may be asked if their parents work or about the reason why they all live under one roof.

Young single mothers experience microaggressions that stem from the assumption that it is undesirable to be a single mother or impossible to have a career if you are a single mom. They may be asked if they had their child "out of wedlock" or how they came to be a single parent. Students of single mothers might be asked questions like, "Does your *dad* play sports with you?" or "Who reads with you, *mom or dad*?" Single fathers also experience microaggressions as their reason for being a hands-on parent might be questioned.

Microaggressions toward adoptive parents or students are also prevalent. Students might hear comments such as, "You're *so lucky* you were adopted." or "What happened to your *real parents*?" Adoptive parents might hear statements such as, "It's great you could adopt since you were *unable to have your own children.*" A birth parent might be told, "I don't know how you did it. It must have been *so hard* to give up your baby."

FAMILY INTERSECTIONALITY

Same-sex families might receive microaggressions that center on the legitimacy of their family. Students of same-sex parents often experience microaggressions at the hands of their peers. They are often inundated with questions about how they can be a family if they don't have a mom and/or dad, what it's like to have two dads/moms, who actually gave birth to them, or they are told they must have a mom to be alive (in the case of two dads).

Farr et al. (2016), in *Microaggressions, Feelings of Difference, and Resilience Among Adopted Children with Sexual Minority Parents,* found "many children adopted by sexual minority couples experience feelings of difference and microaggressions as a result of having same-sex parents" (p. 98). Most of these microaggressions come from peers,

> Children's peers, who often appeared uneducated about sexual minority issues, most commonly initiated microaggressions. For example, one child reported that a peer "didn't know same-sex couples existed" and another said that "most people don't understand" when she tells them about having two mothers (Farr et al., 2016, p. 95).

Reflection: How would you approach situations where students make judgments or assumptions about their peers based on their family structure or dynamic? How would or do you address peer microaggressions?

Families of color also experience numerous types of microaggressions. Many studies have found families of color experience microaggressions at the hands of educators, and other school employees. Posey (2017) found,

> microaggressions were often classed and gendered, and, for a number of parents, re-lived and reinforced in their children's schools. The results reveal both the everyday racism Black parents encountered in the predominantly White suburban community and school district, as well as the dynamic ways they navigated, resisted, and sought to change barriers to Black student and family success.

A study by Yull et al. (2018), found that Black families reported feeling unwelcome in their child's school, dismissed as uncaring and also reported experiencing racial injustice. Families of color may feel excluded by the "whiteness" of schools, and the dichotomy between the predominately white teaching force and families of color lends itself to a lack of understanding that may result in microaggressions in teacher-parent communications.

A list of more microaggressions families experience are educators:

- using the term "illegals" to describe undocumented parents.
- assigning class projects or homework that rely on family engagement, such as the family tree. Some students may not have that information for various reasons.
- assuming that all students have parental support for homework assignments.
- failing to pronounce a student's family name correctly.
- making assumptions about where their family originated based on their last name. This also implies that the family must not be from the United States and therefore does not speak English well or has a native language other than English.

Overall, the most egregious microaggression is the silence that comes from lack of explicit classroom discussions on varied family structures and critical calling out of classroom peer microaggressions. Farr et al. (2017) state teachers are "in a unique position to cultivate positive classroom environments and directly intervene with situations of peer victimization (Troop-Gordon, 2015), teachers could ideally identify microaggressions occurring in schools and construct ways for children to curb and resolve such offenses" (p. 97).

Microaggressions like these have a definite impact on students of diverse family structures.

Reflection: Stop and reflect. Using the table from the beginning of this section, would you change any of your initial definitions? If so, how?.

Figure 11.3 Macro, Micro, Impact, ABE. *Source*: Created by Bouley & Reinking, 2021.

Explicit microaggressions and exclusion from classroom materials, books and discourse have a negative impact on students with varied family structures. Equity and inclusion must not be limited to individual identities, but also include diversity in family structures. Simply put, all students need to see their families represented in all aspects of school and when they do not, they experience an inequitable education. For example, Waters (2017) state,

> Although children in schools across the country experience a variety of living situations and family arrangements, children's books that teachers read in classrooms for young children often do not reflect the family types and living arrangements of students. This situation presents a significant challenge to children who may have trouble connecting with the content of the curriculum. When teachers incorporate children's books that highlight diverse family structures and living arrangements, it can provide an opportunity for students to see themselves and others rep-resented in their everyday lives (p. 132).

Yull et al. (2018) discuss the impact of familial/racial microaggressions in relation to school discipline, "Racial and cultural disconnects—or incompatibility between home and school cultures—produce challenges for students, parents, and school personnel (Coggins & Campbell, 2008) which often lead to disproportionate suspensions and expulsions of students of color" (Gregory, Skiba, & Noguera, 2010, p. 322).

Another side-effect of microaggressions relates to the impact they have on the comfort level and desire for families to engage with teachers and school. Cousins and Mickelson (2011) state that "parents tend to get involved more when they feel welcomed and their traditions and contributions are respected (Brandon, 2007; Mapp, 2003; McKay, Atkins, Hawkins, Brown, & Lynn, 2003), but they are discouraged from involvement when they feel inadequate or feel they do not understand how schools work" (Brandon, 2007; Johnson, 2001; Lawson, 2003, p. 2).

Research on family involvement consistently supports the positive role family involvement plays in student academic success. When families are involved, students benefit in every way, and when families don't feel comfortable or welcome in schools, students suffer in every way, academically, socially, emotionally, and so on.

Maryam Daha (2016) in, *Recognizing and Addressing Microaggressions in Teacher-Family Relationships* discusses the breakdown in communication that can occur when families are met with assumptions and microaggressions from classroom teachers and school personnel.

> These *microaggressions* can be subtle, at times unconscious and without intended harm, but may cause a rift in family-teacher relationships. Communicating with a learning disposition leads to a willingness to learn about the worldview of the family, and focuses on practical strategies that strengthen cross-cultural communication (p. 61).

On a more positive note, and with respect to the impact of microaggressions on students with same-sex parents, a study by Farr et al. (2017) found,

> In addition to indicating experiences of microaggressions and feelings of difference, children in this study demonstrated resilience and conveyed many positive feelings about their families. Consistent with research with older samples of adolescent and adult children with same-sex parents (Gartrell et al., 2012; Goldberg, 2007a, b; Welsh, 2011), nearly three-quarters of children in this sample indicated positive conceptualizations of their families and/or methods of coping with difficulty based on having same-sex parents. Positive feelings were consistently reported more often than both microaggressions and feelings of difference (p. 96).

While in this study students of same-sex families seemed to overcome consistent microaggressions from peers, many students of diverse family structures and families of color are negatively impacted by the ways their families are perceived and treated by educators and peers. Heightening educator awareness and providing a more inclusive and equitable education is imperative for developing an anti-bias school environment for diverse families.

Figure 11.4   Macro, Micro, Impact, ABE. *Source*: Created by Bouley & Reinking, 2021.

As is the case with all CRT, heightening cultural awareness is the necessary beginning for creating anti-bias and equitable environments for students of diverse families. Daha (2016) states, "Self-awareness, including recognizing our own biases that influence our worldview, is important in our interactions with children and families" (p. 62).

Educators must work intentionally and consistently to get to know their families, and their own experiences and biases. Making assumptions about students and their families based on their family dynamic is definitely going to be transmitted to students and families in some way, and likely experienced as microaggressions.

Reflection: What are some things you do to get to know your families? How do you integrate what you learn into your classroom pedagogy, materials, assessments and discourse?

It is critical that educators create environments that are inclusive of every family structure and in every aspect of the classroom/school from books, to curriculum and classroom materials, to the symbolic curriculum (who is on the school/classroom walls), to daily classroom discourse.

The impacts of this inclusion are far-reaching and powerful. "Cultivating inclusive environments that positively promote children's overall development, health and psychological well-being is in the best interest of all individuals working with children" (Farr et al., 2017, p 97). When educators and families have trusting on-going communication, everyone benefits.

In terms of inclusivity in family-school communication and engagement, schools must work to find ways to create a more culturally responsive and inclusive school-wide approach. One way a school could increase family-school partnerships is to develop a Parent Mentor Program similar to that developed and implemented in a study by Yull et al. (2018),

> The Parent Mentor Program seeks to place parents in charge of their school engagement while operating from a race-conscious perspective that acknowledges how the school system often marginalizes and dehumanizes families of color. Rather than focusing solely on the achievement of students of color, the program seeks to organize parents of color as advocates in the school system that collectively push toward structural change in the school's treatment of students of color, with implications for improving the opportunities to learn afforded to these students (p. 320).

All school personnel need to learn about the families they represent in order to not only be inclusive but to be intentional in using family specific language, or in the least, family neutral language. Words matter, and when school personnel address families accurately it is a sign of caring and will have a positive impact on family-school relationships and family engagement--not to mention strengthening students' sense of family pride, identity and belonging.

See Table 11.2 for examples of inclusive language

Table 11.2   Inclusive Language for Families. Created by Bouley, 2021

Exclusive Language	Inclusive Language
"Mom" "Dad" or "Mom and dad"	"Grown-up" or "Grown-ups" "Folks"
"Parents"	"Family"
"Real parents"	"Birth parents"
"Grandmother"	"Caregiver" "Guardian"
"Is adopted"	"Was adopted"
"Step-father" "Step-mother"	"Adults in your family" *find out the specific names individual students use
"Your other mom" or "Your other dad"	Often same-sex parents have unique, discernable names for each mom or dad—learn what they are
"Typical family" or "Normal family"	"Family type" "Family structure"

Altering or lowering expectations for students simply because they have a single parent, divorced parents, a grandparent parent, extended family parent, biracial parents or parents of color, same-sex parents or if they live in multi-generational families, is a dangerous example of educator implicit bias that must be identified, discussed, and eliminated.

Altering how educators engage or communicate with families, or the expectations they have of family members due to family dynamic or identity, is equally dangerous and has a profoundly negative impact on the family's ability to nurture their child's education, and partner effectively with educators in doing so.

Reflection: One Word. What is your one word (figure 11.5) to summarize your thoughts or feelings after reading this chapter? What is your one word?

Examples of one word are provided in this word cloud, which was created by using the words in this chapter.

Figure 11.5   One Word, Chapter 11. *Source:* Created by Bouley & Reinking, 2021.

After reading this chapter, what are some ways you will hold yourself accountable through intentional, thoughtful actions?

Table 11.3 Reflections and Intentions

Reflection Question	Your Answer
My interactions with students…	
My interactions with their families…	
Physical classroom environment…	
Classroom materials and materials used for instruction…	
Lesson planning and curriculum…	
Instructional strategies such as grouping…	
Creating an anti-biased antiracist school climate…	

RESOURCES

Color of Change: The Dangerous Distortion of Families: https://colorofchange.org/wp-content/uploads/2019/05/COC-FS-Families-Representation-Report_Full_121217.pdf

The Benefits of Diversity and Inclusion in the Classroom (American University): https://soeonline.american.edu/blog/benefits-of-inclusion-and-diversity-in-the-classroom

The Harvard Family Research Project https://archive.globalfrp.org

Learning for Justice: Family Diversity https://www.learningforjustice.org/search?query=family%20diversity&f%5B0%5D=facet_content_type%3Aarticle

Rethinking Schools: Reframing the Family Tree https://rethinkingschools.org/articles/framing-the-family-tree/

Chapter 12

School-Wide Approaches to Creating an Equitable, Anti-Bias Education

Administrator Accountability

Multiculturalism compels educators to recognize the narrow boundaries that have shaped the way knowledge is shared in the classroom. It forces us all to recognize our complicity in accepting and perpetuating biases of any kind.

When everyone in the classroom, teacher and students, recognizes that they are responsible for creating a learning community together, learning is at its most meaningful and useful.

—bell hooks

It is well established that students of varying identities experience microaggressions in schools. While, as established, it is important to keep in mind that microaggressions are about the impact not the intent, that impact is harmful to students and must be addressed and minimized. This takes a whole school effort and should not just fall on the shoulders of teachers.

Research supports that teacher implicit bias often comes from lack of self-awareness, knowledge and preparedness. Studies examining teacher bias toward students and families of varying identities reveal lack of knowledge and confidence to adequately support the learning of students with diverse identities as the basis, not teacher desire to do so.

Robin DiAngelo in *White Fragility: Why It's So Hard For White People To Talk About Racism* (2018), states "if I am not aware of the barriers you face, then I won't see them, much less be motivated to remove them. Nor will I be motivated to remove the barriers if they provide an advantage to which I feel entitled."

Teachers are often the first to admit their need for professional development focused on anti-racist, anti-bias teaching and learning, and often request it. This is important since, as established in this book, recent studies show teachers are not immune to the effects of implicit bias (Eberhardt, 2019; Lewis & Diamond, 2017).

According to researchers from the University of Denver (Portman, et al., n.d.),

> It is clear from the literature that microaggressions are often committed by well-intentioned, good people not meaning to hurt anyone. Nevertheless, the outcome of microaggressions is anger, frustration, and withdrawal by those who are the recipients of insensitive comments and actions. Thus, in the case of the class-room, microaggressions are not being committed by spiteful and bigoted pro-fessors (teachers) who want to intentionally hurt students from diverse groups, but rather are undertaken at the unconscious level by well-meaning and caring professors (teachers). The bottom line is that microaggressions result in hostile and unwelcoming classroom environments (p. 1).

Microaggressions do happen because they are commonplace. Furthermore, individuals cannot make changes to practices until awareness and account-ability takes place. Nadal states, "We need to admit when we commit microaggressions, learn from the wrongdoing, and apologize. We all make mistakes, consciously and not, and need to own up to them when we do" (p. 75).

Moreover, Pitts (2020) writes,

> Anti-racist educators understand that they must be lifelong learners. They believe in the power of developing a critical consciousness, which comes from reading, from studying, from deep scholarship, from humility, from listening to and engaging with others, and from constantly examining and re-examining their own ideas, beliefs and truths (para. 7).

So, what do educators need to know? All educators need to know how to interrupt microaggressions in their classrooms and schools.

MICROAGGRESSIONS INTERRUPTED

In order to interrupt microaggressions, educators must know how to rec-ognize them. They need to know how to reflect and recognize their own microaggressions and biases, as well as those of students in the learning envi-ronment. These steps or processes to identify and reflect on personal implicit, or possibly explicit biases, were outlined in each of the chapters focused on individual identities. However, the process of identifying personal implicit biases is often difficult to somewhat impossible. Therefore, we recommend engaging with one or both of these resources focused on assisting in identifying implicit biases within yourself.

First is the resource Project Implicit (2011). Project Implicit is a non-profit, research-based organization whose goal is to "educate the public about implicit biases" and has created a survey to aid individuals in determining and understanding their implicit bias. According to Project Implicit, "The Implicit Association Test (IAT) measures attitudes and beliefs that people may be unwilling or unable to report." If administrators, educators, and other school personnel took the IAT implicit bias test, all of the individuals in a school would get a better understanding, or even a new understanding, of their bias.

Project Implicit states,

> The IAT may be especially interesting if it shows that you have an implicit attitude that you did not know about. For example, you may believe that women and men should be equally associated with science, but your automatic associations could show that you (like many others) associate men with science more than you associate women with science (2011).

This is critical information for minimizing microaggressions in schools.

In addition to offering the IAT, Project Implicit (2011) offers a great deal of education and resources on the topic of implicit bias, prejudice and stereotypes. Based on over 25 million completed IATs, Project Implicit has launched over 3,000 research studies and published over 150 peer-reviewed papers.

Reflection:

1. *After taking the IAT (referenced above), what are your implicit biases? Do you know where they originated? (Website provided in chapter resources.)*
2. *For more work on personal implicit biases and how they impact actions and decisions, successfully complete this open-sourced, 4 module training: http://kirwaninstitute.osu.edu/implicit-bias-training/*

Second is the resource Intercultural Development Inventory, also known as IDI. While Project Implicit is free, IDI does have a cost. Regardless, IDI

> assesses intercultural competence—the capability to shift cultural perspective and appropriately adapt behavior to cultural differences and commonalities. Intercultural competence has been identified as a critical capability in a number of studies focusing on overseas effectiveness of international sojourners, international business adaptation and job performance, international student

adjustment, international transfer of technology and information, international study abroad, and inter-ethnic relations within nations (2021).

Whichever resource you are able to use, it is an imperative part of the interruption process to truly and honestly identify implicit biases. Once implicit biases are identified, a great reflective resource is the Tool: Interrupting Microaggression (Kenney, 2014). In figure 12.1 a snip of the first page is provided. The purpose of "interrupting microaggressions" is to develop communication approaches that address by calling in rather than calling out.

Tool: Interrupting Microaggressions

MICROAGGRESSION EXAMPLE AND THEME	THIRD PARTY INTERVENTION EXAMPLE	COMMUNICATION APPROACH
Alien in One's Own Land To a Latino American: "Where are you from?"	"I'm just curious. What makes you ask that?"	INQUIRE Ask the speaker to elaborate. This will give you more information about where s/he is coming from, and may also help the speaker to become aware of what s/he is saying.
Ascription of Intelligence To an Asian person, "You're all good in math, can you help me with this problem?"	"I heard you say that all Asians are good in math. What makes you believe that?"	KEY PHRASES: "Say more about that." "Can you elaborate on your point?" "It sounds like you have a strong opinion about this. Tell me why."
Color Blindness "I don't believe in race."	"So, what do you believe in? Can you elaborate?"	"What is it about this that concerns you the most?"
Myth of Meritocracy "Everyone can succeed in this society, if they work hard enough."	"So you feel that everyone can succeed in this society if they work hard enough. Can you give me some examples?"	PARAPHRASE/REFLECT Reflecting in one's own words the essence of what the speaker has said. Paraphrasing demonstrates understanding and reduces defensiveness of both you and the speaker.
Pathologizing Cultural Values/Communication Styles Asking a Black person: "Why do you have to be so loud/animated? Just calm down."	"It appears you were uncomfortable when ___ said that. I'm thinking that there are many styles to express ourselves. How we can honor all styles of expression—can we talk about that?"	Restate briefly in your own words, rather than simply parroting the speaker. Reflect both content and feeling whenever possible. KEY PHRASES: "So, it sounds like you think..." "You're saying...You believe..."
Second-Class Citizen You notice that your female colleague is being frequently interrupted during a committee meeting.	Responder addressing the group: "___ brings up a good point. I didn't get a chance to hear all of it. Can ___ repeat it?"	REFRAME Create a different way to look at a situation. KEY PHRASES: "What would happen if...." "Could there be another way to look at this..."
Pathologizing Cultural Values/Communication Styles To a woman of color: "I would have never guessed that you were a scientist."	"I'm wondering what message this is sending her. Do you think you would have said this to a white male?"	"Let's reframe this..." "How would you feel if this happened to your___."

Figure 12.1   Tool: Interrupting Microaggressions. *Source:* (https://academicaffairs.ucsc. edu/events/documents/Microaggressions_InterruptHO_2014_11_182v5.pdf).

Once implicit biases are recognized, reflected upon, and interrupted, creating anti-racist, anti-biased school climates is possible.

SCHOOL-WIDE ANTI-RACIST, ANTI-BIAS CLIMATES

Whether discussing discipline, anti-bullying, family engagement, anti-racist education, or any aspect of schooling, creating an equitable, anti-bias education for all students demands a school and district-wide approach. Anti-racist and anti-bias school policies, protocols and programs must be systemic, systematic, and consistently enforced.

It is imperative then that not only teachers but all school personnel are involved and engaged in all efforts from family to board members, superintendents to cafeteria workers and custodians. Research supports that in order to be effective, important initiatives like these must be developed, implemented and enforced inclusively, and comprehensively.

Yet before doing so, educators need to acknowledge how racism is systemic in schools. According to Pitts (2020), Anti-racist educators recognize that schools are doing *exactly* what they were built to do in this country: Exclude. Silence. Erase. Promote white supremacy. They recognize, therefore, that upending racism in schools will end schooling practices as we have come to know them. (para. 6)

Once recognized, educators need to see themselves working from the ground up toward dismantling the system, as opposed to looking to adopt a published program as a quick fix. While educators are not the ones making policies, educators could view themselves as having the power to create more equitable anti-biased classrooms and schools. When teachers advocate for and demand change, administrators, board members, and politicians need to listen. When school administrators see the pivotal role they play and they work with teachers, change is imminent.

In discussing the need for taking a holistic approach, Pitts (2020) states,

Anti-racist education and anti-racist schooling cannot be packaged or prescribed, arranged into a checklist, rubric or formula. Anti-racist educators understand that anti-racist work begins with the self. They begin by grappling with their beliefs, mindsets, philosophies and biases about the world, education and their students. They work to become conscious of the intentional, multiple ways schools mirror society and how all aspects of school systems are designed to uphold the oppressive aims of the society in which they operate (para. 12).

According to Pitts, this holistic approach involves the following dimensions, which is outlined in table 12.1:

Table 12.1   Holistic Approach Dimensions. *Source:* Pitts (2020)

The demographics of staff, particularly in schools with predominantly BIPOC students	Special education	Professional development and new-teacher training and support
School leadership and paths to school leadership	Definitions and measurements of academic success	The wellness of teachers, staff and students

(Continued)

Table 12.1   Holistic Approach Dimensions (Continued)

School governance (e.g., network and district leadership)	Definitions and measurements of teacher success	School culture and approaches to discipline
School curriculum	School mission and vision statements	School infrastructure
Teaching and learning practices	School, network and district policies	Allocation of resources and budget

Connecting to the concept of creating anti-bias and anti-racist environments in schools through a school-wide approach, Jones (2020), wrote

> Educating and training teachers and administrators on how to enact culturally relevant and inclusive practices is one step toward eliminating racism in schools. Expressing a commitment to anti-racism through school policies, statements, guidelines, or codes takes these efforts a step further.

After examining twenty-five equity or anti-racist policies from several states in the United States and from schools in Australia, South Africa, Ireland and the United Kingdom, Jones (2020) found that most policies address racism through the lenses of:

1. "school environment
2. incident reporting
3. staffing
4. data analysis
5. funding."

According to Jones (2020),

> After addressing these components, policies typically offer guidance or present action steps to support implementation. These guidance documents or action steps often include:

1. providing a clear and accurate definition of racism for consumers of the policy,
2. devising a plan for policy dissemination,
3. appointing an anti-racist committee or point person,
4. coupling equity/anti-racist policy with other school or district-wide policies,
5. partnering with external organizations.

Finally, in figure 12.2 Jones (2020), provides the necessary pieces of an inclusive, anti-racist school policy:

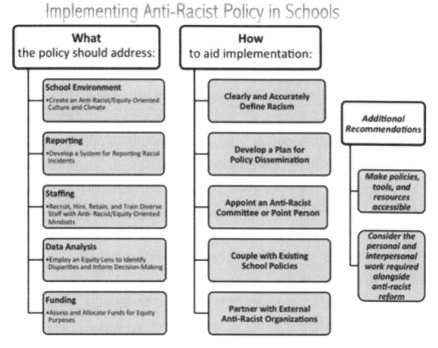

Figure 12.2   Implementing Anti-Racist Policy in Schools. *Source*: (https://education
.uconn.edu/2020/09/22/reducing-racism-in-schools-the-promise-of-anti-racist-policies/).

DISCIPLINE

While discipline and policies overlap, discipline is also a concept that has pulled out for further discussion throughout this book. When discussing holistic, systemic approaches to eradicating racism, implicit bias and microaggressions in schools, it is important to emphasize the need for examining discipline statistics, and creating school-wide, clear and consistent policies and practices. As demonstrated in earlier chapters, racial, gender, income and ability disparities in school discipline outcomes are well documented in the research and are consistent across grades, from preschool to high school.

After an extensive review of the literature on school discipline, Welsh and Little (2018), found that disciplinary disparities are often focused on the student behavior, race, or socioeconomic status. However, it could be more easily explained through teacher and principal behavior, mindsets, and implicit biases. In a TedTalk titled, *School Suspensions Are Adult Behavior*, Dr. Rosemarie Allen stated that "behavior is defined by the person most annoyed by it."

This speaks to the truth that teachers define behavior, both "good" and "bad," which is often determined by implicit bias. Teacher bias has been found to play a role in discipline disparities, "Research suggests that unconscious bias is able to manifest and harm groups that are negatively stereotyped (Gershenson & Dee, 2017), and the lack of a representative bureaucracy may facilitate discrimination through implicit bias (Feistritzer, Griffin, & Linnajarvi, 2011)" (Welsh & Little, 2018, p. 768).

Furthermore, recent evidence suggests that school-level variables are the strongest predictors of disciplinary outcomes, such as school-wide policies and school leadership. As Welsh and Little (2018) state,

> School leadership appears to be an essential component of the rates of and disparities in disciplinary outcomes (Skiba, Chung, Tradchok, Baker, Sheya, & Hughes, 2014). There is substantial variation in the disciplinary philosophies of principals within the same school district, and rates of suspension are linked to principals' attitudes (Mukuria, 2002; Skiba, Edl, & Rausch, 2007; Skiba, Chung et al., 2014) (p. 770).

As established, excessive and disproportionate disciplining is a large part of the systemic racism in schools and has a tremendous impact on students with varying identities—so much so it is referred to as the "school-to-prison pipeline." Schools must develop holistic, district-wide policies and practices that involve all school personnel.

Focus should be on diversifying the teaching force, examining the role of teacher and administrator bias, identifying racial, ethnic, economic, ability and gender disciplining disparities, developing teacher-student relationships and consistent, clear and anti-racist school-wide policies and practices.

School discipline policies and practices, from the purpose they serve, to principal attitudes, to teacher classroom management skills and implicit bias, must be closely examined in order to create equitable anti-racist and anti-bias school climates and educational opportunities.

THE DANGER OF SOCIAL-EMOTIONAL
LEARNING (SEL) PROGRAMS

Social-emotional learning programs are quickly becoming popular in schools across the country. The goal of these programs is to support students to identify, express and manage their emotions, and to assist teachers in developing the knowledge and skills necessary to facilitate that process.

While these are important goals, it is equally important to consider how these SEL programs may serve to perpetuate a hidden curriculum or be focused on white, Eurocentric ideas on social and emotional development and expression. In addition, SEL programs must consider sociopolitical contexts, meaning it is dangerous to focus on teaching students social and emotional skills without taking the school system or climate into consideration.

In discussing school discipline, Welsh and Little (2018) point out,

> The vast majority of the alternative approaches are most concerned with assisting students with assimilating to the school culture rather than crafting the school culture to fit the social, emotional, and cultural needs of students. As such, schools focus more on achieving behavior management through conformity and less on addressing the biases and cultural clashes that may be driving discipline disparities. However, the evidence suggests that remedies to discipline disparities should focus on the disposition and biases of teachers and school leaders' behavior management rather than student misbehavior (p 773).

Long before SEL programs became popular in schools, Daniel Goleman discovered the important role that social and emotional intelligence plays in academic learning and success (Goleman, 1995). Yet, SEL must first consider the long history of discrimination in schools, the disparity between diversity in the teaching force and student/family populations, and the overwhelming research supporting the evidence and role of teacher and administrator bias.

When this context is ignored, SEL becomes one more opportunity for students of diverse and disadvantaged identities to experience microaggressions. In *We Can't Afford White-Washed Social-Emotional Learning*, Dena Simmons (2019), argues that it is the sociopolitical context in which students live that gets in the way of developing social-emotional skills. Telling a student who is hungry because of extreme poverty to manage her emotions "as we discussed" or another student to control and "appropriately express" his anger while he is being racially profiled by the school security, clearly are microaggressions.

While she acknowledges the important role SEL can play in helping students identify and confront prejudice and injustice, Simmons states, "educators often teach SEL absent of the larger sociopolitical context, which is fraught with injustice and inequity and affects our students' lives" (para. 4).

Simmons (2019), goes on to state that fear is a primary reason.

> As an SEL practitioner-researcher who speaks nationally about the intersection of emotional intelligence, equity, and culturally responsive practices, I hear that educators shy away from such discussions for fear that they will be accused of politicization or that they will lose their jobs (para. 4).

Simmons (2019), also believes discomfort and lack of knowledge to be responsible, "Other teachers feel ill-equipped and uncomfortable in addressing topics like poverty, gun violence, racism, sexism, homophobia, transphobia, and other forms of injustice that many students, particularly our most marginalized, experience daily" (para. 5).

Acknowledging students' lived experiences when teaching SEL is the only way schools can teach SEL in an equitable and unbiased way. Additionally, in the process students will be able to develop the skills necessary to advocate for racial and social justice in appropriate and effective ways. Simmons calls these the "ultimate life skills."

Simmons (2019), emphasizes the importance of intentionally having explicit conversations in our schools and classrooms on issues of racial and social justice, and how SEL programs provide an opportunity to do so,

> We can no longer avoid discussing topics that make us uncomfortable. Our students, incessantly inundated with divisive rhetoric and reports of premeditated acts of violence (or even themselves targets of violence), don't have that luxury. SEL has tremendous potential to create the conditions for youth agency and civic engagement and, ultimately, social change. We owe our students an education that centers on their lives and explicitly addresses the sociopolitical context. This will not only prepare our students to engage civically and peacefully across differences, but also to become the changemakers and leaders we need (para. 8).

THE CRITICAL ROLE OF SCHOOL ADMINISTRATORS

Creating anti-bias, anti-racist environments involve every aspect of a school. District and school administrators must take a systemic approach, one that involves environments, curricula, assessment, policies, procedures, family engagement and all aspects of daily life. It must also include on-going opportunities for all school personnel to examine individual and programmatic racism and bias.

Racism and bias exist in many aspects of the education system and administrators must look closely at how they are being perpetuated in their schools. Administrators must analyze discipline data and work with all school personnel to develop and/or analyze school-wide discipline policies and protocol.

All curricula must be scrutinized, including SEL programs, for racism and bias. Administrators, who take a leading role in curriculum selection and development, must work with educators and family members to ensure students have access to a curriculum that centers on justice, equity, inclusion, and diversity.

In building an anti-racist, anti-bias school, administrators need to keep in mind that there is no quick fix or program. Derman-Sparks et al. (2015), remind school leaders to take a slow, comprehensive approach,

> While the urgency to implement anti-bias education is great from the perspective of the children's needs, the process of change happens over time; an anti-bias education leader must plan for the long haul. Successful anti-bias education change needs an intentional and thoughtful strategic approach (para. 2).

In terms of published programs, school leaders who are most often responsible for purchasing programs should rather consider taking a more systemic, ground-up approach that involves school and community members. Likewise, textbook and assessment purchases should be evaluated for bias, as should the procedures around testing.

School administrators should also take the lead in developing and analyzing data for school practices such as tracking and access to various programs. For instance, school members should take a close look at who is in Advanced Placement (AP) classes or gifted and enrichment programs, and more importantly, who isn't. School leaders should ask how students are selected for these programs and how might those assessments be biased.

The same scrutiny should be applied to special education or remedial programs. Administrators should explore if students are being placed in special education services because of their English language proficiency or because the school does not offer the services they actually need. Another area to explore relates to physical bias, and where certain programs such as special education are located within the school.

In addition to membership and location, administrators need to examine policies and procedures around remedial instruction (i.e., pull-out vs. in-classroom remedial instruction) and how they have been informed by the latest research. Analyzing these school programs for racism and bias is critical to developing an equitable anti-bias education for all students.

In addition, administrators should consider how federal and state anti-discrimination policies are addressed and implemented in their schools. Anti-bullying programs should involve school-wide commitment and constant engagement. Rather than posting "zero-tolerance zone" posters in the hallways, educators should have time to discuss ways they are integrating anti-bullying skills in their daily instruction.

Equally important to any school-wide program review relates to family engagement. Research supports that developing and implementing a school-wide family engagement program may be most successful at increasing family involvement. In addition, involving family members in discussions around all other school programs is critical to diversifying ideas and putting into place policies that reflect the community.

Including family and community members in school decision-making becomes even more important when we're reminded that the majority of public-school teachers are white, middle class, able-bodied and monolingual women. When discussing early childhood programs, Derman-Sparks et al. (2015) state,

> Building an anti-bias ECCE program requires shifting the dominant-culture core of a program's thinking, organizational structures, and practice. It means intentionally moving to a many-cultures anti-bias approach. Shifting the culture of a program brings groups at the margin of early childhood theory and practice into the center of all that happens (para. 3).

School and district administrators also need to consider the dangers of including diversity only during assigned months of the year. Surface level multicultural education, such as curriculum inclusions of African Americans only in February, is highly problematic.

In, *Black History Month is Over: Now What?* Simmons (2016) states,

> Sadly, it *still* needs to be restated every year: Limiting sustained, in-depth engagement to Black History Month is problematic. It creates gaps in the curriculum and instruction, and ensures that students—especially Black students—will continue to receive harmful messages about the value of African Americans as a result of those gaps. Every day, not just the days in February, should be an opportunity for students to learn about Black history, experiences and people (para. 4).

Bell (2016) exposes how students as young as six or seven come to understand that contributions by people of color are only discussed or important during certain months of the year. Bell (2016) suggests, "Sure, use heritage months as opportunities to dive deep into the histories and experiences of the months' respective groups, but limiting coverage of diverse cultures and perspectives *only* to the month in question does students a huge disservice—and they know it" (para, 9).

School administrators set the stage and tone in creating an anti-bias, anti-racist equitable school climate. When families enter their child's school, their first encounter is often with members of the school office. A culturally responsive principal will recognize the importance of creating an inclusive and welcoming school office. This should include guiding office school personnel on the importance of the 4C's, which we discussed earlier.

This means that office personnel created an environment where students feel connected, capable, courageous, and cared for. An example of creating a "cared for" environment is welcoming late students with a smile and a comment of "I am so glad to see you today." It is important to remember that tardiness is an adult issue that should be left to adult discussions. Therefore, welcoming students, regardless of when they show up, should be guided by "cared for" and "connected."

Every experience from interacting with the school office administrative assistants to the symbolic curriculum—what and who is on the school walls—makes a critical first impression and sets the tone for inclusion, diversity, and equity.

School leaders can approach all of these suggestions by first developing committees, teams or task forces that include representatives from all aspects of the school community—teachers, paraprofessionals, custodians, family and community members, and so on. Having a school or district-wide justice, equity, diversity and inclusion task force to oversee the work of various committees is an important approach to ensuring anti-bias, anti-racist education.

Most importantly perhaps, and definitely a good starting place, is finding time to consistently reflect on and discuss individual bias. Derman-Sparks et al. (2015) stated,

> Anti-bias leaders provide the necessary time, space, resources, support, and facilitation for teachers and other staff to be part of the process of change. They build a community of learners that enables everyone to explore and grapple with anti-bias issues. A collaborative style of leadership, the preferred early childhood education model, empowers staff members to first begin and then take ownership of their anti-bias work. Anti-bias work grows best in an environment where collegial, mutually respectful relationships among staff and between staff and the program leader are the norm and where a culture exists that fosters open conversation and dialogue, reflection, and risk taking (para. 5).

Doing anti-bias work is critical for creating more equitable classroom experiences and minimizing microaggressions. Implicit bias affects every aspect of teaching and learning from pedagogy to grading of assignments to interacting with family members. Creating a safe space and allocating time for this work may be the most important role of the school administrator.

EDUCATOR AND STUDENT ENGAGEMENT: MAKING TIME FOR TALK

In, *The Anti-Racist Educator,* authors Benson and Fiarmen (2019) discuss the importance of "crucial interactions" in helping teachers to understand their own biases and how they are transmitted to students. The authors discuss how it is crucial that educators have time and space to observe and talk with each other about their teaching practices and expectations, and student engagement.

According to the Benson and Fiarmen (2019),

> These conversations are rare partly because educators, like most Americans, enter the workforce unaware of the influence of unconscious racial bias on their perceptions and actions. Many educators believe that racism is essentially a character trait and that people can be sorted into two distinct categories: you're either racist or you're not (p. 62).

Having time for crucial interactions and critical conversations allows educators the opportunity to build trusting relationships and support each other in growing as anti-racist educators. Benson and Fiarmen (2019) wrote, "Part of that growth, for all teachers, should be confronting the binary mindset and replacing it with a *developmental mindset*. A developmental mindset allows educators to talk to each other productively about possible racial biases, analyze the impact of these biases in a systematic way, and ultimately change their behaviors" (p. 63).

If administrators and educators make time to engage in peer observation and critical dialog, they can discover the impact their biases are having on student engagement, academic success and social-emotional well-being. Creating safe havens for students to recognize and discuss their experiences with educator/peer bias and microaggressions in the classroom is also an important step to creating equitable, anti-bias education.

In the second chapter of "Students, Teachers, and Leaders: Addressing Bullying in Schools" titled, *What are You?: The Hidden Curriculum and Microaggressions Associated With What It Means To Be Different*, Osanloo (2015) discusses her experiences as a student,

> Looking back on my K-12 educational experience, I recognize now the implicit lessons that were being taught to me regarding difference, otherness, and outsiderness. There was an "unwritten" set of rules that governed my socialization into the K-12 educational arena. Concurrently, I was being taught, albeit in an implicit manner, about hegemony, social reproduction, structural racism, and microaggressions (p. 24).

Osanloo (2015), went on to write,

> However, I innately felt the interplay of the hidden curriculum and microaggressions that were circumnavigating me. The two converged, like thunder and lightning, to create a fraught educational experience. I was always able to

sense that something was "not right." That in some way, I did not really fit or belong—that in fact, I was "not right" (p. 24).

Here, Osanloo helps us to see what is perhaps the most significant impact of implicit bias and microaggressions in schools. Schools can do better, we must.

As we close out this book, we encourage you to continue your learning journey. We also want to revisit two quotes we asked you to reflect on at the beginning of this book. Re-read these quotes and reflect on your learning progression throughout this book.

Reflect:

"Inclusion means the structure is made for everyone. Transformation is actually what we need to be doing. Don't focus on inclusion into a broken system but transform the broken system so that inclusion is inevitable."
"Silence is loud. Speak up. Act out. Be bold."

RESOURCES

Intercultural Development Inventory: https://idiinventory.com/
Project Implicit IAT: Take the Test: https://implicit.harvard.edu/implicit/
Project Implicit Resources: https://www.projectimplicit.net
Say Their Name Toolkit: https://myips.org/get-involved/racial-equity/say-their-names
  -toolkit/

Bibliography

9/11 Memorial & Museum. (2021). *Muslims in America After 9/11, Part II.* https://www.911memorial.org/learn/students-and-teachers/lesson-plans/muslims-america-after-911-part-ii.

ACLU. (2021). *School-to-prison pipeline.* https://www.aclu.org/issues/juvenile-justice/school-prison-pipeline.

Adams, M., Bell, L. A., & Griffin, P. (1997). *Teaching for diversity and social justice.* Routledge.

Ahmed, S. (2018). *Implicit bias training for classroom teachers of English language learner students.* Kirwin Institute for the Study of Race and Ethnicity. https://kirwaninstitute.osu.edu/article/implicit-bias-training-classroom-teachers-english-language-learner-students.

Allen, R. (2016, August 1). [Video]. *School suspensions are an adult behavior.* TEDxMileHigh. https://www.youtube.com/watch?v=f8nkcRMZKV4.

American College of Pediatricians. (2018). *Gender dysphoria in children.* American College of Pediatricians. https://acpeds.org/assets/imported/corrected-REVISED-NOV-2018-Gender-Dysphoria-in-Children-1.pdf.

American Psychological Association. (2015). Guidelines for psychological practice with transgender and gender nonconforming people. *American Psychological Association, 70*(9), 832–864.

Anton, M. (2020, December 14). *What is a micro-affirmation?* Educational Equity Resource Portal. https://edequityresources.com/what-is-a-micro-affirmation/.

Argyris, C. (1982). The executive mind and double-loop learning. *Organizational Dynamics. Autumn.*

Association of California School Administrators. (2021). "The arc of the moral university is bent toward justice": An interview with Gary Howard. https://content.acsa.org/articles/interview-with-gary-howard.

Austrew, A. (2021). *Is there a difference between 'calling in' and 'calling out'?* Dictionary.com.

Babad, E., Bernieri, F., & Rosenthal, R. (1989). When less information is more infor-
mative: Diagnosing teacher expectations from brief samples of behaviour. *Journal
of Educational Psychology, 59,* 281–295.

Baldridge, J. (2018, April 11). [Video] *Difficult conversation made easy.* TEDxTalks.
https://www.youtube.com/watch?v=4TkbHLD5Mnw.

Bandura, A. (1977). *Social learning theory.* Prentice-Hall.

Bandura, A. (1994). Self-efficacy. In V.S. Ramachaudran (Ed.), *Encyclopedia of
human behavior, 4,* 71–81. New York: Academic Press. (Reprinted in H. Friedman
[Ed.], *Encyclopedia of mental health.* Academic Press, 1998.

Baptiste, H.P., Ryan, A., & Duhon-Sells, R. (Eds.). (2015). *Multicultural education:
A renewed paradigm of transformation and call to action.* National Association of
Multicultural Education & Caddo Gap Press.

Baquedano-López, P., Alexander, R. A., & Hernandez, S. J. (2013). Equity issues in
parental and community involvement in schools: What teacher educators need to
know. *Review of Research in Education, 37*(1), 149–182.

Barnum, M. (2017, November 28). *As national debate over discipline heats up, new
study finds discrimination in student suspensions.* Chalkbeat. https://www.cha
lkbeat.org/2017/11/28/21103816/as-national-debate-over-discipline-heats-up-new
-study-finds-discrimination-in-student-suspensions.

Barr, R. D., & Gibson, E. L. (2013). *Building a culture of hope: Enriching schools
with optimism and opportunity.* Solution Tree.

Bassett, A. (2020, June 11). *Black lives matter vs. all lives matter: What we say
matters.* MSN News. https://www.msn.com/en-us/news/us/black-lives-matter-vs
-all-lives-matter-what-we-say-matters/ar-BB15l4L4.

Bell, M.K. (2016). *Out of the mouths of babes.* Learning For Justice. https://www.lea
rningforjustice.org/magazine/out-of-the-mouths-of-babes.

Bennett, R. E., Gottesman, R. L., Rock, D. A., & Cerullo, F. (1993). Influence of
behavior perceptions and gender on teachers' judgments of students' academic
skill. *Journal of Educational Psychology, 85*(2), 347–356.

Benson, T.A. & Fiarman, S.E. (2019). The Anti-Racist Educator. *ASCD: Educational
Leadership, 77*(1), 60–65.

Berg, N. (2013, November 18). *Busting ELL myths.* Learning for Justice.

Bettner, B.L. and Lew, A. (1990). *Raising kids who can.* Connexions Press.

Blackburn, S-S. (2019, March 21). *What is the model minority myth?* Learning for
Justice. https://www.learningforjustice.org/magazine/what-is-the-model-minority
-myth.

Blake, S. (2020, June 12). *Why the George Floyd protests feel different --
Lots and lots of mobile video.* Dot.la. https://dot.la/george-floyd-video-2646171
522.html.

Blankenship, M. & Reeves, R. V. (2020, July 10). *From the George Floyd moment to
the Black Lives Matter movement, in tweets.* Brookings.

Billings, E. & Walqui, A. (n.d.). *Dispelling the myth of "English only": Understanding
the importance of the first language in second language learning.* NYSED Office
of Bilingual Education and World Languages. http://www.nysed.gov/common/ny
sed/files/dispelling_myth_rev-2.pdf.

Bouley, T. (2007). That's so gay: Talking about sexual orientation and gender diversity in education. In I. Killoran (Ed.), *The silenced family: Policies and perspectives on the inclusion of children's literature depicting gay/lesbian families in public elementary classrooms* (pp. 140–147). The Association for Childhood Education International (ACEI).

Bouley, T. M. (2011). Speaking up: Opening dialogue with preservice and in-service teachers about the inclusion of LGBT families in early childhood classrooms. *Journal of Praxis in Multicultural Education*, 6(1), pp. 3–20.

Bouley T. M. (2018). Equity Pedagogy: Expanding our notions of gender and sexuality. In A. Esmail (Ed.), *Research studies on educating for diversity and social justice* (pp. 91–102). Rowman and Littlefield.

Bourdieu, P. (1986). The forms of capital. In J. Richardson (Ed.), *Handbook of theory and research for the sociology of education* (pp. 241–258). Westport: Greenwood.

Boyd-Barrett, C. (2020, February 5). *Black maternal mortality rate 2.5 times higher than white in bleak U.S. maternal mortality report.* Babycenter. https://www.bab ycenter.com/pregnancy/health-and-safety/black-maternal-mortality-rate_40006 914.

Brackett, M. (2019). *Permission to feel.* Quercus Publishing.

Brandon, R. (2007). African American parents: Improving connections with their child's educational environment. *Intervention in School and Clinic, 43*(2), 116–120.

Broady, A.S. (2019, December 2). *Schools face questions around gender; here are some definitions.* The Atlanta Journal-Constitution.

Brophy, J. & Good, T. (1970). Teachers' communication of differential expectations for children's classroom performance: Some behavioral data. *Journal of Educational Psychology, 61,* 365–374.

Brown, B. (2013, January 14). *Shame v. guilt.* Brene Brown. https://brenebrown.com /blog/2013/01/14/shame-v-guilt/#close-popup.

Byrne-Haber, S. (2019, October 17). *Disability microaggressions- AKA "ableist things people say".* The Medium. https://sheribyrnehaber.medium.com/disability -microaggressions-aka-ableist-things-people-say-89c3fffd11a1.

Castro, D., Bryant, D., Peisner-Feinberg, E., & Skinner, M. (2004). Parent involvement in Head Start programs: The role of parent, teacher, and classroom characteristics. *Early Childhood Research Quarterly, 19*(3), 413–430.

Challenging Christian Hegemony. (2009). *Practical tools for recognizing and resisting Christian dominance.* https://christianhegemony.org/what-is-christian -hegemony#:~:text=Christian%20hegemony%20as%20a%20system%20of%20d omination%20is,class%20and%20power%20elite.%20Christian%20hegemony %20benefits%20all.

Chemaly, S. (2015, February 12). *All teachers should be trained to overcome their hidden biases.* Time. https://time.com/3705454/teachers-biases-girls-education/.

Cherry, K. (2020, September 18). *How does implicit bias influence behavior?: Explanations and impacts of unconscious bias.* Very Well Mind. https://www.ver ywellmind.com/implicit-bias-overview-4178401.

Clarke, J.A. (2018). Explicit bias. *Northwestern University Law Review, 113*(3), 505–586. https://scholarlycommons.law.northwestern.edu/cgi/viewcontent.cgi?arti cle=1360&context=nulr.

Codeswitch. (2014, March 21). *Black preschoolers far more likely to be suspended.* NPR. https://www.npr.org/sections/codeswitch/2014/03/21/292456211/black-pre schoolers-far-more-likely-to-be-suspended.

Coggins, P., & Campbell, S. D. (2008). Using cultural competence to close the achievement gap. *The Journal of Pan African Studies, 2*(4), 44–59.

Cohen, D. & Passel, J.S. (2018). *A record 64 million Americans live in multigenera-tional households.* Pew Research Center. https://www.pewresearch.org/fact-tank /2018/04/05/a-record-64-million-americans-live-in-multigenerational-households/.

Coleman, A.L. (2019, March 29). *What's intersectionality? Let these scholars explain the theory and its history.* Time. https://time.com/5560575/intersectionality-theory/.

Cousins, L.H. & Mickelson, R.A. (2011). Making success in education: What Black parents believe about participation in their children's education. *Current Issues in Education, 14*(3).

Cristillo, L. (2008). *Religiosity, education and civic belonging: Muslim youth in New York City public schools.* Teachers College Columbia University.

Crossman, A. (2019, August 19). *What is hidden curriculum?* ThoughtCo. https://www .thoughtco.com/hidden-curriculum-3026346.

Crumm, D. (2020, June 6). *What now? Dr. Anni Reinking reminds us it's 'Not Just Black and White'.* Read the Spirit. https://readthespirit.com/explore/what-now-dr -anni-reinking-reminds-us-its-not-just-black-and-white/.

Cuncic, B. (2020, August 29). *What is cultural appropriation?* Very Well Mind. https ://www.verywellmind.com/what-is-cultural-appropriation-5070458.

Daha, M. (2016). *Recognizing and addressing microaggressions in teacher-family relationships.* Child Care Exchange.

Dastagir, A.E. (2017, October 23). *Is it OK for a white kid to dress up as Moana for Halloween? And other cultural appropriate questions.* USAToday. https://www .usatoday.com/story/news/2017/10/23/halloween-cultural-appropriation-quest ions/780479001/.

de Boer, H., Bosker, R.J., Van der Werf, M.P.C. (2010). Sustainability of teacher expectation bias effects on long-term student performance. *Research and Evaluation of Educational Effectiveness, 102*(1), 168–179.

de Boer, H., Timmermans, A.C., & van der Werf, M.P.C. (2018). The effects of teacher expectation interventions on teachers' expectations and student achieve-ment: Narrative review and meta-analysis. *Educational Research and Evaluation, 24*(3–5), 180–200.

De Houwer, J. (2019). Implicit bias is behavior: A functional-cognitive perspective on implicit bias. *Perspectives on Psychological Science, 14,* 835–840.

Delpit, L. (2013). *"Multiplication is for white people": Raising expectations for other people's children.* The New Press.

Derman-Sparks, L., LeeKeenan, D., & Nimmo, J. (2015). *Leading anti-bias early childhood programs: A guide for change (Early childhood education).* Teachers College Press.

DiAngelo, R. (2018). *White Fragility: Why It's so hard for white people to talk about racism.* Beacon Press.

DifferenceBetween.com. (2012, July 10). *Difference between values and morals.* https://www.differencebetween.com/difference-between-values-and-vs-morals/.

Dixon, T.L. (2017). *A dangerous distortion of our families: Representations of families, by race, in news and opinion media.* Color of Change. https://colorofchange.org/wp-content/uploads/2019/05/COC-FS-Families-Representation-Report_Full_121217.pdf.

Druery, D.M., Young, J.L. & Elbert, C. (2018). Macroaggressions and civil discourse. University of Illinois Press, *Spring 2018*, 73–78.

Eberhardt, J. L. (2019). Biased: Uncovering the hidden prejudice that shapes what we see, think, and do.

Education Commission of the States. (2018, January). *Suspension and expulsion.* https://www.ecs.org/wp-content/uploads/Suspension_and_Expulsion.pdf#:~:text=for%20students%20of%20color%20and%20students%20with%20disabilities%2C,as%20white%20students.2%20Similarly%2C%20students%20with%20disabilities%20are.

Ellis, K. & Kent, M. (10 November 2016). Confirming normalcy. 'Inspiration porn' and the construction of the disabled subject? *Disability and Social Media: Global Perspectives.* Taylor & Francis. ISBN 978-1-317-15028-2.

Farr, R.H., Crain, E.E., Oakley, M.K., Cashen, K.K., & Garber, K.J. (2016). Microaggressions, feelings of difference, and resilience among adopted children with sexual minority parents. *Journal of Youth Adolescence, 45*, 85–104.

Feistritzer, C. E., Griffin, S., & Linnajarvi, A. (2011). *Profile of teachers in the U.S. 2011.* National Center for Education Information.

Fergus, E. (2019, January 21). *Confronting our beliefs about poverty and discipline.* Phi Delta Kappan. https://kappanonline.org/confronting-beliefs-poverty-race-school-discipline-fergus/.

Fermoso, J. (2018, May 22). *Why speaking Spanish is becoming dangerous in America.* The Guardian. https://www.theguardian.com/us-news/2018/may/22/speaking-spanish-dangerous-america-aaron-schlossberg-ice.

FindLaw. (2017, September 29). *The Pledge of Allegiance and legal challenges in education.* https://www.findlaw.com/education/student-rights/the-pledge-of-allegiance-and-legal-challenges-in-education.html.

Finley, T. (2016, September 20). *Appears court rules employers can ban dreadlocks at work.* Huffpost. https://www.huffpost.com/entry/appeals-court-rules-dreadlocks-work_n_57e0252ae4b0071a6e08a7c3.

Flannery, M. E. (2015). *When implicit bias shapes teacher expectations.* NEA Today. http://neatoday.org/2015/09/09/when-implicitbias-shapes-teacher-expectations/.

Freedom Project Wa. (2019, April 12). [Video] Implicit bias: Peanut butter, jelly racism. https://www.youtube.com/watch?v=1JVN2qWSJF4.

Gannon, M. (2016, February 5). *Race is a social construct, scientists argue.* Scientific American. https://www.scientificamerican.com/article/race-is-a-social-construct-scientists-argue/.

García, F. & Weiss, E. (2018). *Student absenteeism: Who misses school and how missing school matters for performance.* Economic Policy Institute.

Gartrell, N., Bos, H. W., Peyser, H., Deck, A., & Rodas, C. (2012). Adolescents with lesbian mothers describe their own lives. *Journal of Homosexuality, 59*(9), 1211–1229. doi:10.1080/ 00918369.2012.720499.

Gay, G. (2002). Preparing for culturally responsive teaching. *Journal of Teacher Education 53*(2), 106–116.

Gay, G. (2010). *Culturally Responsive Teaching: Theory, Research, and Practice.* Teachers College Press, 31.

Gehrman, E. (2019, November 20). *Big impact of microaggressions.* The Harvard Gazette. https://news.harvard.edu/gazette/story/2019/11/microaggressions-and-th eir-role-in-mental-illness/.

Gender Equality Law Center. (2015). *Examples of gender stereotypes.* https://www .genderequalitylaw.org/examples-of-gender-stereotypes.

Generations United. (2021). *Family matters: Multigenerational living is on the rise and here to stay.* https://www.gu.org/app/uploads/2021/04/21-MG-Family-Report-WEB.pdf.

Georgetown Law Center on Poverty and Inequality. (2020). *Data snapshot: 2017-2018.* National Data on School Discipline by Race and Gender. https://genderj usticeandopportunity.georgetown.edu/wp-content/uploads/2020/12/National-Data -on-School-Discipline-by-Race-and-Gender.pdf.

Gershenson, S., & Dee, T. S. (2017, March 20). *The insidiousness of unconscious bias in schools.* Brown Center on Education Policy at Brookings.

Gershenon, S., Hart, C., Hyman, J., Lindsay, C., & Papageorge, N.W. (2021). *The long-run impacts of same-race teachers.* National Bureau of Economic Research.

Gibson, E.L. & Barr, R.D. (2017). Building a culture of hope: Exploring implicit biases against poverty. *National Youth-At-Risk Journal, 2*(2), 39–50.

Glock, S., Krolak-Schwerdt, S., Klapproth, F., & Bohmer, M. (2013). Beyond judgment bias: How students' ethnicity and academic profile consistency influence teachers' tracking judgments. *Social Psychology of Education: An International Journal, 16*(4), 555–573.

Gogoi, P. (2020). *Stuck-at-home moms: The pandemic's devastating toll on women.* NPR. https://www.npr.org/2020/10/28/928253674/stuck-at-home-moms-the-p andemics-devastating-toll-on-women.

Gok. S. (2020). *Cultural Bias. Northern New England TESOL.*

Goldberg, A. E. (2007a). (How) does it make a difference? Perspectives of adults with lesbian, gay, and bisexual parents. *American Journal of Orthopsychiatry, 77,* 550–562. doi:10.1037/0002-9432.77.4.550.

Goldberg, A. E. (2007b). Talking about family: Disclosure practices of adults raised by lesbian, gay, and bisexual parents. *Journal of Family Issues, 28,* 100–131. doi: 10.1177/0192513X06293606.

Goldberg, S. (2017). *We are in the midst of a gender revolution: Gender is making headlines around the world.* National Geographic. https://www.nationalgeographic .com/pdf/gender-revolution-guide.pdf.

Goleman, D. (1995). *Emotional intelligence: Why it can matter more than IQ.* New York: Bantam Books.

Goodman, J. (2014). *Flaking out: Student absences and snow days as disruptions of instructional time (No. w20221).* National Bureau of Economic Research.

Gorski, P.C. (2008). *The myth of the 'culture of poverty.'* Educational Leadership. Association for Supervision and Curriculum Development.

Gorski, P. C. (2008a). Peddling poverty for profit: Elements of oppression in Ruby Payne's framework. *Equity & Excellence in Education, 41*(1), 130–148.

Gorski, P. C. (2013). *Reaching and teaching students in poverty: Strategies for erasing the opportunity gap.* Teachers College Press.

Gorski, P.C. (2016a). Poverty and the ideological imperative: A call to unhook from deficit and grit ideology and to strive for structural ideology in teacher education. *Journal of Education for Teaching, 42*(4), 378–386.

Gorski, P. C. (2016b). Re-examining beliefs about students in poverty. *School Administrator, 73*(5), 16–20.

Gottfried, M.A. (2015), Chronic absenteeism in the classroom context: Effects of achievement. *Urban Education, 54*(1), 3–34.

Gottschalk, B. (2019). Holding high, not hurried, expectations for ELLs. *ASCD Education Update Newsletter, 61*(12).

Greene, D.W. (2017). Splitting hairs: the eleventh circuit's take on workplace bans against Black women's natural hair in EEPC v. Catastrophe Management Solutions. *University of Miami Law Review, 71*(4), 987–1036.

Greenberg, J. (2015, February 23). *7 reasons why 'colorblindness' contributes to racism instead of solves it.* Everyday Feminism. https://everydayfeminism.com/2015/02/colorblindness-adds-to-racism/.

Griffith, J. (2020, January 24). *Second black Texas teen told by school to cut dreadlocks, according to his mom.* NBC News. https://www.nbcnews.com/news/us-news/second-teen-suspended-over-dreadlocks-texas-school-n1122261.

Griffith, D. & Tyner, A. (2019). *Discipline reform through the eyes of teachers.* Thomas Fordham Institute Advancing Educational Excellence. https://fordhaminstitute.org/national/research/discipline-reform-through-the-eyes-of-teachers.

Haller, S. (2019, October 18). *A parents' guide to cultural appropriation: An expert breaks down kids' Halloween costumes.* USA Today. https://www.usatoday.com/story/life/parenting/2019/10/18/cultural-appropriation-kids-halloween-costumes-parents-guide/3990124002/.

Hammond, Z. (2015). *Culturally responsive teaching and the brain: Promoting authentic engagement and rigor among culturally and linguistically diverse students.* Corwin.

Harro, B. (2000). *The* cycle of socialization. In M. Adams, W. Blumenfeld, R. Castaneda, H. Hackman, M. Peters, X. Zuniga (Eds.), *Readings for diversity and social justice* (pp. 16–21). New York: Routledge.

Hembree, W.C., Cohen-Kettenis, P.T., Gooren, L., Hannema, S.E., Meyer, W.J., Murad, M.H., Rosenthal, S.M., Safer, J.D., Tangpricha, V., & T'Sjoen, G.G. (2017). Endocrine treatment of gender-dysphoric/gender-incongruent persons: An endocrine society clinical practice guideline. *Journal of Clinical Endocrinology and Metabolism, 102*(11), 3869–3903.

Howard, G. (2010). *7 Principles of Culturally Responsive Teaching*. Gary Howard Equity Institutes.

Human Rights Campaign. (2021a). *Glossary of terms*. https://www.hrc.org/resources/glossary-of-terms.

Human Rights Campaign. (2021b). *Transgender children & youth: Understanding the basics*. https://www.hrc.org/resources/transgender-children-and-youth-understanding-the-basics.

IDEA Data Center. (2021). *Types of disciplinary removals: States and LEAs must report five types of disciplinary removals for children and youth with disabilities*. https://ideadata.org/discipline/.

IDI, LLC (Intercultural Development Inventory). (2021). *The Roadmap to Intercultural Competence Using the IDI*. https://idiinventory.com/.

Igusti, D. (2017, February 22). *Stop saying these microaggressions against Muslim woman*. https://muslimgirl.com/importance-addressing-common-stereotypes-muslim-women/.

Inclusive School Communities. (2021). *Disability microaggressions in education*. https://inclusiveschoolcommunities.org.au/resources/toolkit/disability-microaggressions-education.

Internet Encyclopedia of Philosophy. (n.d.). *Pejorative language*. https://iep.utm.edu/page/5/?cat=-1.

Janicka, A. & Forcier, M. (2016). Transgender and gender nonconforming youth: Psychosocial and medical considerations. *Adolescent Health: Rhode Island Medical Journal*.

Jensen, E. (2009). *Teaching with poverty in mind*. ASCD.

Jervis, R. (2006). Understanding beliefs. *Political Psychology, 27*(5), 641–663.

Johnson, V. (2001). Connecting families and schools through mediating structures. In Sam Redding and Lori Thomas (Eds.), *The Community of the School* (pp. 311–318). Academic Development Institute.

Jones, B. (2020). *Reducing racism in schools: The promise of anti-racist policies*. University of Connecticut: Center for Education Policy Analysis.

Jones, E. & Nisbett, R. (1971). *The actor and the observer: Divergent perceptions of the causes of behavior*. General Learning Press.

Jussim, L (2016). *Self-fulfilling prophecy*. Psychology & Mental Health. Encyclopedia Britannica. https://www.britannica.com/topic/self-fulfilling-prophecy.

Jung, J., Ressler, J., & Linder, A. (2018). Exploring the hidden curriculum in physical education. *Advances in Physical Education, 8(2)*.

Kaiser, B. & Rasminksy, J.S. (2019). Valuing diversity: Developing a deeper understanding of all young children's behavior. *Teaching Young Children, 13*(2).

Kaplin, D. (2017). Microaggressions and macroaggresions in religiously diverse communities. *NYS Psychologist: Special Issue of the NYSPA Notebook. XXIX*(3).

Kattari, S.K. (2017). *Development of the ableist microaggression scale and assessing the relationship of ableist microaggressions with the mental health of disabled adults*. [Dissertation]. https://digitalcommons.du.edu/cgi/viewcontent.cgi?article=2283&context=etd.

Kendi, I.X. (2019). *How to be an antiracist*. One World.

Kenney, G. (2014). Interrupting microaggressions, college of the holy cross, diversity leadership & education. Accessed on-line, October 2014. Kraybill, R. (2008). "Cooperation skills," in M. Armster and L. Amstutz (Eds.), *Conflict transformation and restorative justice manual*, 5th Edition (pp. 116–117). LeBaron, M. (2008). "The open question," in M. Armster and L. Amstutz (Eds.), *Conflict transformation and restorative justice manual*, 5th Edition, pp. 123–124. Peavey, F. (2003). "Strategic questions as a tool for rebellion," in M. Brady (Ed.), *The Wisdom of Listening* (pp. 168–189). Boston: Wisdom Publ..

Killerman, S. (2015, March 27). *The Genderbread Person v3.3.* https://www.gen derbread.org/wp-content/uploads/2017/02/Breaking-through-the-Binary-by-Sam-Killermann.pdf.

Kim, L. (2021). A review of the literature on teachers' beliefs about English language learners. *International Journal of Educational Research Open, 2*(2).

Kosciw, J. G., Greytak, E. A., Zongrone, A. D., Clark, C. M., & Truong, N. L. (2018). *The 2017 National School Climate Survey: The experiences of lesbian, gay, bisexual, transgender, and queer youth in our nation's schools.* GLSEN. https ://www.glsen.org/sites/default/files/2019-10/GLSEN-2017-National-School-Cli mate-Survey-NSCS-Full-Report.pdf.

Kramer, S. (2019). *U.S. has world's highest rate of children living in single-parent households.* Pre Research Center. https://www.pewresearch.org/fact-tank/2019 /12/12/u-s-children-more-likely-than-children-in-other-countries-to-live-with-just-one-parent/.

Krogstad, J.M. (2019). *A view of the nation's future through kindergarten demographics.* Pew Research Center. https://www.pewresearch.org/fact-tank/2019/07 /31/kindergarten-demographics-in-us/.

Kyung Hee, K., & Zabelina, D. (2015). Cultural bias in assessment: Can creativity assessment help? *International Journal of Critical Pedagogy, 6*(2), 129–148.

Lakhani, N. (2020). *Black babies more likely to survive when cared for by black doctors - US study.* Guardian News & Media. https://www.theguardian.com/world/2 020/aug/17/black-babies-survival-black-doctors-study.

Lawson, M. (2003). School-family relations in context: Parent and teacher perceptions of parent involvement. *Urban Education, 38*(1), 77–133.

Lee, J., & Zhou, M. (2015). *The Asian American achievement paradox.* Russell Sage Foundation.

Leibowitz, S. & de Vries, A.L.C. (2016). Gender dysphoria in adolescence. *International Review Psychiatry, 28*(1), 21–35.

Lewis, A. E., & Diamond, J. B. (2015). Despite the best intentions: How racial inequality thrives in good schools. New York: Oxford University Press.

Lexico. (2021). *Diversity.* https://www.lexico.com/en/definition/diversity.

Lilienfeld, S.O. (2017). Microaggressions: Strong claims, inadequate evidence. *Perspectives on Psychological Science, 12*(1), 138–169.

Lippert, L.B. (2017). How mainstream teacher attitudes affect English language learner student learning in the mainstream classroom. *School of Education Student Capstone Projects,* 119.

Livingston, G. & Brown, A. (2017). *Intermarriage in the U.S. 50 years after Loving v. Virginia.* Pew Research Center: Social & Demographic Trends. https://www .pewresearch.org/social-trends/2017/05/18/intermarriage-in-the-u-s-50-years-after -loving-v-virginia/.

Lloyd, C. (2020, July 15). *Black adults disproportionately experience microaggressions.* Gallup News. https://news.gallup.com/poll/315695/black-adults-disproporti onately-experience-microaggressions.aspx.

López, N. (2003). *Hopeful girls, troubled boys: Race and gender disparity in urban education.* Psychology Press.

Los Angeles County Office of Education. (2011). https://www.lacoe.edu/Accounta bility/State-Federal-Programs/SFP-Publications.

Lu, W. (2016, September 26). *13 microaggressions people with disabilities face.* Bustle. https://www.bustle.com/articles/186060-13-microaggressions-people-with -disabilities-face-on-a-daily-basis.

Lynch, M. (2019). *33 microaggressions that educators commit daily.* The Advocate. https://www.theedadvocate.org/45-microaggressions-that-educators-commit -daily/.

Mapp, K. (2003). Having their say: Parents describe why and how they are engaged in their children's learning. *The School Community Journal, 13*(1), 35–64.

Marshall, M. (2018, January 31). *21 microaggressions to steer clear of.* Raising Self Awareness. https://raisingselfawareness.com/microaggressions-steer-clear-of/.

McKay, M., Atkins, M., Hawkins, T., Brown, C., & Lynn, C. (2003). Inner-city African American parental involvement in children's schooling: Racial socialization and social support from the parent community. *American Journal of Community Psychology, 32*(1/2), 107–114.

Michael-Luna, S. (2015, November). *What parents have to teach us about their dual language children.* NAEYC. https://www.naeyc.org/resources/pubs/yc/nov2015/ what-parents-have-teach-us-about-their-dual-language-children.

Migdol, E. (2019, October 24). *4 types of microaggressions people with disabilities are tired of hearing.* The Mighty. https://themighty.com/2019/10/disability-micr oaggressions-how-to-respond/.

Miller, C.C. (2018). Does teacher diversity matter in student learning? *NY Times.*

Mogilevsky, M. (2016, June 4). *5 microaggressions secular people often hear - And why they're wrong.* Everyday Feminism. https://everydayfeminism.com/2016/06/ microaggressions-against-secular-people/.

Momene, R. (2015, December 18). *Negative stereotypes and attitudes linked to disability.* Atlas Corps. https://atlascorps.org/negative-stereotypes-and-attitudes-li nked-to-disability/.

Moody, A. T. & Lewis, A. J. (2019). Gendered racial microaggressions and traumatic stress symptoms among black women. *Psychology of Women Quarterly, 43(2),* 201–214.

Morin, A. (2020, July 14). *Pros and cons of zero tolerance policies in schools.* Very Well Family. https://www.verywellfamily.com/the-pros-and-cons-of-zero-toleranc e-policies-1094916.

Morning Edition. (2021, March 24). *New data highlight disparities in students learning in person.* NPR: Education. https://www.npr.org/2021/03/24/980592512/new-data-highlight-disparities-in-students-learning-in-person.

Mukuria, G. (2002). Disciplinary challenges: How do principals address this dilemma? *Urban Education, 37,* 432–452. doi:10.1177/00485902037003007.

Nadal, K.L. (2014). A guide to responding to microaggressions. *CUNY Forum, 2*(1), 71–76. https://advancingjustice-la.org/sites/default/files/ELAMICRO%20A_Guide_to_Responding_to_Microaggressions.pdf.

Nadal, K.L. (2018). *Microaggressions and traumatic stress: Theory, research, and clinical treatment.* American Psychological Association. https://www.apa.org/pubs/books/Microaggressions-and-Traumatic-Stress-Series-Forward-and-Intro-Sample.pdf.

Nadal, K.L., Griffin, K.E., Hamit, S., Leon, J., & Tobio, M. (2012). Subtle and overt forms of Islamophobia: Microaggressions toward Muslim Americans. *Journal of Muslim Mental Health, VI*(2).

Nadal, K.L., Griffin, K.E., Wong, Y., Hamit, S., Rasmus, M. (2014). The impact of racial microaggressions on mental health: Counseling implications for clients of color. *Journal of Counseling & Development, 92*(1), 57–66.

National Alliance to End Homelessness. (2018). *Family homelessness in the United States: a State-by-State snapshot.* Data and Graphics. https://endhomelessness.org/resource/family-homelessness-in-the-united-states-state-by-state-snapshot/.

National Center for Cultural Competence at Georgetown University. (n.d.a) *It's how we are wired.* https://nccc.georgetown.edu/bias/module-3/3.php.

National Center for Cultural Competence at Georgetown University. (n.d.b). *Two types of bias.* https://nccc.georgetown.edu/bias/module-3/1.php.

National Center for Education Statistics. (2020, May). *Characteristics of public school teachers.* https://nces.ed.gov/programs/coe/indicator_clr.asp.

National Center for Education Statistics. (2020a, May). *English Language Learners in public schools.* https://nces.ed.gov/programs/coe/indicator_cgf.asp.

National Conference for Community and Justice. (2021). *Colorism.* https://www.nccj.org/colorism-0.

National Council of Teachers of English. (2016, May 31). *CCC Statement on Ebonics.* [Position Statement]. https://ncte.org/statement/ebonics/.

National Council of Teachers of English. (2017). *Antiracist ELA Educators' Actions.* [Infographic].

National Council of Teachers of English. (2020). *NCTE position paper on the role of English teachers in educating English language learners (ELLs).* https://ncte.org/statement/teaching-english-ells/.

National School Boards Association. (2019, August 1). *Special Ed discipline disparities: The numbers reveal the need for positive practices.* https://nsba.org/ASBJ/2019/August/Special-Education-Disparities.

Nittle, N.K. (2020, December 14). *Persistent racial stereotypes in TV shows and movies.* ThoughtCo. https://www.thoughtco.com/common-racial-stereotypes-in-movies-television-2834718.

Nittle, N.K. (2021, February 28). *The roots of colorism, or skin tone discrimination: This bias was boarn in the practice of human enslavement.* ThoughtCo. https://ww w.thoughtco.com/what-is-colorism-2834952.

Noguera, P. A. (2001). Transforming urban schools through investment in the social capital of parents. In S. Saegert, J. P. Thompson, & M. R. Warren (Eds.), *Social capital and poor communities* (pp. 189–212). Russell Sage.

Nosowitz, D. (2016, August 23). *Is there a place in America where people speak without accents?: Newscasters and Stephen Colbert seem to think so.* Atlas Obscura.

Ochieng, A. (2017, March 29). *Muslim schoolchildren bullied by fellow students and teachers.* NPR: Codeswitch. https://www.npr.org/sections/codeswitch/ 2017/03/29/515451746/muslim-schoolchildren-bullied-by-fellow-students-and -teachers.

Ochoa, G. L. (2013). *Academic profiling: Latinos, Asian Americans, and the achievement gap.* University of Minnesota Press.

Open Education Sociology Dictionary. (2021). *Gender Role.* https://sociologydic tionary.org/gender-role/.

Osanloo, A. (2015). *The hidden curriculum and microaggressions associated with what it means to be "different"* In editor book Students, Teachers, and Leaders Addressing Bullying in Schools. Eds. Christa Boske and Azadah Osanloo (pp. 23–32).

Overland, M.K., Zumsteg, J.M., Lindo, E.G., Sholas, M.G., Montenegro, R.E., Campelia, G.D., & Mukherjee, D. (2019). Microaggressions in clinical training and practice. *PM&R, 11*(9), 1004–1012.

Oxford University Press. (2021). *Cultural capital.* https://www.oxfordreference.com /view/10.1093/oi/authority.20110803095652799.

Papillon, K. (n.d.). *Two types of bias.* National Center for Cultural Competence at Georgetown University. https://nccc.georgetown.edu/bias/module-3/1.php.

Patient Worthy. (2017, February 17). *Changing the use of "special needs".* Pfeiffer Syndrome. https://patientworthy.com/2017/02/17/changing-use-special-needs/.

Perina, K. (2019, September 29). *Understanding name-based microaggression.* Psychology Today. https://www.psychologytoday.com/us/blog/underdog-psycho logy/201909/understanding-name-based-microaggressions.

Perry, D. G., Pauletti, R. E., & Cooper, P. J. (2019). Gender identity in childhood: A review of the literature. *International Journal of Behavioral Development, 43*(4), 289–304.

Petrilli, M.J. (2017, December 8). *How to think about discipline disparities.* Thomas B. Fordham Institute Advancing Educational Excellence. https://fordhaminstitute. org/national/commentary/how-think-about-discipline-disparities.

Pew Research Center. (2012). *The rise of intermarriage, Chapter 1: Overview.* https ://www.pewresearch.org/social-trends/2012/02/16/chapter-1-overview/.

Pew Research Center. (2015). *Parenting in America: The American family today.* http://www.pewsocialtrends.org/2015/12/17/1-the-american-family-today/.

Pew Research Center. (2021). *Religion & public life: Religious landscape study.* https ://www.pewforum.org/religious-landscape-study/.

Pew Research Center. (2019, May 14). *Majority of public favors same-sex marriage, but divisions persist. U.S. politics & policy.* https://www.pewresearch.org/politic s/2019/05/14/majority-of-public-favors-same-sex-marriage-but-divisions-persist/.

Pfizer. (2020, August 26). *Understanding racial microaggressions and its effect on mental health.* https://www.pfizer.com/news/hot-topics/understanding_racial_ microaggression_and_its_effect_on_mental_health#:~:text=How%20racial%20mi croaggressions%20impact%20mental,disease%20and%20type%202%20diabetes.

Pitlick, N.E. (2015). Alternatives to zero tolerance policies affecting students of color: A systematic review. *Clinical research paper.* https://ir.stthomas.edu/ ssw_mstrp/500/#:~:text=Zero%20tolerance%20policies%20in%20schools%20ha ve%20had%20many,funneled%20from%20schools%20into%20the%20criminal %20justice%20system.

Pitts, J. (2020, September 11). *What anti-racism really means for educators.* Learning for Justice. https://www.learningforjustice.org/magazine/what-antiracism-really -means-for-educators#:~:text=Anti%2Dracist%20educators%20believe%20in%2 0the%20intellectual%20power%20of%20teaching,to%20oppress%20or%20to %20liberate.

Population Reference Bureau. (2021). *American attitudes about poverty and the poor.* https://www.prb.org/americanattitudesaboutpovertyandthepoor/.

Portman, J., Bui, T.T., Ogaz, J., & Trevino, J. (n.d.) *Microaggressions in the classroom.* University of Denver: Center for Multicultural Excellence. http://otl.du.edu/ wp-content/uploads/2013/03/MicroAggressionsInClassroom-DUCME.pdf.

Posey, L. (2017). Race in place: Black parents, family-school relations, and multispatial microaggressions in a predominantly white suburb. *Teachers College Record, 119*(12).

Pride Legal. (2021, January 12). *Gay divorce and straight divorce: The difference.* Pride Legal Law at Your Command. https://pridelegal.com/gay-divorce-versus-str aight-divorce/.

Project Implicit. (2011). *Implicit Harvard.* https://implicit.harvard.edu/implicit/takeat est.html.

PsychologyToday. (2021). *Bias.* https://www.psychologytoday.com/us/basics/bias.

Public Broadcasting Station. (2005). *Spanish in the U.S.: Correcting myths.* https:// www.pbs.org/speak/seatosea/americanvarieties/spanglish/usa/.

Rea, S. (2015, June 8). *Researchers find everyone has a bias blind spot.* Carnegie Mellon University. https://www.cmu.edu/news/stories/archives/2015/june/bias-bl ind-spot.html.

Reach Out & Read Minnesota. (2020). When it comes to children's books, representation matters in a big way. https://reachoutandreadmn.org/news-events/blog/div erse-childrens-books.html.

Ready, D.D. (2010). Socioeconomic disadvantage, school attendance, and early cognitive development: The differential effects of school exposure. *Sociology of Education, 83*(4), 271–286.

Ready, D.D. & Wright, D.L. (2011). Accuracy and inaccuracy in teachers' perceptions of young children's cognitive abilities: The role of child background and classroom context. *American Educational Research Journal, 48*(2), 335–360.

Reichert, M., Hawley, R., & Tyre, P. (2010). *Reaching boys teaching boys: Strategies that work -- and why*. Jossey-Bass.

Reinking, A.K. & Bouley, T.M. (2021). *The economic and opportunity gap: How poverty impacts the lives of students*. Rowman & Littlefield.

Romero, M., & Lee, Y. S. (2007). *A national portrait of chronic absenteeism in the early grades*. Columbia Academic Commons. https://academiccommons.columbia .edu/doi/10.7916/D89C7650.

Rosenthal, R. & Babad, E.Y. (1985). Pygmalion in the gymnasium. *Educational Leadership, 43*(1), 36–39.

Rosenthal, R, & Jacobsen, L. (1968). *Pygmalion in the classroom: Teacher expectation and pupils' intellectual development*. Holt, Rinehart and Winston.

Rowe, C. (2015, June 23). *Race dramatically skews discipline, even in elementary school*. Seattle Times. https://www.seattletimes.com/education-lab/race-dramatically-skews-discipline-even-in-elementary-school/.

Rubie-Davies, C.M. (2007). Classroom interactions: Exploring the practices of high- and low-expectation teachers. *British Journal of Educational Psychology, 77*(2), 289–306.

Rudat, A. (2020, November 9). *Debunking three myths about English learners*. UnboundEd. https://blog.unbounded.org/debunking-three-myths-about-english-learners/.

Ruiz, R. (1984). Orientations in language planning. *The Journal for the National Association of Bilingual Education, 8*(2), 15–34.

Samson, J.F. & Collins, B.A. (2012). *Preparing all teachers to meet the needs of English language learners*. Center for American Progress.

Scafidi, S. (2005). *Who owns culture?: Appropriation and authenticity in American law*. Rutgers University Press.

Schafft, K.A. (2009). Poverty, residential mobility, and student transiency within a rural New York school district. *Rural Sociology, 71*(2), 212–231.

Schrader, J. (2011, December 27). Colorblind ideology is a form of racism. *Psychology Today*. https://www.psychologytoday.com/us/blog/culturally-speaking/201112/col orblind-ideology-is-form-racism.

Schumer, L. (2020, June 29). *What white privilege really means - and how to work on it*. Good Housekeeping. https://www.goodhousekeeping.com/life/a32948548/ what-is-white-privilege/.

Schunk, D.H. (2003). Self-efficacy for reading and writing: Influence of modeling, goal setting, and self-evaluation. *Reading and Writing Quarterly, 19*, 159–172.

Senge, P. M. (2006). *The fifth discipline: The art of practice of the learning organization*. Doubleday.

Sherouse, B. (Ed.) (2015). Schools in transition: A guide for supporting transgender students in K-12 schools. *Human Rights Campaign*. https://assets2.hrc.org/files/ assets/resources/Schools-In-Transition.pdf?_ga=2.125822922.1960350513.15791 97337-2043928797.1578168412.

Shim, J.M. (2017). Self-identified linguistic microaggressions among monolingual pre-service teachers: Why they matter for English language learners. *Multicultural Learning and Teaching 12*(2).

Simmons, D. (2016). Black history month is over. Now what? Learning for Justice. https://www.learningforjustice.org/magazine/black-history-month-is-over-now -what.

Simmons, D. (2019). Why we can't afford whitewashed social-emotional learning. *ASCD Education Update, 61*(4).

Simmons University. (2021). *Anti-Oppression: Anti-Islamomisia.* https://simmons .libguides.com/anti-oppression/anti-islamomisia#Islamophobia.

Skiba, R. J., Chung, C. G., Trachok, M., Baker, T. L., Sheya, A., & Hughes, R. L. (2014). Parsing disciplinary disproportionality: Contributions of infraction, student, and school characteristics to out-of-school suspension and expulsion. *American Educational Research Journal, 51*, 640–670. doi:10.3102/0002831214541670.

Skiba, R. J., Edl, H., & Rausch, M. K. (2007, April). *The disciplinary practices survey: Principal attitudes towards suspension and expulsion.* Paper presented at the annual meeting of the American Educational Research Association.

Sleeter, C. E. 2004. Context-conscious portraits and context-blind policy. *Anthropology & Education Quarterly, 35*(1), 132–136.

Smith, A. (2020, June 11). *What to know about microaggressions.* Medical News Today. https://www.medicalnewstoday.com/articles/microagressions.

Smith, K. (2019, August 12). *There's nothing 'micro' about the impact of microaggressions.* Philadelphia College of Osteopathic Medicine. https://www.pcom.edu /about/departments/marketing-and-communications/digest-magazine/digest-feat ured-stories/theres-nothing-micro-about-the-impact-of-microaggressions.html.

Solomon, A. (2019, September 2). The dignity of disabled lives. *The New York Times.* https://www.nytimes.com/2019/09/02/opinion/disabled-human-rights.html.

Spanish Tutor DC. (2021). *Why English isn't the official language of the U.S. Federal Government.* https://www.spanishtutordc.com/news/why-english-isnt-the-official -language-of-the-u-s-federal-government/.

Stanford Encyclopedia of Philosophy. (2016, May 23). *Disability: Definitions, models, experience.* https://plato.stanford.edu/entries/disability/.

Staats, C. & Capatosto, K. (2017). *State of the science: Implicit bias review.* W.K. Kellogg Foundation. http://kirwaninstitute.osu.edu/wp-content/uploads/2017/11 /2017-SOTS-final-draft-02.pdf.

Stapleton, L. (2016). Audism and racism: The hidden curriculum impacting Black d/ Deaf college students in the classroom. *The Negro Education Review, 67,* 149–168.

Statista Research Department. (2021). *Number of married couples in the U.S. 1960-2020.* https://www.statista.com/statistics/183663/number-of-married-couples-in -the-us/.

Steele, C. M. (1997). A threat in the air: How stereotypes shape intellectual identity and performance. *American Psychologist, 52*(6), 613–629. https://doi.org/10.1037 /0003-066X.52.6.613.

Steele, C. M. (2011). *Whistling Vivaldi: How stereotypes affect us and what we can do (Issues of our time).* W.W. Norton & Company.

Steele, C. M. & Aronson, J. (1995). Stereotype threat and the intellectual test performance of African American. *Journal of Personality and Social Psychology, 69,* 797–811.

Stokes, B. (2017). *What it takes to truly be 'one of us'.* Pew Research Center: Global Attitudes & Trends. https://www.pewresearch.org/global/2017/02/01/what-it-t akes-to-truly-be-one-of-us/.

Sue, D.W. (2010, October 5). Racial microaggressions in everyday life. *Psychology Today.* https://www.psychologytoday.com/us/blog/microaggressions-in-everyday -life/201010/racial-microaggressions-in-everyday-life.

Sue, D.W., Capodilupo, C.M., Torino, G.C., Bucceri, J.M., Holder, A.M.B., Nadal, K.L., & Esquilin, M. (2007). *Racial microaggressions in everyday life: Implications for clinical practice.* Teachers College, Columbia University. https ://www.cpedv.org/sites/main/files/file-attachments/how_to_be_an_effective_ally-l essons_learned_microaggressions.pdf.

Sy, S. & Nagy, L. (2021, March 16). *Asian American community battles surge in hate crimes stirred from COVID-19.* PBS NewsHour. https://www.pbs.org/newsh our/show/asian-american-community-battles-surge-in-hate-crimes-stirred-from -covid-19.

Szewczyk-Sokolowski, M., Bost, K.K., & Wainwright, A.B. (2005). Attachment, temperament, and preschool children's peer acceptance. *Social Development,* *14*(3), 379–397.

Tam, R. & Diaz-Ochu, (2020, August 19). *Commit to confronting the microaggres-sions that are affecting your learners.* University of Utah Health. https://accelerate .uofuhealth.utah.edu/explore/commit-to-confronting-the-microaggressions-that-are-affecting-your-learners.

Teaching Tolerance. (2018). *Social justice standards: The teaching tolerance anti-bias framework.* Learning for Justice. https://www.learningforjustice.org/sites/defa ult/files/2020-09/TT-Social-Justice-Standards-Anti-bias-framework-2020.pdf.

The Annie E. Casey Foundation. (2017, July 26). *New study: The 'Adultification' of Black girls.* https://www.aecf.org/blog/new-study-the-adultification-of-black -girls/#:~:text=Adultification%20is%20a%20form%20of%20dehumanization%2C %20robbing%20black,decision%20making%20%E2%80%94%20a%20key%20c haracteristic%20of%20childhood.

The Glossary of Education Reform. (2013, August 29). *Stereotype threat.* https://www .edglossary.org/stereotype-threat/.

The Glossary of Education Reform. (2015, July 13). *Hidden curriculum.* https://www .edglossary.org/hidden-curriculum/.

The Graide Network. (2018, August 27). *Teacher bias: The elephant in the class-room.* https://www.thegraidenetwork.com/blog-all/2018/8/1/teacher-bias-the-el ephant-in-the-classroom.

The Kirwan Institute. (2012). *Understanding implicit bias.* Kirwan Institute for the Study of Race and Ethnicity. https://kirwaninstitute.osu.edu/article/understanding -implicit-bias.

The National Association for Multicultural Education. (2021). *Definitions of multi-cultural education.* https://www.nameorg.org/definitions_of_multicultural_e.php.

The Washington Post. (2021, April 17). *982 people have been shot and killed by police in the past year.* https://www.washingtonpost.com/graphics/investigations/ police-shootings-database/.

Timmermans, A.D., Kuyper, H., van der Werf, G. (2015). Accurate, inaccurate, or biased teacher expectations: Do Dutch teachers differ in their expectations at the end of primary education? *British Journal of Educational Psychology, 85*(4), 459–478.

Timpf, K. (2018, March 14). *'God Bless You' listed among anti-muslim 'microaggressions'*. National Review. https://www.nationalreview.com/2018/03/god-bless-you-microaggression-against-muslims/.

Todres, J. (2018). The Trump effect, children, and the value of human rights education. *Family Court Review, 56,* 331–343.

Torres-Mackie, N. (2019, September 29). *Understanding name-based microaggressions*. Psychology Today. https://www.psychologytoday.com/us/blog/underdog-psychology/201909/understanding-name-based-microaggressions.

Troop-Gordon, W. (2015). The role of the classroom teacher in the lives of children victimized by peers. *Child Development Perspectives, 9*(1), 55–60. doi:10.1111/cdep.12106.

Turner, C. (2016, September 28). *Bias isn't just a police problem, It's a preschool problem*. Illinois Public Media: NPR, PBS. https://will.illinois.edu/news/story/bias-isnt-just-a-police-problem-its-a-preschool-problem.

Tyner, A.R. (2019, August 26). *Unconscious bias, implicit bias, and microaggressions: What can we do about them?* American Bar Association. https://www.americanbar.org/groups/gpsolo/publications/gp_solo/2019/july-august/unconscious-bias-implicit-bias-microaggressions-what-can-we-do-about-them/.

U.S. Bureau of Labor Statistics. (2021). *Economic news release*. https://www.bls.gov/news.release/empsit.t01.htm.

U.S. Department of Education. Office of Civil Rights (2016, June 7). *2013-2014 Civil Rights data collection: A first look*. https://www2.ed.gov/about/offices/list/ocr/docs/2013-14-first-look.pdf.

U.S. Department of Health and Human Services Office of Minority Health. (2019). *Mental and behavioral health - Asian Americans*. https://www.minorityhealth.hhs.gov/omh/browse.aspx?lvl=4&lvlid=54.

U.S. Department of Education. (2016). Chronic Absenteeism in the nation's schools: An unprecedented look at a hidden educational crisis (online fact sheet). https://www2.ed.gov/datastory/chronicabsenteeism.html.

Umansky, I. & Dumont, H. (2019). *English learning labeling: How English learner status shapes teacher perceptions of student skills & the moderating role of bilingual instructional settings*. EdWorkingPaper No. 19-94. Annenberg Brown University.

Umansky, I. & Dumont, H. (2019a). *Do teachers have biased academic perceptions of their English learner students?* Brookings: Brown Center Chalkboard.

United States Census Bureau. (2014). *10 percent of grandparents live with grandchild, Census Bureau reports*. https://www.census.gov/newsroom/press-releases/2014/cb14-194.html.

University of Michigan. (n.d.). LSA Inclusive Teaching Initiative. https://sites.lsa.umich.edu/inclusive-teaching/wp-content/uploads/sites/355/2018/12/Social-Identity-Wheel-3-2.pdf#:~:text=The%20Social%20Identity%20Wheel%20can%20be

%20used%20in,or%20reflective%20writing%20on%20identity%20by%20using %20the.

University of Michigan. (2018, July 17). *Black children subjected to higher discipline rates than peers.* Phys.org. https://phys.org/news/2018-07-black-children-subje cted-higher-discipline.html.

Vassell, N. (2020, June 17). *'Like death by a thousand cuts': How microaggressions play a traumatic part in everyday racism.* Independent. https://www.independent.c o.uk/life-style/microaggression-meaning-definition-racism-black-lives-matter-geo rge-floyd-a9568506.html.

Warkentin, S. (2019, March 22). *Both parents and kids want more diverse books, new reading report finds.* Tinybeans Red Tricycle. https://redtri.com/scholastic-kids-family-reading-report-more-diverse-books/.

Ware, L. (2016, December 14). *'Blue lives' don't matter because blue lives don't exist.* Huffpost. https://www.huffpost.com/entry/blue-lives-dont-matter-because -blue-lives-dont_b_5849b659e4b0afda6e983f20.

Washington, E.F., Birch, A.H., Roberts, L.M. (2020, July 3). *When and how to respond to microaggressions.* Harvard Business Review. https://hbr.org/2020/07/ when-and-how-to-respond-to-microaggressions.

Waters, K.J. (2017). Children's books featuring diverse family structures and liv-ing arrangements: Recommendations for elementary teachers. *Interdisciplinary Journal of Undergraduate Research, 6*(21), 126–134.

Welsh, M. G. (2011). Growing up in a same-sex parented family: The adolescent voice of experience. *Journal of GLBT Family Studies, 7*(1–2), 49–71. doi:10.1080 /1550428X.2010.537241.

Welsh, R.O. & Little, S. (2018). The school discipline dilemma: A comprehensive review of disparities and alternative approaches. *Review of Educational Research, 88*(5), 752–794.

White, M.C. (2014, November 17). *One in 30 American children is homeless, Report says.* NBC News. https://www.nbcnews.com/business/economy/one-30-american -children-homeless-report-says-n250136.

Williams, M.T. (2011, December 27). *Colorblind ideology is a form of racism.* Psychology Today. https://www.psychologytoday.com/us/blog/culturally-spea king/201112/colorblind-ideology-is-form-racism.

Woolley, Susan W. (2019). "When you don't believe something is real, you can't actually advocate for or support it": Trans* inclusion in K-12 schools. *Intersections: Critical Issues in Education, 3*, 25–43. https://digitalrepository.unm. edu/intersections/vol3/iss1/5.

Yull, D., Wilson, M., Murray, C., & Parham, L. (2018). Reversing the dehumaniza-tion of families of color in schools: Community-based research in a race-conscious parent engagement program. *School Community Journal, 28*(1), 319–347.

Zdanowicz, C. (2017). *No, where are you really from?* CNN. https://www.cnn.com/ interactive/2017/08/opinion/where-im-really-from/.

Zulman, N. (2018, November 23). *Why we need to dispatch "differently abled": Moving past euphemisms for disability.* Honi Soit. https://honisoit.com/2018/11/w hy-we-need-to-ditch-differently-abled/.

About the Authors

Theresa M. Bouley, PhD, is a professor of education at Eastern Connecticut State University and the president of the Connecticut chapter of the National Association for Multicultural Education (NAME). Her research and teaching center on justice, equity, diversity, and inclusion in education. This is her second book coauthored with Dr. Reinking. *The Economic and Opportunity Gap: How Poverty Impacts the Lives of Students* was published in spring 2021.

Anni K. Reinking, EdD, is an education consultant, professor, and the director of Development and Education Research at CSedresearch.org. Her research and teaching center on equity, diversity, and inclusion in education and community organizations. This is her fifth book and second book co-authored with Dr. Bouley.

Made in United States
Troutdale, OR
08/01/2023

11727851R00130